The Early Childhood Education Playbook

The Early Childhood Education Playbook

Kateri Thunder

John Almarode

Alisha Demchak

Douglas Fisher

Nancy Frey

FOR INFORMATION:

Corwin

A SAGE Company

2455 Teller Road

Thousand Oaks, California 91320

(800) 233-9936

www.corwin.com

SAGE Publications Ltd.

1 Oliver's Yard

55 City Road

London EC1Y 1SP

United Kingdom

SAGE Publications India Pvt. Ltd.

B 1/I 1 Mohan Cooperative Industrial Area

Mathura Road, New Delhi 110 044

India

SAGE Publications Asia-Pacific Pte. Ltd.

18 Cross Street #10-10/11/12

China Square Central

Singapore 048423

President: Mike Soules

Vice President and
  Editorial Director: Monica Eckman

Publisher: Jessica Allan

Content Development
  Editor: Mia Rodriguez

Editorial Assistant: Natalie Delpino

Project Editor: Amy Schroller

Copy Editor: Diane DiMura

Typesetter: C&M Digitals (P) Ltd.

Proofreader: Dennis Webb

Cover Designer: Scott Van Atta

Marketing Manager: Olivia Bartlett

Library of Congress Cataloging-in-Publication Data

Names: Thunder, Kateri, author. | Almarode, John, author. | Demchak, Alisha, author. | Fisher, Douglas, author. | Frey, Nancy, 1959- author.

Title: The early childhood education playbook / Kateri Thunder, John Almarode, Alisha Demchak, Douglas Fisher, Nancy Frey.

Description: Thousand Oaks, California : Corwin, [2023] | Includes bibliographical references and index.

Identifiers: LCCN 2022028309 | ISBN 9781071886526 (spiral bound) | ISBN 9781071886533 (epub) | ISBN 9781071886540 (epub) | ISBN 9781071886564 (pdf)

Subjects: LCSH: Visible learning. | Early childhood education. | Effective teaching. | Affective education.

Classification: LCC LB1078 .T48 2023 | DDC 370.15/23—dc23/eng/20220706

LC record available at https://lccn.loc.gov/2022028309

This book is printed on acid-free paper.

22 23 24 25 26 10 9 8 7 6 5 4 3 2 1

CONTENTS

Visit the companion website at
resources.corwin.com/theearlychildhoodeducationplaybook
for downloadable resources.

ABOUT THE AUTHORS

Kateri Thunder, PhD, has the pleasure of collaborating with learners, families, and educators from school divisions and early learning centers around the world to translate research into practice. Previously, Kateri served as an inclusive early childhood educator, an Upward Bound educator, a mathematics specialist, an assistant professor of mathematics education at James Madison University, and Site Director for the Central Virginia Writing Project. Then, Kateri followed her passion back into the classroom where she spent each day learning with her prekindergartners and coaching mathematics specialists in Charlottesville City Schools. Kateri researches, writes, and presents on equity and access in early childhood and mathematics education and the intersection of literacy and mathematics for teaching and learning. She has partnered with thousands of educators to catalyze change in their classrooms, centers, and schools. Kateri is chair of NCTM's Research Committee, co-creator of The Math Diet, board member for Barrett Early Learning Center, and a best-selling author for Corwin's *Teaching Mathematics in the Visible Learning Classroom* Series, the *Success Criteria Playbook*, and *Visible Learning in Early Childhood*.

Dr. John Almarode is a professor of education in the College of Education at James Madison University, teaching in the Elementary and Inclusive Early Childhood Education Programs. In 2015, John was awarded the inaugural Sarah Miller Luck Endowed Professorship. In 2021, John was honored with an Outstanding Faculty Award from the State Council for Higher Education in Virginia. At James Madison University, he continues to work with pre-service teachers, graduate students, and teacher leaders and was recently named a Madison Scholar in the College of Education. He has published numerous articles on teaching and learning as well as books such as *Clarity for Learning, The Success Criteria Playbook, PLC+, Visible Learning for Science, Visible Learning in Early Childhood, Inclusive Teaching in the Early Childhood Science Classroom*, and most recently, *How Learning Works*.

Alisha Demchak, MEd, is an early childhood educator and researcher whose passion for improving reading outcomes for all learners is visible across her work. Alisha has taught in early childhood classrooms and mixed-age settings, served as a reading specialist and interventionist, and coached early childhood educators, administrators, and literacy coordinators. Currently, she is researching evidenced-based instructional practices in early childhood reading and striving to ensure those practices enter into classrooms by working with pre-service and in-service teachers to build their skill set and confidence in reading instruction.

Douglas Fisher, PhD, is a professor of educational leadership at San Diego State University and a teacher leader at Health Sciences High. At Health Sciences High, he currently oversees a child development and preschool program with Nancy Frey. Previously, Doug was an early intervention teacher and elementary school educator. He is the recipient of an International Reading Association William S. Grey citation of merit and an Exemplary Leader award from the Conference on English Leadership of NCTE. He has published numerous articles on teaching and learning as well as books such as *The Teacher Clarity Playbook, PLC+, Visible Learning for Literacy, Comprehension: The Skill, Will, and Thrill of Reading, How Tutoring Works*, and most recently, *How Learning Works*. Doug loves being an educator and hopes to share that passion with others.

Nancy Frey, PhD, is a professor in educational leadership at San Diego State and a teacher leader at Health Sciences High and Middle College where she oversees a child development and preschool program with Douglas Fisher. Nancy started her career as special educator for young children. Later, as a reading specialist, she directed an intervention clinic that supported language and literacy development in children. She is a member of the International Literacy Association's Literacy Research Panel. Her published titles include *Visible Learning in Literacy, This Is Balanced Literacy, Removing Labels*, and *Rebound*. Nancy is a credentialed special educator, reading specialist, and administrator in California and learns from teachers and students every day.

WELCOME!

When we share space, time, and interactions with our youngest learners, we have the opportunity to shape the beginning of their journeys as explorers, inventors, problem solvers, communicators, and collaborators. We can create learning spaces full of rich interactions that intentionally grow Visible Learners who own their learning journeys.

Whether you work with children from birth through age eight, children with exceptional needs, and children speaking English as an additional language, whether you work in a daycare center, school system, preschool, or family care program, whether you are a paraprofessional, a lead teacher, a special educator, or a director, and whether you have years of experience or you are a novice, we are thrilled to share this learning journey with you.

 **THE LEARNING INTENTION FOR THIS PLAYBOOK**

We are learning about implementing instructional approaches and strategies that have the potential to positively impact young children's learning and development.

Like you, we come from a broad range of early childhood teaching experiences. Kateri has taught preschool through high school as well as pre-service and in-service inclusive early childhood educators. She currently coaches early learning educators and administrators as they strive to form partnerships with families and to implement research. John Almarode, drawing from his work with schools and classrooms across the globe, teaches methods courses in the Inclusive Early Childhood and Elementary Education Programs at James Madison University. This allows him the opportunity to bridge the gap between theory and practice for the next generation of early childhood educators. Alisha taught kindergarten and second grade and served as a reading specialist and instructional coach for PreK-4 elementary schools. Currently, she is researching instructional practices in early childhood reading as she continues to translate research into practice to improve reading outcomes for all learners. Doug started his career as an early childhood educator and language development specialist. He taught in the early childhood and inclusive education programs at San Diego State University and currently oversees a child development and preschool program that enriches the lives of the children of the staff at Health Sciences High. Nancy started her career as special educator for young children. Later, as a reading specialist, she directed an intervention clinic that supported language and literacy development in children.

We feel privileged to learn with and from our youngest learners and, you, their educators. And, we are passionate about growing your expertise as early childhood educators so that you can maximize the learning opportunities of young children.

You likely selected this Playbook for both personal and professional reasons. Maybe you are a lifelong learner seeking to explore new ways of thinking about early childhood teaching, learning, and development. You might be seeking to grow in a specific area of your teaching practice. Either way, your reason for engaging in this learning journey matters. With that being said, take a few moments and formulate a few goals you are striving for through the work in this Playbook. You will notice there are two columns in the space below. For now, list your goals in the left column. We will return to the column on the right later in this introduction.

REFLECTION

Goals for Engaging in This Work	
1.	
2.	
3.	
4.	

VISIBLE EARLY CHILDHOOD LEARNING

Early childhood is a developmental stage uniquely sensitive to growth across multiple domains in ways that are interwoven and concurrent. Our instructional decisions can maximize this development by using research to identify what works best in teaching, learning, and development. Furthermore, we take our teaching and children's learning and development seriously. We hold ourselves highly accountable for space, time, and interactions with our youngest learners, and thus strive for a year's worth of developmental growth or learning gains for each of our learners. John Hattie's research, the research that spawned the concept of *Visible Learning* (see Hattie, 2008), yielded many insights into how we *might* do this in early childhood.

There are three overarching ideas that will support our work moving forward in this Playbook:

1. There are things that we do in our early childhood centers or classrooms that do not move learning and development forward.

2. There are also things that we do in our early childhood centers or classrooms that have a fairly insignificant impact on learning and development.

3. Finally, there are things that we do in our early childhood centers or classrooms that have a very large positive impact on learning and development.

 # REFLECTION

Using the space below, what are the things in your early childhood center or classroom that take time and energy, but you do not see an impact on children's learning and development? What are those things that take time and energy, but you see only a small positive impact? And what are those things that take time and energy, and you see a large positive impact on learning and development?

No Visible Impact	Small Visible Positive Impact	Large Visible Positive Impact

John Hattie engaged in a similar process, but not from a list of things he does in his own classroom; he drew from the large body of educational research. To date, he has accumulated more than 1,800 meta-analyses, a compilation of over 100,000 studies involving 300 million students across the globe, which comprises the Visible Learning database. Meta-analyses are collections of individual studies that include an overall effect size. We will report effect sizes throughout this Playbook so that you can see how powerful each of our recommendations are. In the Visible Learning database, the average effect size of all things that impact learning is 0.40. By definition, influences above 0.40 are above average and, when implemented well, are very likely to positively impact learning.

Big Ideas

However, this body of educational research is not a list of dos and don'ts. In fact, this synthesis of research leads to a powerful conclusion about what happens in our centers and classrooms that gives us the potential to maximize learning and development in young children. This conclusion is that the greatest gains in learning and development occur when *early childhood educators see learning through the eyes of their learners and learners see themselves as their own teachers*. This is what is meant by Visible Learning.

REFLECTION

Use the space provided to rewrite the above conclusion as though you are talking about your learners in your center or classroom. In other words, write the above conclusion in the first person. We will get you started.

> I maximize learning and development in my classroom or center when . . .

VISIBLE LEARNING LEADS TO VISIBLE EARLY CHILDHOOD LEARNERS

Knowing what works best allows us to be purposeful and deliberate in how we create learning spaces full of rich interactions that intentionally grow Visible Learners. When we implement Visible Learning research, we grow Visible Early Childhood Learners. Visible Learners share six characteristics that reflect many of the hallmarks of early childhood education, where teaching and learning is child centered and where children drive instruction, eventually taking ownership over their own learning. Visible Early Childhood Learners

- know their current level of understanding; they can communicate what they do and do not yet know;

- know where they are going next in their learning and are ready to take on the challenge;

Big Ideas

- select tools to move their learning and development forward;

- seek feedback about their learning and recognize errors as opportunities to learn;

- monitor their learning and make adjustments when necessary; and

- recognize when they have learned something and serve as a teacher to others (Frey et al., 2018).

With Visible Learning research at our side, we can intentionally, purposefully, and deliberately develop each of these characteristics in our young learners— *all* of our young learners. We strive to offer *all* learners the equity of access and opportunity to achieve at the highest levels of learning possible. The development of Visible Early Childhood Learners must be intentionally equitable and inclusive.

Before closing out this introduction and diving into the modules of this Playbook, let's look at the characteristics of Visible Early Childhood Learners and reflect on our own centers and classrooms. Using the space below, describe what each of these characteristics would look like in your specific environment and what you currently do to support each characteristic. If you have to leave any of the spaces blank, that is OK. That is why we are engaged in this Playbook.

REFLECTION

Visible Early Childhood Learners . . .	What this means in my center or classroom . . .	How I can support this in my center or classroom . . .
Know their current level of understanding; they can communicate what they do and do not yet know.		
Know where they are going next in their learning and are ready to take on the challenge.		
Select tools to move their learning and development forward.		
Seek feedback about their learning and recognize errors as opportunities to learn.		
Monitor their learning and make adjustments when necessary.		
Recognize when they have learned something and serve as a teacher to others.		

THE WAY FORWARD

We know that despite our best efforts, when children move to primary or elementary school, many of our learners do not maintain the growth trajectories established in preschool programs (Cooper et al., 2010; Durkin et al., 2022; Gilliam & Zigler, 2000). In other words, the effects of preschool fade over time. We can counter this fade effect by creating a seamless, strong foundation that sustains gains and leads to better long-term learning outcomes (Stipek et al., 2017). To establish this foundation, we need to identify what works best when, implement coherent practices across learning contexts, and maintain developmentally appropriate alignment.

Our time with young children is precious. Every child deserves the very best start to becoming lifelong learners. "Every child deserves a great teacher, not by chance, but by design" (Fisher et al., 2016). And so, we must start this work right now.

WAYS TO USE THIS PLAYBOOK

The purpose of this Playbook is to examine how the Visible Learning research can guide our decisions as we plan, teach, document, and partner with families and colleagues so that we can have the greatest possible impact on young children's learning and development. The modules of this Playbook will unpack unique characteristics of early childhood education as well as coherent practices, called *teacher clarity*, that form a strong foundation for learning over time.

A playbook is filled with tools and methods to support a team as they work toward a common goal. As you work on this Playbook, you may collaborate with your fellow teachers, your program team, your grade level, or your teaching partners. Together, we will work toward this common goal: We are learning about implementing instructional approaches and strategies that have the potential to positively impact young children's learning and development.

 # REFLECTION

Before we move into Module 1, there is one more task to complete. You may recall that at the beginning of this introduction you were asked to identify goals. You did this in the left column of the table on page 6. **Now, let's return to the right column.** That column is set aside for you to articulate the evidence that will convince you and others

(Continued)

(Continued)

that you have met the specific goals in the left column. Remember, if our goal is Visible Learning in early childhood, then we must generate *visible* evidence to make that learning visible to both us and our young learners.

Take a moment and return to page 6. In the column on the right, please describe what evidence would convince you and others that you have met each of the goals on the left. For example, if you are aiming to increase the amount of talking interactions in your early childhood classroom, the evidence might be the percentage of your day devoted to children talking with other children and adults.

When you are finished with this task, we will summarize the next steps in this Playbook.

This Playbook is made up of five parts. Part 1 examines a significant aspect of early childhood education: the partnerships among educators, families, and learners. The purpose of Part 1 is to value each person we partner with—teachers, administrators, teaching assistants, family members, and learners—for their critical contributions to learning and development.

With a better sense of who we are as a learning community, we next examine teacher clarity in early childhood. Teacher clarity has four critical components: clarity of organization, explanation, examples and guided practice, and assessment. Part 2 begins the process of learning about, modeling, practicing, and implementing clarity in early childhood. First, we develop clarity around our learning goals. Then, in Part 3, we use this clarity as a guide to plan tasks, learning strategies, and scaffolds to help learners meet those goals. Finally, Part 4 examines the relationship between formative evaluation and feedback practices. We see every interaction as an opportunity to elicit evidence of learning and to use feedback that strengthens our partnerships and maximizes learning and development.

As we orient ourselves to the progression of learning within this Playbook, we appreciate that we all bring incredible strengths and critical questions to this work. Together, we intend to learn about implementing instructional approaches and strategies that have the potential to positively impact young children's learning and development. At the beginning and end of each module, we will evaluate where we are along the path toward mastery of this learning. Our strengths and questions will inform our next steps and the lens through which we engage and move forward.

Let's take that next step together.

PART I

WHO BEFORE DO

BECOMING EXPERT EDUCATORS

Positive teacher-student relationships are critical to learning and development. Therefore, in our work with learners, we put *who* before *do*. We discover *who* is learning with us *before* we make decisions about what we will *do* related to teaching, learning, and development.

Part 1 is all about *who before do*. In this module, we focus on getting to know YOU. We begin by inviting you to reflect on your teacher identity, teacher credibility, and teacher efficacy. Then, we explore the seven characteristics of expert early childhood educators and set aims to intentionally grow these characteristics in *all* our young learners.

 ## LEARNING INTENTION AND SUCCESS CRITERIA FOR MODULE 1

Before you engage with the learning in this module, read what we intend to learn (LI, the learning intention) and what it'll look and sound like when we've learned this (SC, the success criteria). Next, read the levels, descriptions, and images of the path to mastery (the rubric). Evaluate where you are right now for each success criteria. At the end of the module, we'll return to this self-evaluation and document the ways we've intentionally grown our teaching practice over time.

LI: We are learning about the importance of growing our credibility and self-efficacy so that we can build our expertise as early childhood educators.

SC: I'll know I've learned this when I can

(Continued)

(Continued)

Beginning	Emerging	Developing	Expanding	Bridging
Becoming aware 	Initially trying	Deliberately practicing	Intentionally stretching	Transferring and generalizing

Icon source: istock.com/rambo182

- Reflect on my teacher identity, credibility, and self-efficacy.

_____

_____

_____

_____

_____

- Explain the importance of my teacher identity, credibility, and self-efficacy for positively impacting children's learning and development.

_____

_____

_____

_____

- Make sense of the relationship between growing my credibility and self-efficacy and growing my expertise in the big ideas of teaching, learning, and development for early childhood.

_____

_____

_____

_____

_____

- Identify ways to grow my credibility and efficacy as an early educator.

_____

_____

_____

_____

_____

 # REFLECTION

The teaching, learning, and development of our youngest learners unite us. There are so many occupations, and in education, quite a variety of roles. So, why are you an early childhood educator? What keeps you returning each day? Take a moment to pause and reflect on who you are as an educator and what insights and strengths you bring to this work.

Your Teacher Identity

Why do you choose to work with this unique age of young learners?	What draws you to your specific role at your specific program?
What makes you a great early educator?	What is your hope for your young learners?

 **REFLECTION**

We began by reflecting on who we are as educators. And now, we reflect on who we are to the children we work with, their families, and our colleagues. How do they see us?

Teacher Credibility

How would your **learners** respond to the following question: *How would you describe your teacher?*	How would your learners' **families** respond to the following question: *How would you describe your child's teacher?*	How would your **colleagues** respond to the following question: *How would you describe (your name) as a teacher?*

These answers represent teacher credibility. Teacher credibility is the learner's belief that they can and will learn from you. In early childhood, our partnerships with learners, families, and colleagues are central to teaching, learning, and development so we consider all their perspectives. Teacher credibility has a very strong effect size of 1.09 (www.visiblelearningmetax.com); it is worth our time and energy to grow our teacher credibility because when children believe they can learn from us, they are more likely to.

There are four characteristics of teacher credibility:

➢ Trust

➢ Competence

➢ Dynamism

➢ Immediacy

These characteristics are the ways that we communicate to learners that they can and will learn from us.

Trust: Children and families want to trust us to keep our word and to follow through. They want us to genuinely care for and respect each child and trust that we always work to do our best for them as learners, friends, and family members.

Competence: Children and families want to know we are competent educators by experiencing well-organized, accurate, and clearly communicated instruction. They want to be assured that we hold expertise from both experience and education about early childhood learning and development and that we apply this knowledge thoughtfully as we interact with children.

Dynamism: Children and families want to feel our passion for working with young children and for being a part of their learning and development. They want to be meaningfully engaged in their interactions with us and know that we will be positive, energetic, and active.

Immediacy: Children and families want us to be accessible and relatable. They want to know we are moving learning and development forward with purpose, not wasting time, and that we are responsive to who they are as individuals.

REFLECTION

Now that you've read about the four characteristics of teacher credibly, choose a color, a symbol, or an image to represent each one. Briefly explain the reasoning behind your representations.

Trust	Competence
Dynamism	Immediacy

Through words and actions, we make sure our children and their families believe they will experience success as learners because we are their teachers. One pivotal way to grow our teacher credibility is by viewing every interaction we share with our learners and their families as a learning opportunity. Every interaction occurs by design, not by chance. Rather than simply engaging in free play or mere observation, we engage in interactions for learning where we communicate trust, competence, dynamism, and immediacy.

 **REFLECTION**

What are other ways we can strengthen our credibility?

Ways I can strengthen my credibility with my **learners** this school year	Ways I can strengthen my credibility with **families** this school year	Ways I can strengthen my credibility with my **colleagues** this school year

CASE IN POINT

Emelie Mendoza promised to give her children's families a schedule for the week. But she forgot. She sits fairly far away from her learners when reading aloud to them because she thinks that they can see her better. And she often calls a child by another child's name. Her skill level in terms of instructional repertoire is very strong, and she is often asked to share her teaching strategies with others.

Ms. Mendoza means well. She loves her role and wants to see her learners flourish. In reflecting on her teaching with her director, Ms. Mendoza said, "I'm just not seeing the growth that I thought I would get. The children are a little distant from me, but they seem warmer with other staff. They are so happy to see the other people who work here and they are nice to me, but it's just not the same."

The program director asked Ms. Mendoza to analyze her actions to identify if there were possibilities for increasing her credibility with children and their caregivers. Immediately, she said that she really needed to learn names and get them right. When asked how she might do that, Ms. Mendoza said that she could put their pictures on index cards and practice them every night. As she noted, "I have three different classes that I'm with at different parts of the day. So I'm seeing about 50 children a day and that's hard. But I want to be better."

What else might Ms. Mendoza do to improve her credibility?

Trust	Competence
Dynamism	Immediacy

TEACHER SELF-EFFICACY

The potential for learning begins with both teacher credibility and self-efficacy. Just as learners must believe they can learn from us, we must believe we can teach them effectively. Teacher self-efficacy is the belief that our work matters and that we can and will be effective educators. Most significantly, teacher self-efficacy is the belief that we can have a positive impact on *every* learner. In early childhood, this belief is critical because we lay the foundation that thwarts achievement gaps from forming. Teacher self-efficacy has a large effect size of 0.65 (www.visiblelearningmetax.com); it is worth our time and energy to grow our teacher self-efficacy because when we believe we can move *all* learners forward, we are more likely to.

There are four influences that develop our self-efficacy: experiences of mastery, modeling, social persuasion, and physiological factors (Bandura, 1977).

Important Vocabulary

Experiences of Mastery

When we take on a new challenge and we are successful, this experience of mastery builds our belief that we can learn new skills or improve. As early educators, these experiences of mastery occur when we try something new in our planning, teaching, and assessment and when we directly see the positive impact it has on our learners. As we see evidence that each learner grows and develops because of our interactions, we expand our experiences of mastery and we come to more deeply believe we are capable of having a positive impact on *every* learner's development.

Modeling

When our colleagues and educator friends take on new challenges and are successful, their modeling also positively influences our self-efficacy. They serve as a model to us; we see someone we can relate to and connect with trying new strategies and positively impacting every learner. And then, we transfer their success to the possibility of success in our own teaching. Their modeling grows our belief that we can do it too.

Social Persuasion

When we are told that we can help every child grow and develop, this verbal encouragement builds our belief that our teaching is impactful. Social persuasion can come from messages we hear and read that describe the importance of early childhood experiences, from feedback based on observations by coaches or administrators, from compliments and encouragement from colleagues and our children's families, and from words and actions of gratitude from our young learners themselves. All this positive feedback tells us we are capable of reaching *every* child, which becomes a message we remember and rely on as we work to improve our practice.

Physiological Factors

When we are healthy, happy, and safe, we are more willing to take risks, to expend our energy while trying, and to seek new challenges. This physiological well-being opens us to believing that our efforts to meet each child where they are and help move them forward will result in successful learning and development; in other words, it helps us believe the work is worth it. Many personal, professional, and community factors can influence how we perceive risk and challenge as professionals. We need to be in a mental, emotional, and physical space that energizes and facilitates honing our craft.

REFLECTION

Return to the descriptions of the four influences on self-efficacy.

- For each influence, underline or highlight one **sentence** that most clearly captures its meaning for you.
- Next, select a **phrase** that captures its meaning and write it in the appropriate box below. The phrase may be in the sentence you identified or it may be a phrase from elsewhere in the description.
- Finally, select a single **word** that captures its meaning and write it in the appropriate box below. Again, the word may be in the sentence or phrase you identified or it may be a word from elsewhere in the description.

When you read the sentence, phrase, and word, you should have a more complete understanding of each influence.

Experiences of Mastery	Modeling
Sentence	Sentence
Phrase	Phrase
Word	Word
Social Persuasion	Physiological Factors
Sentence	Sentence
Phrase	Phrase
Word	Word

While we phrased each of the influences on self-efficacy in positive terms, you may recall experiences that had either positive or negative effects on your self-efficacy. Being aware of experiences that build and deplete our self-efficacy is important so that we can intentionally engage in building experiences and avoid depleting experiences.

 **REFLECTION**

Take a moment to reflect on each of the four influences on self-efficacy and your specific experiences with them. What experiences have built or depleted your teacher self-efficacy?

Experiences that **build** my teacher self-efficacy	Experiences that **deplete** my teacher self-efficacy

The collective work of a team of educators is incredibly powerful for positively impacting young children's learning and development. In fact, collective teacher efficacy has an effect size of 1.36 (www.visiblelearningmetax .com), which is off the charts! Working collaboratively has the potential to considerably accelerate learners' development. With that said, you may have started work in this Playbook alone, but we highly encourage you to collaborate with a colleague or a team of colleagues for the remainder of the Playbook.

One of our favorite ways to think of collective teacher efficacy is in terms of our strengths. Each of us brings unique strengths of perspective, experience, and ideas to our work. In this module, we have reflected on our strengths through our teacher identity, credibility, and self-efficacy. Now, we need to leverage those strengths for the benefit of our collective team.

In this Playbook, we protect time and space to learn with and from each other, we model for each other, we give each other positive feedback, and we share the challenging journey to mastery. It's worth our time, energy, and effort to work as a team of educators to build our efficacy and to develop our teaching practice. It's worth it to build our expertise together.

BUILDING OUR EXPERTISE TOGETHER

If you're like us, you ask a lot of questions about what you can do that is best for your children's learning and development. There are so many decisions to make each day that sometimes we find ourselves in the weeds, surrounded by questions and unsure how to move forward. This is when we need to refocus our questions on what really matters, what is really worth it, what is likely to have a large positive impact on our learners. To build our expertise together, we must refocus our efforts on seven big ideas for effective teaching, learning, and development in early childhood.

 # REFLECTION

1.1 **Big Ideas for Effective Teaching, Learning, and Development in Early Childhood**

7 Big Ideas for Effective Teaching, Learning, and Development in Early Childhood		My Goals
Early childhood educators and their learners work together as evaluators of learning growth for all.	Effect Size = 1.32	
Early childhood educators and learners have high expectations for learning that communicate equity of access and opportunity to the highest level of learning possible.	Effect Size = 0.90	

(Continued)

(Continued)

7 Big Ideas for Effective Teaching, Learning, and Development in Early Childhood		My Goals
Learning experiences move learning toward explicit and inclusive success criteria.	Effect Size = 0.77	
Learning experiences and tasks have the developmentally appropriate level or right level of challenge for all young learners.	Effect Size = 0.74	
Trust is established with all learners so that errors and mistakes are viewed as opportunities for new learning.	Effect Size = 0.72	
Early childhood educators are continually seeking feedback about their impact on all their children's learning.	Effect Size = 0.72	
There is the right balance of surface and deep learning in the early childhood classroom.	Effect Size = 0.69	

As you read these seven big ideas, some may be familiar and others new. Some language may reflect how you and your colleagues talk about your teaching practice while other language may be novel. In this Playbook, we will unpack these seven big ideas and make them actionable in our early childhood contexts. Together, let's set our shared aim to intentionally implement these big ideas in our early childhood contexts.

REFLECTION

In the introduction, you shared your goals for working in this Playbook as well as the evidence that would make meeting those goals visible to you. Return to page 2 and review those goals. What connections do you see between your goals and the seven big ideas for effective teaching, learning, and development in early childhood? Now look back at the table on the previous page to record these connections. Highlight, circle, or underline anything that overlaps with your goals. You can use the empty column on the right to record connections between your goals and the big ideas.

LEARNING INTENTION AND SUCCESS CRITERIA FOR MODULE 1

Now that you have engaged with the learning in this module, reread what we intended to learn (LI, the learning intention) and what it looks and sounds like to have mastered learning this (SC, the success criteria). Next, reread the levels, descriptions, and images of the path to mastery (the rubric). Reevaluate where you are right now for each success criteria. Use the space to document the evidence you have of where you are and where you are headed next.

LI: We are learning about the importance of growing our credibility and self-efficacy so that we can build our expertise as early childhood educators.

SC: I'll know I've learned this when I can

(Continued)

(Continued)

Icon source: istock.com/rambo182

- Reflect on my teacher identity, credibility, and self-efficacy.

_____

_____

_____

_____

_____

- Explain the importance of my teacher identity, credibility, and self-efficacy for positively impacting children's learning and development.

_____

_____

_____

_____

_____

- Make sense of the relationship between growing my credibility and self-efficacy and growing my expertise in the big ideas of teaching, learning, and development for early childhood.

_____

_____

_____

_____

_____

_____

- Identify ways to grow my credibility and efficacy as an early educator.

_____

_____

_____

_____

_____

2

PARTNERSHIPS WITH AND FOR LEARNERS

Let's return to the seven big ideas for effective teaching, learning, and development in early childhood introduced in the last module (p. 21). Each of the big ideas relies on establishing partnerships with learners, families, and fellow educators.

In fact, the following four big ideas include specific language about partnerships:

Big Ideas

> Early childhood educators **and** their learners **work together** as evaluators of learning growth for all.

> Early childhood educators **and** learners have high expectations for learning that communicate equity of access and opportunity to the highest level of learning possible.

> **Trust is established** with all learners so that errors and mistakes are viewed as opportunities for new learning.

> Early childhood educators **continually seek feedback** about their impact on all their children's learning.

Partnerships are a central component of early childhood. We form partnerships to create inclusive, anti-racist, anti-bias learning settings, where every child and every family is welcomed and included. We do not do this work alone; we must partner with learners, families, and fellow educators. In this module, we continue our reflection of *who before do* by valuing those we partner with in order to create effective learning contexts for every learner.

LEARNING INTENTION AND SUCCESS CRITERIA FOR MODULE 2

Before you engage with the learning in this module, read what we intend to learn (LI, the learning intention) and what it'll look and sound like when we've learned this (SC, the success criteria). Next, read the levels, descriptions, and images of the path to mastery (the rubric). Evaluate where you are right now for each success criteria. At the end of the module, we'll return to this self-evaluation and document the ways we've intentionally grown our teaching practice over time.

LI: We are learning the importance of partnering with our learners, their families, and our fellow educators, so that we can create inclusive, anti-racist, anti-bias learning spaces where educators and learners work together, trust is established, and feedback is valued.

SC: I'll know I've learned this when I can

Icon source: istock.com/rambo182

• Explain why partnerships with our learners, their families, and fellow educators are central to effective, inclusive, anti-racist, and anti-bias teaching, learning, and development in early childhood.

_____

_____

_____

_____

_____

• Describe what partnerships that are inclusive, anti-racist, and anti-bias look and sound like.

_____

_____

_____

_____

_____

_____

- Identify and implement ways to build these partnerships that are inclusive, anti-racist, and anti-bias.

_____

_____

_____

_____

_____

- Make connections among the big ideas for effective teaching, learning, and development in early childhood, these partnerships, and the characteristics of Visible Early Childhood Learners.

_____

_____

_____

_____

_____

So how do we create these partnerships? And what should they look like and sound like? We begin by reflecting on partnerships with our learners.

PARTNERSHIPS WITH LEARNERS

Our work throughout this Playbook centers around partnering with learners to develop Visible Early Childhood Learners. This is central to the big ideas for effective teaching, learning, and development in early childhood. Throughout this Playbook, we will examine ways to partner with learners to communicate clarity, implement tasks and learning strategies, evaluate learning, make decisions about next steps, and give and seek feedback. But to begin, in this module, we will focus on an important first step: knowing our learners.

Partnering with infants, toddlers, preschoolers, and primary schoolers begins with knowing each learner well. We get to know learners by spending time with each one and discovering: _What are their ways of communicating, noticing, wondering, and interacting? What sparks their excitement as well as other emotions? What is familiar and unfamiliar to them?_ Knowing learners means we notice and value who each learner is and we believe each learner is already ready to meaningfully join and contribute to the learning community.

LEARNING ABOUT LEARNERS PROTOCOL

As early childhood educators, we should set aside time to get to know our learners. Getting to know our learners will ensure we see each child's value and we capitalize on their strengths so they contribute to the learning community. The *Learning About Learners Protocol* gives us the opportunity to spend time with learners, to observe learners as they engage with their peers and interact in the learning environment, and to document our noticings so they become actionable. The information generated from this structure will provide the foundation for our partnerships with both families and colleagues.

Here is the *Learning About Learners Protocol*:

> **Get to know all learners.** Intentionally spend time playing and working with each learner. Observe each learner and notice who they are. Remember, this protocol is designed to help us grow in our understanding of our learners, not to formally assess them. You do not need to spend time with every learner on the same day or for the same amount of time. Decide on a process that works for you and your colleagues and incorporate the process into your week.

> **Notice how, what, and who.** Essentially, the *Learning About Learners Protocol* asks us to gather information about how the learner is communicating, what they are doing, and who they are working with during the day. This includes looking at specific artifacts that learners create. Furthermore, this should include transitions and experiences outside of the classroom (e.g., outdoor play, snack and meals).

> **Be intentional and open.** While we want to know what children know, understand, and can do, the power of this protocol comes from the information gathered about who learners are, the processes they go through during their learning journeys, and the ways they interact and make sense of the world around them. By paying attention to how young children learn, we gather information needed to include each of them. Observing with these questions in mind may help you be intentional while remaining open to children's in-the-moment decisions, language, and actions:
> - *What are learners doing to make meaning of concepts and skills?*
> - *How do learners make meaning of the learning environment?*
> - *How do learners interact with other members of the classroom community?*
> - *What are learners gravitating toward? What is a popular material or choice and why?*

- *Who typically works or plays in this space? Do all children eventually work or play here?*
- *Do learners engage in a balance of independent and collaborative work or play?*
- *Do learners work or play for a sustained time period in one area or on one task?*

▶ **Communicate your genuine wonder and your desire to understand and know each learner.** As you spend time playing with, working with, and noticing each child, the actions and words you choose should convey your genuine interest in who they are and in creating space for them to bring their whole selves into the learning context. Remember to be quiet and just listen. Taking the time to actively listen communicates that you value the child.

▶ **Stay.** Rather than moving from child to child and space to space, stay in one area with one learner or one group of children. The depth and breadth of children's thinking is often revealed over time as they engage more deeply in a task.

▶ **Keep a record.** Recording our interactions, noticings, and observations makes them visible and therefore actionable. We suggest the following template to organize your noticings:

TEMPLATES

Learning About Learners Protocol

Date _____

Description of the Task or Experience	Noticed Doing	Heard Saying	Saw Creating

online resources Source: Adapted from Sweeney, D., & Harris, L. S. (2017).

Protocol guidance adapted from Thunder & Demchak (2018).

What makes the *Learning About Learners Protocol* so powerful is the information the protocol provides. It empowers us to take an asset-focused stance with each child and family. Every child brings valuable knowledge and expertise to our settings. When we spend time getting to know our learners and noticing their strengths, we can intentionally leverage these strengths for the benefit of our whole learning community. The *Learning About Learners Protocol* can help facilitate our partnerships with families and leverage their strengths for the benefit of our learning community as well.

This work to know each of our learners is worth our time and energy. Knowing learners builds positive teacher-student relationships, which has the potential to accelerate learning and development (effect size = 0.47) (www.visiblelearn ingmetax.com). Acting on these relationships to create meaningful partnerships can grow our teacher credibility. To effectively partner with our learners, we also need to partner with families.

PARTNERSHIPS WITH FAMILIES

Our young learners are already confident members of their family communities, and as they enter our centers and schools, they begin to see themselves as members of new communities—our learning communities. Our partnerships with families can help maximize children's learning and development by building a two-way bridge between home and school.

We know children's achievement has the potential to accelerate when families are involved in their children's education (effect size = 0.42) (www.visiblelearn ingmetax.com). This does not mean waiting for families to come to our schools and centers, but rather it means that we must actively engage families, meeting families where they are, and creating family partnerships.

Let's look back at the specific language that describes partnerships within the big ideas for teaching, learning, and development in early education (p. 29). These big ideas provide us with a vision for meaningful family partnerships: We work together as evaluators of learning growth, together we have high expectations for learning, we establish trust, and we continually seek feedback from families about our impact.

Big Ideas

The first step to forming a partnership with families is genuinely believing that every family is an expert about their own child and that every family has "funds of knowledge" (Vélez-Ibáñez & Greenberg, 1992). Funds of knowledge are ways of showing and knowing that are unique, brilliant, and important to children's learning and development.

From our beliefs, we develop expectations and actions. When we believe that we should partner with every family to learn from and with them, then we expect to grow this partnership with every family and we take actions to intentionally form this partnership.

Intentionally communicating with families is one way to form a partnership. Communication has two directions: us telling or sharing *and* us listening. Let's begin by reflecting on what we already do.

REFLECTION

		What I Already Do
Who?	• Who do you communicate with in your learners' families and who communicates with you?	
How?	• How do you communicate with your learners' families? How do they communicate with you?	
When?	• When, during the year and during each week or day, do you communicate with your learners' families? When do families respond?	
Where?	• Where do you talk with or meet with families? Where do families prefer to talk or meet?	
What?	• What do you share or tell? What do you listen for? What do families share or tell? What do they want to know?	

Look back at what you already do and note the following:

● How much of what you already do is focused on you—what works for you, what you tell and share, what you initiate?

● How much of what you already do is focused on families—what works for them, what they tell and share, what they initiate?

● How much of your communication involves you telling and sharing? How much is focused on listening and learning?

● How are you meeting families where they are?

Take a moment to write what you noticed about your current practices:

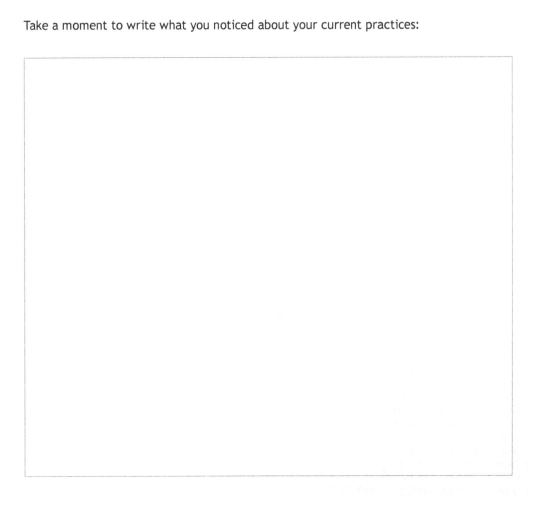

By listening to and learning from families, we can rely on families as resources to help us create continuity of context for our learners. Continuity of context means that home and school share familiar aspects. This continuity can be found in routines, language, songs and stories, and traditions and celebrations. When we create continuity between home and school, the familiarity allows learners to show what they know readily and enables each learner to see themself as having valuable knowledge. This intentional cohesiveness from home to school is one aspect of culturally responsive teaching (Hammond, 2014). To create this continuity, we need to rely on families as resources.

Families have much to contribute to our learning community as fellow learners and even as teachers. When we ask families to teach our learning community about their everyday routines, heritage languages, stories and songs, and traditions and celebrations, then we position every family as an expert. When we rely on families as resources, we leverage their strengths to benefit our learning community and we grow our appreciation of children's rich home lives. The following figure provides examples of each of these areas.

Component and Definition	Examples From Hazel Roblero, an Early Childhood Educator
Routines. When we ask, *What is a typical day like for you and your child?* we learn which school routines are familiar and unfamiliar, which home routines are significantly connected to school, and which home routines could be translated to school in order to improve our school day.	**Routines.** Hazel learns some families do not wear any shoes in their home and others regularly change into house shoes. This routine becomes a powerful area of expertise for children to lead and teach when the class learns to change into rain and snow boots and to tie shoes. Hazel also learns some families use the routine of packing snack or lunch as a special time to discuss the upcoming school day and some families regularly engage in a family meal with shared dishes. As a result, Hazel checks with every family about food allergies, and her class has none! Hazel and her teaching assistant create shared plates of snack while also allowing children to bring and enjoy their individual snacks.
Language. For some of our learners, school is a space where they are learning and speaking a new or additional language. We need to protect space for children to practice and connect their heritage languages by including books, songs, and labels in these languages. We can model being language learners by asking children and their families to teach our learning community words, phrases, and songs in their heritage languages. We can also empower families by communicating the value of deepening and expanding their children's heritage language.	**Language.** Hazel has books, board games, song books, and recipes in multiple languages that children borrow. Families help her create labels for classroom materials with photos and multiple languages. When Hazel's class studies plants, she takes a video of herself exploring her backyard, pointing to plants and naming them. She shares this video with families and asks them to share what they discover around their homes. One family, who speaks Karenni, makes a video of Mom pointing to different plants and parts of plants naming each in Karenni.
Songs and Stories. Often in early childhood, we use familiar children's songs and stories to create community and to contextualize and explore concepts and skills. However, what we consider familiar may not be familiar to all learners and their families. We need to discover the familiar songs and stories of each family, their favorite songs to sing and books to read together, their oral storytelling traditions, and the music of their homes. Sharing stories, books, songs, and music will help to ensure that our learning community welcomes and includes every learner and that our exploration of concepts and skills takes place in truly familiar contexts.	**Songs and Stories.** Hazel partners with her Spanish-speaking families to identify traditional children's songs and stories in Spanish and to pair them with traditional children's songs and stories in English. Some songs are familiar in both languages but others are unique. For example, when the class reads and sings variations of *There Was An Old Woman* to practice sequencing, they also read and sing variations of *La Rana Cantaba Debajo Del Agua*, a traditional children's song in Spanish that also practices sequencing. After singing the counting song *One Elephant*, a child's father teaches the class to sing *Un Elefante Se Balanceaba* with actions while a grandma teaches the class the same song in French.
Traditions and Celebrations. Every culture, religion, and family have their own unique traditions and celebrations that young children are learning about, looking forward to, and talking about. Learning about and respecting families' traditions and celebrations deepens our relationship with them and helps children to see difference as an opportunity to learn as well as to see commonalities among us all. To truly be a community of learners, we need to be a community.	**Traditions and Celebrations.** Hazel learned about *Gotcha Day* from a family who celebrates this special day each year to commemorate the day her family "got her" and she was adopted. On Eid-al Fitr, Hazel's learners of the Muslim faith celebrate with family visits and special meals. On the days before and after, her children are abuzz with excitement about seeing relatives, and Hazel intentionally engages her children in sharing and talking about this celebration.

CASE IN POINT

Darren Tinajero is a new educator having recently joined the staff of Lakeview Preschool. He is fluent in English and Spanish and has basic proficiency in sign language. Darren wants to learn more about his children and their families. When he meets with his first family, they ask why he wants to work with young children. He responds that he has a talent for languages and hopes to share that with his learners. He also notes that observing learning is magical and he enjoys the lightbulb moments when children acquire knowledge and skills. The family asks why he doesn't work with older children and he responds that he went to school to become an early childhood educator because his mother owned a childcare center.

> What advice do you have for new educators, like Darren, as they join the profession so that families develop trust with them?

Darren learns that this family values play time, especially sports. He also learns that they allow their children to eat with their fingers and have not yet taught them to use silverware. Further, this family has a lot of stories about their ancestors and they often reference extended family members in their conversations, such as "That reminds me of Uncle Leo who said . . ." or "Remember when Grandma Alma made the fudge and forgot the chocolate?"

> What can Darren do with this information? What advice do you have for the integration of this information into the classroom?

Learning about families' routines, languages, stories and songs, and traditions and celebrations are powerful starting points for building a two-way bridge between home and school. Our next step is to deepen this work by applying what we learn within our teaching, thus creating continuity of context through relying on families as resources. With this foundation, we can move toward the vision of working together as evaluators of learning growth, together we have high expectations for learning, we establish trust, and we continually seek feedback from families about our impact. In this way, we deepen our engagement with families to form true partnerships for learning.

PARTNERSHIPS FOR INCLUSION AND EQUITY

Another vital partnership within early childhood spaces is with our fellow educators—special educators, paraprofessionals, and specialists such as music teachers or physical therapists. Through partnership, our decisions ensure all our learners have equity of access and opportunity to the highest level of growth and learning. *This means all learners, regardless of their personal or social circumstances, have the access and opportunity to achieve their potential.*

Thus, we must seek to provide an inclusive environment for all learners—an environment that actively engages all learners, welcomes and embraces every learner as an important member of the community, and provides the necessary support to each learner so that they have an equal opportunity for success (see Jimenez et al., 2012; Spooner et al., 2011).

> *Early childhood inclusion embodies the values, policies, and practices that support the right of every infant and young child and his or her family, regardless of ability, to participate in a broad range of activities and contexts as full members of families, communities, and society. The desired results of inclusive experiences for children with and without disabilities and their families include a sense of belonging and membership, positive social relationships and friendships, and development and learning to reach their full potential. The defining features of inclusion that can be used to identify high quality early childhood programs and services are access, participation, and supports.* (DEC/NAEYC, 2009, p. 1)

REFLECTION

What is inclusion? Describe inclusion in your own words.	Compare and contrast this with what you witnessed or experienced as a learner yourself.

For us as early childhood educators, inclusion means that we must provide a wide range of experiences, tasks, and interactions that are accessible to every learner regardless of their unique identity profile. The experiences, tasks, and interactions must engage learners beyond compliance, but with a strong sense of belonging and efficacy. And finally, we must have strategic supports in place to ensure every learner's access and participation (DEC/NAEYC, 2009; NAEYC, 2019). Inclusion is based on the belief that all learners have the right to equity of access and opportunity to the highest level of learning possible.

We must also create an anti-racist, anti-bias learning community for all our members—a learning community that celebrates diversity, is asset focused, and is safe and supportive for every child and their family. As early childhood educators, we must start with ourselves and our reflections on our teacher identity, credibility, and self-efficacy; we began this work in Module 1. From a space of awareness and intentionality, we can work to actively disrupt injustice by taking an anti-racist and anti-bias stance and by actively building our partnerships with learners, families, and fellow educators.

All children have the right to equitable learning opportunities that help them achieve their full potential as engaged learners and valued members of society. Thus, all early childhood educators have a professional obligation to advance equity. They can do this best when they are effectively supported by the early learning settings in which they work and when they and their wider communities embrace diversity and full inclusion as strengths, uphold fundamental principles of fairness and justice, and work to eliminate structural inequities that limit equitable learning opportunities. (NAEYC, 2019, p. 1)

 **REFLECTION**

What is educational equity? Describe educational equity in your own words.	Compare and contrast this with what you witnessed or experienced as a learner yourself.

In early childhood, our learning communities can be intentionally anti-bias spaces, where children develop positive social identities, experience and celebrate diversity through caring connections, recognize and make sense of justice and injustice through empathy, and express activism to help others through agency and confidence (Derman-Sparks & Edwards, 2019; NAEYC, 2019). Much of this work mirrors the work to create an inclusive learning environment, and it relies on knowing and valuing our learners and their families. It also relies on our partnerships with fellow educators.

Our partnerships with fellow educators empower us to make this vision of inclusion and equity a reality in our early learning spaces. Like our partnerships with learners and families, we must begin from an asset-focused stance, believing each colleague brings strengths, perspectives, and experiences to be leveraged for the benefit of the whole teaching and learning community. Communication through both talking *and* listening is critical among partners. It is also important to have a common understanding of the partners' shared roles and unique responsibilities within those roles. Table 2.1 delineates the five roles within partnerships among educators as they work together to create inclusive and equitable learning spaces.

2.1   5 Roles and 4 Partners

Partner	Instruction	Assessment	Communication	Leadership	Recordkeeping
Roles of the General Educator	Teaching individuals, small groups, and whole class Monitoring learners' progress Implementing adaptations designed with special educator Implementing integrated concepts and skills with specialist	Conducting and documenting formative and summative evaluations Identifying significant junctures for self-, peer, and family feedback Implementing structures and routines for effective formative evaluation and feedback practices	Collaborating with special educator and specialist on curriculum Collaborating to analyze the effectiveness of implemented strategies, tasks, and adaptations Attending IFSP/IEP meetings Partnering with families	Designing structure and routines of the class Supervising paraprofessional and volunteers in class Providing partners with information on standards and curriculum	Recording daily and unit plans Maintaining attendance and assessment records Attending problem-solving meetings
Roles of the Special Educator	Teaching individuals, small groups, and whole class Adapting materials and instruction Coordinating supports for individual children	Administering educational tests Monitoring learners' progress through formative evaluation Identifying significant junctures for self-, peer, and family feedback	Collaborating with general educator and specialist on curriculum Collaborating to analyze the effectiveness of implemented strategies, tasks, and adaptations Attending IFSP/IEP meetings Partnering with families	Training and supervising paraprofessionals Facilitating the use of related service personnel	Developing IFSP/IEP Maintaining formative evaluation records Maintaining records of curricular adaptations

(Continued)

(Continued)

Partner	Instruction	Assessment	Communication	Leadership	Recordkeeping
Roles of the Paraprofessional	Following the instructional plans as implemented by the general educator Implementing adaptations designed by special educator Providing specialized assistance, including personal care Reteaching and facilitating deliberate practice	Assisting and supporting with formative evaluation Collaborating with general and special educators to monitor learners' progress	Collaborating to analyze the effectiveness of implemented strategies, tasks, and adaptations Assisting teachers in communication with families Maintaining communication with school personnel Honoring confidentiality of learners' information	Facilitating social relationships among children Creating a positive environment for learners Modeling effective communication strategies for other staff	Maintaining logs and time sheets as required to document contact time
Roles of the Specialist	Teaching whole class Monitoring learners' progress Implementing adaptations designed with special educator Implementing integrated concepts and skills with general educator	Collaborating with educators to monitor learners' progress Identifying significant junctures for self-, peer, and family feedback	Collaborating with general educator and special educator on integrated curriculum Collaborating to analyze the effectiveness of implemented strategies, tasks, and adaptations Attending IFSP/ IEP meetings Partnering with families	Designing structure and routines that complement the specialized class taking place within the class Supervising paraprofessional and volunteers in class Providing partners with information on specialized standards and curriculum	Recording daily and unit plans Maintaining attendance and assessment records Attending problem-solving meetings

Source: Adapted from Frey, N. (2003).

CASE IN POINT

Lizbeth Sandoval and Cynthia Pacheco are educators who have just started to collaborate; Cynthia was just hired as the new special educator for the preschool program. The previous special educator used a pull-out model and removed learners with disabilities from the class to provide specialized services. Lizbeth was worried that the children were missing interactions with peers and language development opportunities, not to mention that she did not know what the focus was and thus could not reinforce the skills that the special educator was providing. In addition to the two teachers, Tina Le is a paraprofessional in the class. The three of them had a planning meeting and quickly agreed that they could provide services to the learners in the regular classroom during centers, small groups, and whole group.

A few weeks later, the three teachers met to discuss their progress in meeting learners' needs. Lizbeth noted that she had a better sense of the needs of the children and she also saw a change in her own teaching to meet learners' needs when they were with her. Cynthia said that she really enjoyed being in the classroom and that the children in her small groups were really making progress. Tina shared that she wasn't sure what she was supposed to be doing during small groups and centers; she felt that she was just walking around and supervising and not doing anything that really helped the children.

Using the roles from Table 2.1, identify areas of clarity that the team might need to address.

Educator	Instruction	Assessment	Communication	Leadership	Recordkeeping
Lizbeth Sandoval					
Cynthia Pacheco					
Tina Le					

REFLECTION

Who do you partner with currently?

Return to Table 2.1 outlining *5 Roles and 4 Partners*. Which roles are **strengths** in your partnerships: instruction, assessment, communication, leadership, and recordkeeping? Circle or highlight these in the table. Then look below the roles and circle or highlight the responsibilities that are examples or evidence of these strengths.

Looking at the remaining roles, which one is priority for your team to bolster in order to achieve effective inclusion?

This is where your next conversation with your partners needs to begin.

CASE IN POINT

Sam Brooks, Maria Montiel, and Emma Vest have worked together for several years. Sam is a general educator, Maria is a paraprofessional, and Emma is a special educator. When he reflects on their partnership's roles and responsibilities, Sam notes many strengths in what they get done together as a team, but he also notes that they tend to talk about their children from a deficit point of view; "can't," "won't," and "don't" are frequently used. Their collaboration meetings follow a familiar pattern: Sam shares his frustrations about not reaching the same families, Maria lists off all the things she says the children can't, won't, or don't do; and Emma engages only when she can talk about "her kids." This pattern leaves all three educators feeling exasperated, defeated, and alone. Furthermore, Sam is seeing the impact of these conversations bleed over into their interactions with the children and their families. Sam has stopped trying to contact some families, Maria assumes learners can't or won't complete certain tasks or that they won't know something and will behave in a particular manner, and Emma only engages with the kids on her caseload. The children are now reacting to these assumptions by withdrawing.

Sam wants to disrupt his team's meeting pattern. He wants to operate from an asset-based mind frame during collaboration meetings. He reviews their collaborative roles and responsibilities and decides to begin with assessment. To help guide the conversation, Sam creates checklists for the whole team to use during choice time. They will each use the checklists to be on the lookout for specific concepts and skills that the children demonstrate. Every child is on every teacher's list. In this way, Sam, Maria, and Emma are intentionally looking for and documenting the strengths every child brings to learning. The checklist helps focus the collaboration meetings on sharing these strengths and seeing every learner as a critical part of the learning community. The checklist also reminds all three teachers that they share all of the learners and provides Sam with specific, strength-based celebrations of learning to share with families.

There is more work for this team to do in order to create an inclusive, anti-bias learning space. Using the roles from Table 2.1, identify other areas that could help create inclusivity and equity by shifting to an asset-based stance.

Instruction	Assessment	Communication	Leadership	Recordkeeping

 **REFLECTION**

Who else might be a powerful asset to your instructional practice for your children's learning and development? Perhaps a music teacher, occupational therapist, speech/language pathologist, community counselor, community activist, or a local bicycling initiative coordinator.

Brainstorm someone whose specialized knowledge could inform your teams' decisions for inclusion and equity, someone whose strengths could be leveraged for the benefit of the learning community in order to more effectively create access, participation, and supports and to intentionally take an anti-racist, anti-bias stance.

And now, let's consider our work specifically in this Playbook to learn about implementing instructional approaches and strategies with the potential to positively impact young children's learning and development. Think about the educators you already partner with. How can we invite those we partner with into this work? How can we share our current thinking and our deliberate practice? What might you do or say?

Our partnerships with fellow educators are a critical piece of collective teacher efficacy. Remember, working collaboratively has the potential to considerably accelerate learners' development. By building our expertise together, we can create inclusive, anti-racist, anti-bias learning spaces where *every* learner is valued and has the access and opportunity to become a Visible Learner.

VISIBLE LEARNERS

Knowing and valuing our learners as individuals is where we begin our partnerships. Let's also keep the goal of our partnerships in mind. Why are we intentionally working to develop these meaningful partnerships?

One of the hallmarks of early childhood education is child-centered or child-directed learning, where children's interests, discoveries, and questions lead the learning. Developing self-regulation, autonomy, and agency are often critical emphases of early childhood settings.

Our hope for young learners takes this core value a step further and deeper by making explicit young children's ownership of their learning journey. Our ultimate goal is to grow Visible Learners. In our Welcome, we first introduced the six characteristics of Visible Learners and you reflected on ways you are already intentionally growing these in your children (p. 5).

It may seem like too lofty of a goal to grow Visible Learners with infants and toddlers. But our work in early childhood is about laying the foundation for growing Visible Learners over time with *every* child. We can begin this work even with infants and toddlers by partnering with families.

Together, we should all intentionally model through our language and actions what it means to be Visible Learners. In other words, across all of our partnerships from learners to families to special educators and specialists, we need to take on the characteristics of Visible Learners ourselves.

 # REFLECTION

Let's return to the six characteristics of Visible Learners. Where do you see yourself within these characteristics? You may see yourself embodying these characteristics now, as you engage in learning about implementing instructional approaches and strategies with the potential to positively impact young children's learning and development. You may see yourself embodying these characteristics in other areas of your life—do you have a hobby you're learning more about? Are you attending school yourself while also teaching? In the right column, record the examples or evidence of when and how you demonstrated these characteristics.

(Continued)

(Continued)

We Are Visible Learners

Visible Learners	I Am a Visible Learner When I . . .
Know their current level of understanding; they can communicate what they do and do not yet know	
Know where they are going next in their learning and are ready to take on the challenge	
Select tools to move their learning forward	
Seek feedback about their learning and recognize errors as opportunities to learn	
Monitor their learning and make adjustments when necessary	
Recognize when they have learned something and serve as a teacher to others	

As you continue working in this Playbook and working toward your other projects and goals in life, keep noticing ways you are a Visible Learner. The more we notice, the more we can be intentional in implementing the characteristics ourselves. And the more we live as Visible Learners, the more we'll see opportunities to develop these characteristics in our young learners.

These characteristics of Visible Learners bring the concept of Visible Learning into focus. Visible Learning is about *seeing learning through the eyes of our young learners and our learners seeing themselves as their own teachers.* When we intentionally grow Visible Learners, we are constantly seeing and communicating learning through the eyes of learners, and our learners develop self-regulation, autonomy, and agency to own their learning. This does not mean that we sit back and watch as children teach themselves; it means we learn from and partner with children to maximize their learning and development.

Big Ideas

LEARNING INTENTION AND SUCCESS CRITERIA FOR MODULE 2

Now that you have engaged with the learning in this module, reread what we intended to learn (LI, the learning intention) and what it looks and sounds like to have mastered learning this (SC, the success criteria). Next, reread the levels, descriptions, and images of the path to mastery (the rubric). Reevaluate where you are right now for each success criteria. Use the box to reflect on the evidence you have of where you are and where you are headed next.

LI: We are learning the importance of partnering with our learners, their families, and our fellow educators, so that we can create inclusive, anti-racist, anti-bias learning spaces where educators and learners work together, trust is established, and feedback is valued.

SC: I'll know I've learned this when I can

Icon source: istock.com/rambo182

- Explain why partnerships with our learners, their families, and fellow educators are central to effective, inclusive, anti-racist, and anti-bias teaching, learning, and development in early childhood.

_____

_____

_____

_____

_____

- Describe what partnerships that are inclusive, anti-racist, and anti-bias look and sound like.

_____

_____

_____

_____

_____

(Continued)

(Continued)

- Identify and implement ways to build inclusive, anti-racist, and anti-bias partnerships.

_____

_____

_____

_____

_____

- Make connections among the big ideas for effective teaching, learning, and development in early childhood, these partnerships, and the characteristics of Visible Learners.

_____

_____

_____

_____

_____

3

INTENTIONAL INTERACTIONS FOR EQUITY AND INCLUSION

Children are always learning, both at home and at school. In our early childhood settings, we intentionally grow Visible Early Childhood Learners through our partnerships and through our interactions.

Interactions are the heart of early childhood education. Our intentional use of language within these interactions is critical to children's learning and development. This is where we should focus our time and energy as early childhood educators. To maximize the positive impact of our interactions, we take on the roles of conversational partner and language facilitator.

But we can't stop there.

We must intentionally use these roles of conversational partner and language facilitator to create equitable and inclusive spaces for *all* children. We do this important work by being intentionally inclusive, anti-racist, and anti-bias in our interactions. We do this by being culturally responsive. We do this by selecting language that reflects to *all* children a vision of themselves as confident, capable, and metacognitive learners. In other words, we reflect to *all* children a vision of themselves as Visible Learners.

This work is founded on the theme for Part 1: *who before do*. To intentionally interact with all children for equity and inclusion, we must know ourselves as educators, have a vision for who we want to become as expert educators, know our learners and their families, and value their partnerships with us.

LEARNING INTENTION AND SUCCESS CRITERIA FOR MODULE 3

Before you engage with the learning in this module, read what we intend to learn (LI, the learning intention) and what it'll look and sound like when we've learned this (SC, the success criteria). Next, read the levels, descriptions, and images of the path to mastery (the rubric). Evaluate where you are right now for each success criteria. At the end of the module, we'll return to this self-evaluation and document the ways we've intentionally grown our teaching practice over time.

LI: We are learning about the power of intentional interactions so that we can create equitable, inclusive early childhood spaces.

SC: I'll know I've been successful learning this when I can

Beginning	Emerging	Developing	Expanding	Bridging
Becoming aware 	Initially trying	Deliberately practicing 	Intentionally stretching	Transferring and generalizing

Icon source: istock.com/rambo182

- Describe what a conversational partner and a language facilitator are.

_____

_____

_____

_____

_____

- Analyze how being an intentionally inclusive, anti-racist, and anti-bias conversational partner and language facilitator can grow every child's identity, agency, positionality, and authority.

_____

_____

_____

_____

_____

- Identify strategies to take on the roles of conversational partner and language facilitator in order to create equitable, inclusive early childhood spaces.

_____

_____

_____

_____

_____

REFLECTION

Using the blank pie chart below, color in the percentage that reflects your beliefs about **conversations** in your classroom or center: **Who does most of the conversing? You or your learners?** If possible, use two different colors. For example, you may believe that 90 percent of the conversations are between your learners or led by your learners and 10 percent are led by you.

(Continued)

(Continued)

Let's do this one more time. Only this time, the pie chart reflects **the nature of the conversations**. What percentage of the conversations in your classroom or center are **around learning**? What percentage of the conversations are **around management and behavior**?

We hope your classroom space is filled with the voices of your learners. Language is the linchpin of early childhood. Every early childhood setting should be filled with talk, and not just any talk. They should be full of intentional talk, intentional language, and intentional interactions. Both conversational partners and language facilitators intentionally use interactions to positively impact children's learning and development.

CONVERSATIONAL PARTNERS

Important
Vocabulary

A conversational partner participates in tasks or play in order to intentionally engage children in talk. A conversational partner engages in co-play. By simply joining the existing talk, a conversational partner does not place any constraints or demands on language. As an insider and fellow participant, a conversational partner elicits responses from children within a familiar and safe space.

In this way, children more readily express their ideas using their preferred nonverbal and verbal communication strategies. All children have rich informal and nonverbal knowledge that may not be linked to formal language yet. Engaging in the role of conversational partner provides important insight into children's rich informal knowledge.

In the role of conversational partner, educators use three primary strategies to intentionally interact with children and elicit their language use. A conversational partner models language, asks questions, and engages in back-and-forth exchanges. Table 3.1 shows examples of these conversational partner strategies from across early childhood settings.

3.1 Conversational Partner Strategies

Conversational Partner Strategy	Model Language	Ask Questions	Engage in Back-and-Forth Exchange
With Infants	The teacher rolls a car into a block saying, "Roll. Boom! Roll. Boom!"	Playing Peek-a-Boo together, the teacher asks, "Where is Lincoln? Peek-a-Boo! There's Lincoln!"	Sitting facing each other, the child squeals, "aaaaaa" and the teacher repeats with the same tone. The child repeats, then the teacher repeats getting a little louder each time and then getting a little quieter each time.
With Toddlers	The teacher talks while stacking cups, "Up, up, up." The child knocks the tower over. The teacher says, "Down, down, down."	Playing with a toy barn, the teacher asks, "Time to eat! What do we have to feed the animals?" The child holds out a toy apple and signs "apple." The teacher says and signs, "Apple!" and then adds, "Animals love to eat apples!"	While putting clothes on stuffed animals, the teacher holds a hat saying, "Here's a hat." The child points to the pig and says, "Pig hat." The teacher responds, "Time to put your hat on, Pig."
With Preschoolers	While outside, the teacher bends down and points to a large leaf, "Wow! This is a large leaf. It is larger than my hand!" Children begin to compare their hands to the leaf.	The teacher joins the art center where multiple children are painting on one blue background. The teacher asks, "What are you painting?" Children respond, "Ocean. I make fishies!" "I make shark." "Jellys." The teacher summarizes, "So we have fish, shark, jellyfish. What could I paint?" Children make suggestions, "Dolphin." "Whale." "Ocka-, ocka-, I forget," Ilias suggests and gets stuck. The teacher responds, "Wow, you know so many ocean animals. I'm going to paint an *octopus*! Thank you for the idea, Ilias."	While building with blocks, the teacher says, "I'm going to build a grocery store right here in our town." The child says, "I go grocery shopping with my mommy. And I get popsicles from the other place next door." The teacher responds, "You can build the popsicle store next to the grocery store!"

(Continued)

Conversational Partner Strategy	Model Language	Ask Questions	Engage in Back-and-Forth Exchange
With Primary Schoolers	Two children are looking at an *Elephant and Piggie* book by Mo Willems. The teacher sits down and says, "This book must be very hilarious! Elephant and Piggie sure do get into some funny situations! They make me laugh!"	At the counting jar center, the teacher says, "I can't see all the marbles in the jar so I'm trying to estimate how many there are. How many marbles do you estimate are in the jar?" The child responds, "Maybe 15?" The teacher replies, "You estimate 15 marbles. How did you think of that?" The child replies, "I can see 10 but I can't see some."	The child has written a letter to grandma and reads it to the teacher. The teacher says, "I can see spaces between your words!" The child explains, "That's so Grandma can read my words." The teacher confirms, "Yes, those spaces help us read your writing. What are you working on next?" The child responds, "I am going to make sure I have big letters at the starts." The teacher replies, "Capital letters will help your grandma know when a new sentence begins. While you check the beginnings, also check for end marks."
My Examples			

CASE IN POINT

Araceli Camacho is seated at a table with three children. They each have a toy and she asks each child to talk about their toy. As the first student shares, the other two become very distracted. One of the children is banging the toy on the table and the other starts talking about going home. Ms. Camacho regains the attention of her learners and they listen to their peer for a short time. When the second child is invited to share, the first child gets out of the chair and begins to walk again. The other learner begins to bang their toy on the table.

How might Ms. Camacho revise this learning experience by being intentional with modeling language, asking questions, or engaging in a back-and-forth exchange?

LANGUAGE FACILITATORS

A language facilitator can remain an outsider or can be a participant in the task or play; however, a language facilitator explicitly supports the use of specific, often novel, language involved in the task or play. By being present in the moment, a language facilitator is able to assist the practice and transfer of certain vocabulary, language structures, and language functions. A language facilitator is also able to give feedback in the moment to refine and clarify language use.

Important Vocabulary

In the role of language facilitator, educators use four primary strategies to intentionally interact with children and assist in their language practice and transfer. A language facilitator narrates actions, thinks aloud, and prompts and scaffolds language as children engage in a task or play alone or with peers. Table 3.2 shows examples of these language facilitator strategies from across early childhood settings.

3.2 Language Facilitator Strategies

Language Facilitator Strategy	Narrate Action	Think Aloud	Prompt Language	Scaffold Language
With Infants	The child is shaking a rattle and the teacher narrates, "Shake, shake. Shake, shake."	The child covers a stuffed animal with a blanket. The teacher models thinking aloud, "Where's elephant now? Is elephant under the blanket? Peek-a-Boo! There's elephant!"	The child picks up a monkey toy and shows it to the teacher. The teacher says, "Monkey. What does a monkey say? Eee Eee Eee." The teacher waits for the child to make any sound and then says, "Yes! The monkey goes eee eee eee."	Tapping plastic donuts together, the teacher sings and models, "Tap, tap, tap your toys. Tap along with me." The teacher then asks, "Can you tap?" When the child does not start tapping, the teacher uses hand-over-hand to help the child tap toys while singing again.

(Continued)

(Continued)

Language Facilitator Strategy	Narrate Action	Think Aloud	Prompt Language	Scaffold Language
With Toddlers	The child puts shapes into the sorter and the teacher narrates, "In. In. In. Putting shapes in." The child dumps shapes out of the bucket and the teacher narrates, "Ouuuuuut! Pouring shapes out!"	The child bounces to music. The teacher models thinking aloud, "Dancing! Dancing! I love dancing when I hear music! Music makes me happy!"	The child is looking at a book and pointing to pictures, sometimes saying sounds, signs, or words for familiar pictures. The teacher points to the sun and prompts, "What's that?" The child says, "Sun." The teacher extends, "Sun. Remember when we looked for the sun in the sky but it was hiding behind clouds?"	The child is outside standing, pointing to the slide and grunting. The teacher says and signs, "Slide. Do you want to go on the slide?" The child calms down and reaches for the teacher's hand. The teacher says and signs, "Slide. Slide. Slide. Your turn." The child moves their hands like the sign as the teacher repeats, "Slide," and then celebrates, "Yes! That's how you say slide. Let's walk to the slide!"
With Preschoolers	The child is building a marble run and the teacher narrates, "That marble has to travel down the long yellow tube, through the spinner, and out the chute! I can't wait to see it!"	While reading aloud a nonfiction book about whales, the teacher pauses to share his thinking, "I wonder if whales ever sleep. They could be diurnal, like us—they sleep at night. Or they could be nocturnal, like the coyotes we read about—they sleep during the day. Maybe this book will tell us if whales sleep at night or during the day."	The child is waiting by the teacher with a coat on, looking at the zipper. The teacher asks, "Do you need help with your coat?" She waits for the child to respond. The child shakes his head yes. The teacher prompts, "Yes, you do need help with your coat. It looks like something is stuck. What's stuck?" The child says, "My zipper."	The child is playing at the pretend kitchen and the teacher asks, "What is for dinner tonight?" The child responds, "baghetti!" The teacher replies, "I love /SSS/paghetti! Let's say that fun word together. Look at my mouth and make your mouth look like mine. We are going to sound like snakes. Ready? /SSSSSS/paghetti!"
With Primary Schoolers	The child is making a pattern using different kinds of buttons. "I notice you are building an ABC pattern. I see a large button, a medium button and then a small button. Large, medium, small, large medium, small."	Children and the teacher are getting ready to go outside. The teacher says, "Oh no! I have a problem and I'm frustrated! I lost my clipboard. Let me take a deep breath. (*dramatic deep breath*) Now, I'm going to think about the last place I saw my clipboard. (*pause*) Oh I remember! It is over by the door."	The child comes up to the teacher crying and pointing to the sidewalk. The teacher asks, "Oh no, did something happen on the sidewalk?" The child replies, "I fell and hurt my knee!"	At morning circle, the teacher says, "Today we are pretending to go on a trip to a mountain and you can bring three things that begin with the /mmm/ sound. You will start your sentence like this, 'I am going to the mountain and I will bring . . .'"

Language Facilitator Strategy	Narrate Action	Think Aloud	Prompt Language	Scaffold Language
My Examples				

REFLECTION

Reflect on your classroom or center. Think back to times when you recently took on each of the roles—conversational partner and language facilitator. Or think about a typical time of day in your classroom or center when you could take on one of the roles. **Record examples of what you said or could say in the last row of Table 3.1 and Table 3.2.** *Remember, the key difference between the two roles is whether you are a participant in the task or play eliciting language (conversational partner) or whether you are an observer or participant explicitly supporting specific language (language facilitator).*

IDENTITY, AGENCY, POSITIONALITY, AND AUTHORITY

Through our intentional interactions, we can purposefully take an inclusive, anti-racist, and anti-bias stance. We can grow *every* child's positive identity, who they are and who their family is. We can develop *every* child's agency, or initiative, self-regulation, and problem-solving. We can position *all* children as competent or capable members of our learning community. And, we can share our authority with *all* children so that they become active decision-makers who own their learning (Berry & Thunder, 2012).

Important Vocabulary

From singing songs to reading books, from pretending to building, from sharing meals to getting dressed to go outside, and from counting to drawing, we need to examine the decisions we make in each interaction as we take on the roles of conversational partner and language facilitator. How are we using these interactions to intentionally grow children's identity, agency, positionality, and authority?

REFLECTION

Let's look at some examples from early childhood classrooms and centers. In the column on the right, identify how the teacher is using the roles of conversational partner and language facilitator to grow *every* child's identity, agency, positionality, or authority. In the final row, add your own example of a time when you did or when you could intentionally interact with your learners to promote equity and inclusion.

Examples of Intentional Interactions for Equity and Inclusion	How is the teacher using the roles of conversational partner and language facilitator to grow every *child's identity, agency, positionality, and/or authority?*
With Infants: *Ms. Brittney is reading* The Family Book *by Todd Parr (2019) with two infants. As she reads, she thinks aloud making connections between the different types of families and their families, "This family looks like my tiny family—just me and my doggie. This family looks like Anna's family." Ms. Brittney also asks questions as she reads, "'All families like to hug each other!' I love to hug my doggie. Anna gives her daddy a hug every day when he comes to pick her up. Who do you like to hug, Jayden? I see you hug your sister and your grandma. I like to give you both hugs!"*	
With Toddlers: *Ms. Gaffney sees two toddlers pulling a garden hose and asks, "What did you discover?" Luna shrugs and Noah says, "Long." Ms. Gaffney replies, "It is long! Muy largo como una serpiente o una cuerda! Long like a snake or a rope. Have you seen one before? Has visto antes?" Ms. Gaffney purposefully speaks in both children's heritage languages. They both say yes. Ms. Gaffney scaffolds, "How do you use it? Como lo usas?" Noah says, "Wash car." Luna holds the hose and pretends to aim it while making a whoosh sound. Ms. Gaffney confirms their ideas in a mixture of English and Spanish, "This is a hose. Una manguera. You can use it to wash a car! Noah dice que puedes usarlo para llavar un auto. I use it to wash my dog. Lo uso para lavar a mi perro. Luna, esa es la forma correcta de sostener una manguera para lavar—you hold it just like that! Hose. Manguera." The children*	

repeat the word in both English and Spanish. Ms. Gaffney asks in Spanish, "Luna, can you show Noah how to hold the hose to wash his car?"	
With Preschoolers *Eli is working on several self-help skills, including pulling up his pants after using the bathroom, putting his shoes on, and putting on and zipping up his coat. One day after successfully getting his pants up all by himself, Ms. Harrison says, "Eli! You have learned how to pull up you pants all by yourself!" She shows him the visual chart with pictures of the three skills he needs to learn. Then she says, "Now it's time to choose which skill you want to work on next. You can choose: putting on you shoes or your coat. Which would you like to work on next?" "Shoes!" Eli replies. "Ok, you want to work on putting on your shoes. Let's make a plan!" replies Ms. Harrison.*	
With Primary Schoolers *Mr. James is outside with his class when two children run to him, clearly upset and yelling at each other. "I can see there is a problem and that you are upset. Please tell me what is wrong." Shiane points and yells, "It's my turn with the pogo stick! She's had it the whole time!" Margo replies, "I need to have it longer because I can't do it yet! I'm trying but I keep falling over!" Mr. James gives both girls a chance to explain their perspective and then reflects back to them the problem by saying, "It seems Shiane wants a turn and Margo is feeling frustrated trying to learn how to use the pogo stick. Unfortunately, we only have one pogo stick to share. How can we make this work?" Mr. James pauses to give thinking time. When the girls don't say anything, Mr. James offers, "Shiane, do you think you could give Margo some tips on using the pogo stick?" Shiane says, "Sure. And then after you have practiced a few times, I can take my turn." "Margo, do you think this plan sounds fair?" Mr. James asks. Margo replies, "Yes! I would love some help. And watching you do it may help me too!"*	
My Example	

CASE IN POINT

Shana Mawyer is getting ready to read aloud *The Hike* by Alison Farrell (2019), but she tells her paraprofessional, "Our kids don't know what a hike is. They don't have the experiences that everyone else has, like going on a hike, so they don't have the background knowledge to make sense of this book." The paraprofessional, Rae Davis, points out, "I had never been on a hike until last year. My family didn't have a car so we walked everywhere. I think that's really similar to many of our kids. They do a lot of walking and looking around and observing while they walk. I bet they've gotten lost and had to find their way back too. Those are all important parts of hiking."

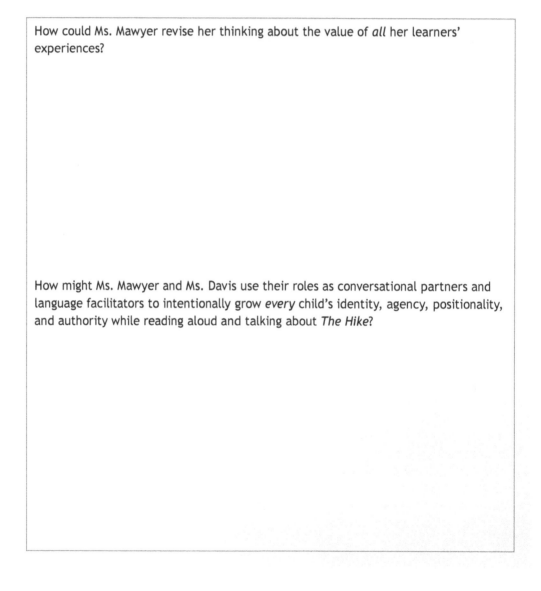

How could Ms. Mawyer revise her thinking about the value of *all* her learners' experiences?

How might Ms. Mawyer and Ms. Davis use their roles as conversational partners and language facilitators to intentionally grow *every* child's identity, agency, positionality, and authority while reading aloud and talking about *The Hike*?

Our early childhood settings are richly filled with culturally, linguistically, and ability diverse children. When we see our interactions through the lens of equity and inclusivity, we can intentionally plan for language-based interactions that welcome, value, and include *every* child.

LEARNING INTENTION AND SUCCESS CRITERIA FOR MODULE 3

Now that you have engaged with the learning in this module, reread what we intended to learn (LI, the learning intention) and what it looks and sounds like to have mastered learning this (SC, the success criteria). Next, reread the levels, descriptions, and images of the path to mastery (the rubric). Reevaluate where you are right now for each success criteria. Use the box to reflect on the evidence you have of where you are and where you are headed next.

LI: We are learning about the power of intentional interactions so that we can create equitable, inclusive early childhood spaces.

SC: I'll know I've been successful learning this when I can

Beginning	Emerging	Developing	Expanding	Bridging
Becoming aware 	Initially trying	Deliberately practicing 	Intentionally stretching	Transferring and generalizing

Icon source: istock.com/rambo182

- Describe what a conversational partner and a language facilitator are.

_____

_____

_____

_____

- Analyze how being an intentionally inclusive, anti-racist, and anti-bias conversational partner and language facilitator can grow every child's identity, agency, positionality, and authority.

_____

_____

_____

_____

_____

(Continued)

- Identify strategies to take on the roles of conversational partner and language facilitator in order to create equitable, inclusive early childhood spaces.

_____

_____

_____

_____

_____

PLAYFUL LEARNING

4

Who before do means we know ourselves, our early childhood partners, and the significance of our interactions for welcoming, valuing, and including every child. Now, we begin to make sense of how knowing *who* informs what we *do*.

We have a unique role in children's lives. We are their teachers. And with this role comes awesome responsibility. We make decisions in partnership with families and learners, and yet, with a different lens than families and learners. Our decisions are instructional decisions. Our goal is to maximize children's learning and development within the settings of our classrooms and centers. We aim for at least a year's worth of developmental growth or learning gains for each of our learners.

We are engaged in this Playbook because we know we can use research to identify what works best in teaching, learning, and development. We are seeking to understand and know what works best when, what really matters in early childhood, and what is worth our time and energy as early educators.

In early childhood, one thing we all do is play.

REFLECTION

Using the space provided, what do you mean by "play" in your learning environment? How does play support growth and development in your learners?

Let's consider these questions as we examine play in early childhood education.

LEARNING INTENTION AND SUCCESS CRITERIA FOR MODULE 4

Before you engage with the learning in this module, read what we intend to learn (LI, the learning intention) and what it'll look and sound like when we've learned this (SC, the success criteria). Next, read the levels, descriptions, and images of the path to mastery (the rubric). Evaluate where you are right now for each success criteria. At the end of the module, we'll return to this self-evaluation and document the ways we've intentionally grown our teaching practice over time.

LI: We are learning about the intersection of play and our intentional interactions so that we can enter children's play in ways that value and maximize playful learning.

SC: I'll know I've learned this when I can

Beginning	Emerging	Developing	Expanding	Bridging
Becoming aware 	Initially trying	Deliberately practicing	Intentionally stretching	Transferring and generalizing 

Icon source: istock.com/rambo182

- Explain the significance of playful learning by design, not by chance.

_____

_____

_____

_____

- Describe the three characteristics of guided play that make play particularly impactful for learning.

_____

_____

_____

_____

- Intentionally enact our roles as conversational partner and language facilitator within playful learning.

_____

_____

_____

_____

- Value what children bring to play and what they learn within play while also intentionally maximizing learning through our instructional decisions.

_____

_____

_____

_____

_____

As we start our conversation about play, we begin with *who*. We center our thinking around our learners and the rich experiences and knowledge they bring to play. And then we consider how we enter their play, a space that is natural and precious. As educators, how are we part of children's play?

REFLECTION

In your mind's eye, step into your classroom or center while your children are engaged in play and reflect on these questions:

Where are your children and what are they doing?

What is in the play space and how are the materials chosen?

Where are you and what are you doing?

Where are the other adults and what are they doing?

What happens right before your children begin play?

What happens right after they end play?

How do you decide if play time is successful?

We can remember when our classrooms' play time involved us watching from the side, occasionally circulating and observing. We measured success by a lack of arguments and injuries. Some children learned something during play time but not every child, and we didn't know who learned what. Does this sound familiar to you? In this case, the learning during play was by chance, not by design. But as educators, we should ensure *every* child learns and that we know what they each learned throughout our day.

PLAYFUL LEARNING BY DESIGN, NOT BY CHANCE

Learning through play experiences requires more than simply time and space to play. In fact, when researchers examined the relationship between pretend play and learning, they could not find evidence that merely engaging in pretend play *causes* any significant development in children (Lillard et al., 2013). Play is typically motivating, which helps create a context for positive engagement and interactions. Learning can happen in pretend play because it is often rich with positive adult-child interactions and language; it is a context for a lot of talk. However, the researchers found that the critical link did not exist between play and learning but between adult-child interactions and learning. It is the language-based interactions that *cause* learning.

So, what really matters in play? What should we spend our time and energy planning, implementing, and building our expertise about? Our language-based interactions with children—the way we enter children's play with talk.

Early childhood programs should strive to create intentional, rich, positive, language-based interactions. It is our language within our interactions that matters most. As we examined in Module 3, it is through our interactions that we create inclusive and equitable learning spaces for every child. This includes our play spaces. Our interactions in play have the potential to accelerate learning.

And so, we must reframe what we emphasize about play. At the intersection of play and our intentional interactions with children is playful learning.

Playful learning includes all forms of play and encompasses all the learning experiences of early childhood. In playful learning, the adult is intentionally interacting with the child while maintaining a sense of playfulness.

Playful learning has been described as mindset, where learning is approached as empowering, meaningful, and joyful (Mardell et al., 2021). This means that even deliberately and explicitly teaching a concept or skill should harness the playful curiosity of our youngest learners. In playful learning, we intentionally cultivate multiple strategies, perspectives, and surprises through reasoning, creativity, and problem-solving. We enter playful learning with the expectation that children will bring their funds of knowledge, wonder, and unique ideas.

Playful learning can be both child and adult initiated. Playful learning can include pretend play, inquiry and exploration, and direct instruction. In each of these settings, language makes learning explicit; by naming objects, processes, and ideas, we make them retrievable and transferable to new contexts. Our intentional interactions as conversational partners and language facilitators transform nonverbal learning into verbal inquiry, placing new information in memorable chunks that can be accessed and applied.

In order to create opportunities for *every* learner to meaningfully and joyfully learn through play, we must engage in playful learning by design and not by chance. We must shift to focus on intentional playful learning in all early childhood contexts rather than merely creating opportunities for open play or free play (Hirsh-Pasek et al., 2009; Lillard et al., 2013; Skene et al., 2022).

 # REFLECTION

Playful learning can be a mindset, a way of thinking about all learning in early childhood.

> In your own words, how would you describe **playful learning** and why it's important?

Let's take a moment to reflect on the ways we are already successfully creating a sense of playful learning in our classrooms and centers. And then, let's use our partnerships with learners, our *who before do*, to expand or deepen our playful learning.

(Continued)

(Continued)

How is playful learning already evident in your classroom or center? How are you harnessing the creativity of your young learners?	How do you already encourage multiple strategies, perspectives, and surprises from your learners?	What do you know about your learners' interests, curiosities, and senses of humor that you could leverage to expand or deepen playful learning?

THE PLAY CONTINUUM

The mindset of playful learning is one way to consider the way we enter play. Another is the play continuum, where the roles of the adult and child change as you move from one end to the other end. At one end of the play continuum is free play or open play, where the play is completely child directed and the adult is, at most, an observer. At the other end of the play continuum is direct instruction, where the play is completely adult directed and the child is a participant.

It may seem strange to include direct instruction on the play continuum, but sometimes in play, adults direct what and how to engage in playful activities. For example, learning to play a game or a sport or to manipulate a toy can begin with direct instruction. With practice and continued play, the roles of the children and the adult may shift. Eventually the game, sport, or toy may become part of free play, where the adult steps completely out of play and becomes merely an observer throughout.

In the middle of this continuum is guided play.

4.1 Play Continuum

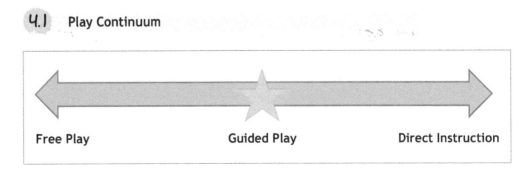

Free Play   Guided Play   Direct Instruction

Guided play includes all forms of play: physical play, object play, and pretend and sociodramatic play in indoor and outdoor environments. In guided play, both the adult and the child have significant roles: the adult engages with the child, either in co-play or by facilitating the play, and the child is an active decision-maker in the play. Guided play has also been called *facilitated play* and *enhanced play*.

REFLECTION

Using the blank continuum below, take a moment and review the Play Continuum by labeling the three broad types of play. Try to do this without looking back in the module.

4.2 **Blank Continuum**

Before moving on, provide specific examples from your own learning environment for each part of the continuum. List these below each type of play. Be specific in describing where this appears in your classroom.

There is value in every form of play along the continuum. In this Playbook, we are learning to enter children's play in ways that value and maximize playful learning; therefore, let's look closer at guided play. There are three defining characteristics of guided play (Skene et al., 2022):

1. The adult has a clear learning goal in mind and makes choices about setting up the play space and the playful activity based on that goal.

2. The child has opportunities to make choices and share their unique voice within the playful activity.

3. The adult engages with the child intentionally and responsively as a conversational partner and/or as a language facilitator.

Guided play capitalizes on the motivating and engaging parts of play while also creating an optimal learning experience within play. The child has voice and choice, which values what learners bring to and learn through play. At the same time, the adult intentionally creates the play space and playful activity with a particular learning goal in mind. And, the adult intentionally interacts with the child to maximize their learning. Guided play can maximize the potential of learning through play by ensuring *every* child learns and that the adult knows what is learned. In other words, in guided play, playful learning takes place by design and not by chance.

 **CASE IN POINT**

Daria Quintana has free play time in her early childhood classroom several times per day. She places items in various areas for children to interact with. Many of the items align with learning goals, such as blocks or items represented in the books that she reads aloud, and others are for "free imagination" as she says. Daria also has time allotted for practicing name writing, letter formation, and numeral formation. The children trace dotted lines on worksheets each day, and Daria uses letter and numeral flashcards for rote practice. However, the director of the program sent all the educators an article about playful learning and guided play and invited a conversation about the types of play that were being used in the classrooms.

Daria reflected on the playful learning approach and the three defining characteristics of guided play. She noted that children in her class played or practiced. When they played, the three conditions for guided play were not present. And when they practiced, there was nothing playful about the learning. In fact, as she told her colleague, "I supervise the play to make sure that no one gets hurt and that they get along. And I make sure everyone is seated practicing their letters and numbers every day. I think we need to revise our play time and our practice time to make them both more meaningful for learning."

What might be the first steps Daria and her colleagues could take to make the play more meaningful and move to a focus on guided play? What might Daria and her colleagues do to harness children's playful curiosity and make the direct instruction about letters and numbers reflect playful learning?

Priority Level (low, medium, high)	Action Step	Who Might Be Involved

Now, let's examine even more closely this intersection where play meets our intentional interactions and our instructional decisions. How can we intentionally take on the roles of conversational partner and language facilitator in guided play? How can our language-based interactions value what children bring to play and what they learn within play while also intentionally maximizing learning?

A CLEAR LEARNING GOAL

Children's play is valuable, and we must enter play with intentionality. In guided play, the adult has a clear learning goal in mind and makes choices about setting up the play space and the playful activity based on that goal. This is the first defining characteristic of guided play. We will dive deeply into setting learning goals and communicating these to learners and families in Part 2. We use the same planning process when we are planning for all forms of play (such as physical, object, and sociodramatic play both indoors or outdoors). We also use this planning process for all learning experiences because they should all be playful learning.

Big Ideas

Our eyes are always focused on our ultimate goal: to grow Visible Learners. Visible Learners are empowered with language, problem solving, self-regulation, and metacognition to own their learning journeys far beyond their early childhood experiences. Therefore, we focus on the teaching, learning, and development of overarching concepts and skills, also known as unconstrained skills (Durkin et al., 2022), that have vertical significance for Visible Learners. In Part 2, we will explore the ways discrete or constrained skills fit within the bigger picture of developing these overarching concepts and skills as well as the importance of making children's learning process visible through our interactions.

CASE IN POINT

Example	Reflection
Matías Castillo's toddlers are about to go outside. Before they leave the morning circle, Matías tells them with excitement, "Outside, there is something new to play with! There is a tent! It is next to the mud kitchen." Matías shows the class a picture of the tent next to the mud kitchen outside.	What do you notice about the example?

Example	Reflection
"We are learning about words to describe where we are. We can walk in the tent. We can walk out of the tent," Matías signs *in* and out *as he speaks. "Let's use our words with our hands and our mouths to say where we are when we play with the tent.* In. Out."	How does this example exemplify the role of a clear learning goal? How could you use this example in your own classroom?

PLAYFUL ACTIVITIES OR TASKS

Our planning process enables us to have a clear learning goal in mind, which guides our choices about setting up the play space and the playful activity. As we move forward, we will use *tasks* to refer to the different types of play and work young children engage in, including guided play and all playful learning. Tasks can be child or adult initiated, pretend, inquiry, exploration, or direct instruction. For example, tasks can be clapping toys together, stacking blocks, pretending to be the Three Billy Goats Gruff, singing a song, reading a book, sorting shells, putting together a puzzle, beading a necklace, and drawing a picture.

We know our learners and their families before we make decisions about what tasks we will do. Thus, with every task, we intentionally create opportunities to make meaningful choices and share learners' unique voices. This is the second defining characteristic of guided play. In Module 9, we will examine the characteristics of high-quality tasks for playful learning, including guided play. Voice and choice are central to high-quality tasks.

CASE IN POINT

Example	Reflection
Outside, Matías Castillo's toddlers can choose where they play within the fenced yard. Each space has materials and tools to support talk about where they are and where their toys are: in, out, around, next to, on, off.	What do you notice about the example?
Some children choose to go immediately to explore the new tent and begin walking in and out, waving from the windows. Others work at the mud kitchen, cooking on the stove, filling the sink with water, or stirring mixtures of mud and rocks to put in the oven. And others begin at the sandbox, digging holes and putting sand into buckets and dump trucks. The children move freely from space to space, delivering sand to the chefs, "eating" mud cakes in the tent, and rolling toy trucks from space to space. As they move and play, they talk.	How does this example exemplify the role of learners' choice and voice?
	How could you use this example in your own classroom?

THE GOLDILOCKS PRINCIPLE

The way the adult engages in guided play (and all playful learning) is paramount. This is the third defining characteristic of guided play. What really matters are the language-based interactions that are critical to learning and development. Intentional language is the center. Like all playful learning, guided play is rich with verbal inquiry. In Module 3, we began making sense of how we can intentionally take on the roles of conversational partner and language facilitator. We should assume these roles in all playful learning.

Whether we are insiders co-playing (conversational partners) or outsiders inserting, prompting, and scaffolding language (language facilitators), our interactions must be intentional and responsive. Intentional and responsive interactions meet each learner where they are, welcoming, valuing, and including every child, and then moving them toward the learning goal. Through our interactions, we create optimal learning experiences that fit the Goldilocks Principle (Hattie, 2008). The learning experiences are not too hard; too hard learning experiences place levels of cognitive demand on learners that exceed the limits of their working memory capacity. The learning experiences are not too easy; too easy learning experiences allow for mindless or passive engagement. Optimal learning experiences are just right, where children learn by design and not by chance. In guided play and all playful learning, the role of the adult is to help maintain this "just right" level of cognitive demand through their intentional interactions. In Parts 3 and 4, we delve into the strategies we use to create these just right learning experiences.

CASE IN POINT

Example	Reflection
Today, Matías Castillo is co-playing with the children at the tent while Isla Gerby, a paraprofessional, is facilitating language at the mud kitchen and sandbox.	What do you notice about the example?
Matías is a little pig along with Kieran. They are hiding in the tent while Azalea looks in the windows and huffs and puffs. Matías engages as a conversational partner. He models language, "Kieran, we are *in* the tent. Look at Azalea! She is *out* of the tent. She's huffing and puffing!" Azalea shouts, "Down!"	How does this example exemplify the role of adult as a conversational partner and/or language facilitator?
Matías asks a question, "Azalea, did you blow the tent *down* like the Big Bad Wolf?" Azalea shakes her head yes with a big smile. "We need to get *out* of the tent before she eats us! Where should we go, Kieran?"	How could you use this example in your own classroom?
Kieran points to the sandbox. Matías models, "Let's run *out* of the tent and go to the sandbox!" Kieran shouts, "Go out!" They hold hands and run out while Azalea chases them.	

CASE IN POINT

Courtney Melton's team has been struggling with behavior during recess. The teachers feel like they are constantly pausing their chats to break up arguments and attend to injuries. Upon returning from a field trip to an outdoor playscape, they all comment on how much smoother their time outside was and how many discoveries each child was excited to share. After some reflection, they decide to make their recess time more like the field trip experience: All the teachers will engage and interact with children during outdoor play.

Courtney's team makes this shift slowly over several weeks. First, they make a small change. They change the name of their play time outside from "Recess" to "Outdoor Choice Time" and their play time inside from "Centers" to "Indoor Choice Time." They communicate to children that both play times are spaces to make choices, whether indoors or outdoors. They also commit to engaging and interacting throughout both play times, rather than just watching and taking a break.

During lunch, Courtney and her teammates share that investing time interacting with the children outside has resulted in more joy for everyone. Moments that would have otherwise resulted in arguments or injuries have become learning moments because the teachers are immediately present to facilitate conversations and scaffold self-regulation. They start to notice common challenges and collaborate to plan mini-lessons to address them.

The next change begins when Courtney hears three children talking about what they will do together outside. They are making a plan. This reminds Courtney of their centers' routine: Plan-Do-Review. At the beginning, every child makes a plan for centers time. Then they all go to centers. At the end, the children review what they actually did by sharing. Courtney and her teammates decide to try using Plan-Do-Review for Outdoor Choice Time as well. Vocalizing plans and sharing their review allows the teachers to notice activities of interest and to scaffold joining play so all kids find a friend.

The team also realizes the depth and breadth of the children's outside play plans are lacking compared to their indoor play plans. Outside, they have access to playground equipment—a jungle gym, swings, and a sandbox. Courtney's team decides to try bringing additional play materials outdoors. They put some high-interest items (a crate of dinosaurs, several toy vehicles, sand tools, and chalk) on an old computer cart and roll it outside during Outdoor Choice Time. They take photos of the supplies and tape the images to the side of the cart. They assign three children to be supply managers—in charge of rolling the cart in and out and checking that everything is returned to the cart.

Now, children are beginning to request items be added to the cart based on their plans. Courtney's team agrees to spend the next Outdoor Choice Time noticing using the *Learning About Learners Protocol* (p. 30). Then they will meet as a team to share their noticings and decide next steps.

Courtney's team is shifting their outdoor time from free play to guided play, but they're not done yet. Based on the three defining characteristics of guided play, give Courtney's team feedback. *What have they implemented well?* These are their **glows**. *Where do you see opportunities to continue their work toward full implementation of guided play? How can they use their noticings from the* Learning About Learners Protocol *to implement the three defining characteristics?* These are their **grows**.

Grows	Defining Characteristics of Guided Play	Glows
	The adult has a clear learning goal in mind and makes choices about setting up the play space and the playful activity based on that goal.	
	The child has opportunities to make choices and share their unique voice within the playful activity.	
	The adult engages with the child intentionally and responsively as a conversational partner and/or as a language facilitator.	

Whether we work toward adopting a playful learning mindset or implementing the three defining characteristics of guided play, we need to reframe how we think about play. We need to bring intentionality to the ways we enter children's play, and especially, to our language-based interactions. We need to engage in playful learning by design, not by chance.

LEARNING INTENTION AND SUCCESS CRITERIA FOR MODULE 4

Now that you have engaged with the learning in this module, reread what we intended to learn (LI, the learning intention) and what it looks and sounds like to have mastered learning this (SC, the success criteria). Next, reread the levels, descriptions, and images of the path to mastery (the rubric). Reevaluate where you are right now for each success criteria. Use the box to reflect on the evidence you have of where you are and where you are headed next.

LI: We are learning about the intersection of play and our intentional interactions so that we can enter children's play in ways that value and maximize playful learning.

SC: I'll know I've learned this when I can

Icon source: istock.com/rambo182

- Explain the significance of playful learning by design, not by chance.

_____

_____

_____

_____

_____

- Describe the three characteristics of guided play that make play particularly impactful for learning.

_____

_____

_____

_____

_____

- Intentionally enact our roles as conversational partner and language facilitator within playful learning.

_____

_____

_____

_____

_____

- Value what children bring to play and what they learn within play while also intentionally maximizing learning through our instructional decisions.

_____

_____

_____

_____

_____

PART II

COMMUNICATING CLARITY

5

STANDARDS AND INTEGRATION

When we have clarity about our teaching, we can make impactful decisions about what children are learning, why, and how we'll know when they've learned it. And, we can help make sense of what they do and do not yet know and where they are going next in their learning. This decision-making process requires deep understanding of standards and learning expectations.

Big Ideas

LEARNING INTENTION AND SUCCESS CRITERIA FOR MODULE 5

Before you engage with the learning in this module, read what we intend to learn (LI, the learning intention) and what it'll look and sound like when we've learned this (SC, the success criteria). Next, read the levels, descriptions, and images of the path to mastery (the rubric). Evaluate where you are right now for each success criteria. At the end of the module, we'll return to this self-evaluation and document the ways we've intentionally grown our teaching practice over time.

LI: We are learning to deeply understand standards so that we can make decisions about what to teach when. To grow this expertise, we are analyzing standards and learning foundations, making sense of them in the early childhood context, and finding connections across developmental domains.

SC: I'll know I've learned this when I can

(Continued)

87

(Continued)

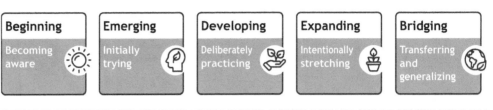

Icon source: istock.com/rambo182

- Analyze standards and learning foundations to identify concepts and skills.

_____

_____

_____

_____

_____

- Analyze standards and learning foundations for considerations of developmental variability, opportunity, access, and context, and cultural, linguistic, and ability diversity.

_____

_____

_____

_____

- Identify related standards and learning foundations for meaningful integration.

_____

_____

_____

_____

_____

- Brainstorm options for multidisciplinary, interdisciplinary, and transdisciplinary integration.

_____

_____

_____

_____

_____

Standards are sometimes called learning outcomes, learning foundations, goals, desired results, or learning expectations. We must know which significant and developmentally appropriate concepts and skills children should be learning and when, in order to know which concepts and skills to intentionally teach. Quality, early learning standards describe significant, developmentally appropriate content and outcomes. Your program may use its own learning expectations, curriculum-based standards, state early-learning goals, foundations, or progressions, national organizations' standards, Head Start Early Learning Outcomes, or Common Core State Standards for Grades K-2.

 # REFLECTION

Take a few minutes to identify the learning expectations your preschool, program, or center uses to make instructional decisions. For example, in one program where Kateri taught, they used the state-created early childhood standards supplemented by their adopted curriculum's standards. Kateri had to know where these two sets of standards aligned and where they differed as she made decisions about what to teach when. In the preschool that Doug and Nancy lead, the focus is on the California Preschool Learning Foundations.

What standards, learning outcomes, goals, desired results, or learning expectations do you rely on? Where are the standards located or how do you access them?

As we engage with any standards, we must also be informed about and appreciate the ways in which early childhood standards pose both opportunities and challenges (NAEYC/NAECS, 2002).

Important Vocabulary

Developmental Variability: Our youngest learners' development varies greatly, which means children may not meet learning outcomes at the pace set by the standard. Standards describe general and average milestones, yet deviation from that timeline is expected.

Opportunity, Access, and Context: Our youngest learners' development depends upon opportunity and access to experiences within familiar and unfamiliar contexts. Discontinuities in contexts as well as lack of opportunity and access may camouflage our youngest learners' capabilities. It is our responsibility to create continuity, opportunity, and access.

Cultural, Linguistic, and Ability Diversity: Our youngest learners are culturally and linguistically diverse learners, which means the ways children demonstrate learning expectations may look and sound different across cultures and languages. Early childhood programs also include children with different abilities and developmental delays, who also demonstrate learning expectations at different paces and in different ways. We will fail to recognize children who demonstrate standards if we're not aware of and actively working to notice their different ways of showing and knowing.

Standards can be tools to guide and help us discover learning opportunities. They can inspire family partnerships in order to learn about children, cultures, and language. And they can empower us to ensure opportunity, access, and experience across contexts. Standards, however, should never be used to label, exclude, or restrict access to learners (NAEYC/NAECS, 2002).

To effectively use standards, we must first grow our expert knowledge of them. We must deeply understand the standards across developmental domains. We must grow our appreciation of and professional noticing of different ways to experience, show, and know the standards. In this module, we intentionally grow our expertise by analyzing standards, making sense of them in the early childhood context, and finding connections across developmental domains.

ANALYZING STANDARDS

Analyzing standards involves identifying and making sense of the concepts (or nouns) and the skills (or verbs). This is the first step in a planning process that we will learn about, model, and practice throughout Part 2.

Standards make explicit what children will typically be able to do by a particular age or developmental milestone. For example, this is one learning goal for infants from birth to 9-months-old in the socioemotional domain:

Child communicates needs to familiar adults by using a variety of behaviors, such as, crying, looking, smiling, pointing, dropping, reaching, or banging objects. (Office of Head Start, 2021)

First, we must identify a standard to intentionally teach. Often, we select a standard based on our knowledge of our learners—what they are ready for, what they are interested in, what they are curious about. In one program, the teacher knows her infants have wants and needs and that both she and her infants would benefit from intentionally developing behaviors to communicate these.

Infant: Birth to 9 Months (Standards from *Head Start Early Learning Outcomes Framework*, Office of Head Start, 2021)

Domain	Social and Emotional Development
Standard	Child communicates needs to familiar adults by using a variety of behaviors, such as crying, looking, smiling, pointing, dropping, reaching, or banging objects.

YOUR TURN!

What have you noticed your learners are ready for, interested in, or curious about?	What standard best encompasses this?

Standards describe the concepts children are making sense of as they learn and grow. The standards' nouns and noun phrases are the concepts.

Important Vocabulary

In the above infant socioemotional learning goal, the nouns or concepts are "familiar adults as resources" and "needs." Our youngest learners are making sense of the ways familiar adults can be resources to help them meet their needs.

Standards also describe the skills children are learning and practicing as they engage with the concepts. The standards' verbs and verb phrases are the skills.

In our example, the skills are "communicate" and "crying, looking, smiling, pointing, dropping, reaching, banging." *Communicate* is an unconstrained skill learners will engage with and expand upon throughout their learning journey and into adulthood. The other verbs are ways to enact the skill of communicating needs—subskills that are developmentally appropriate ways of communicating as an infant.

Domain	Social and Emotional Development
Standard	Child communicates needs to familiar adults by using a variety of behaviors, such as crying, looking, smiling, pointing, dropping, reaching, or banging objects.
Concepts (Nouns)	• Needs • Familiar adults
Skills (Verbs)	• Communicate

YOUR TURN!

Look back at the standard you identified for your learners.

Concepts (Nouns)
What nouns do you see in the standard? These are the concepts.
•
•
•

Skills (Verbs)
What verbs do you see? These are the skills.
•
•
•

As we analyze the standard, we also make sense of the meaning of the standard within the context of early childhood:

- **Developmental Variability:** In our example, the standard allows for variation in development by giving a range of ages from birth to 9-months-old. When learners do not appear to be approaching the standard within that age range, we should also consider the two other challenges for standards in early childhood.

- **Opportunity, Access, and Context:** Opportunity and access to experiences with familiar adults vary. For some infants, familiar adults may be few or many and may include other children. When infants join a new context with unfamiliar adults, we may not see the behaviors described in the standard *yet*; we must allow time to become familiar adults first.

- **Cultural, Linguistic, and Ability Diversity:** In addition, there are other behaviors not listed but used by infants to communicate their needs, depending on the infants' culture, language, and abilities, such as hearing and seeing abilities. To deeply understand, appreciate, and notice the diverse ways our learners may show this skill, we must collaborate with families and colleagues.

Considerations	Developmental Variability	Birth to 9 months
	Opportunity, Access, & Context	Who is familiar? How many familiar adults or older children do they engage with? Am I *familiar* yet?
	Cultural, Linguistic, & Ability Diversity	Ways of communicating beyond the standard: signs, grunting. Ask families what the child does already to communicate needs and wants.

 YOUR TURN!

Consider the standard you are analyzing.

Considerations	Developmental Variability	
	How does the standard allow for variation in development? Does it describe an age range?	
	What developmental variation might you expect?	

(Continued)

(Continued)

Considerations	Opportunity, Access, & Context What opportunities and access do each of your learners have to experiences, people, objects, etc., described in the standard? What are individual learners' familiar contexts for engaging in the standard's concepts and skills?	
	Cultural, Linguistic, & Ability Diversity How do your learners' already express the concepts and skills? What does it look like and sound like to demonstrate these concepts and skills in their family culture, using their family language, and/or with their unique abilities? What are different ways learners could show and know these concepts and skills?	

CASE IN POINT

Samantha Towers reviewed the California Preschool Learning Foundations (2008), specifically in the area of social and emotional learning. One expectation reads, "Children respond sympathetically to a distressed person and are more competent at responding helpfully" (p. 9). Ms. Towers analyzed the standard and noted that learners needed the skills to *respond sympathetically* and *helpfully*. And that they needed to recognize a *distressed person*. In talking with her team, Ms. Towers said, "None of our kids do this. Not a one. They are so self-centered. I'm not even sure where to start with this one. I've been so focused on their language development." Ms. Towers works in a federally funded program and enrolls children who live in poverty, most of whom speak Spanish at home.

If you were her colleague, how might you respond to help Ms. Towers? Consider the developmental variability, opportunity and access issues, as well as the cultural significance.

INTEGRATION

While early childhood standards are often organized into developmental domains, young children's growth occurs across domains simultaneously and interconnectedly. When we analyze standards, we also look for meaningful integration of standards across developmental domains. What standards have strong and meaningful connections? What standards would make sense to teach intentionally at the same time? While many standards could overlap, we typically look for between two and four standards to inform a unit of study. More than four standards are hard to teach with the same level of intentionality all at the same time.

When we look across the other standards in other developmental domains, we noticed many standards that could overlap with our original standard (shaded in green). But we focused on standards with strong, meaningful connections that could be intentionally taught simultaneously. With these criteria, we found three related standards. Then we analyzed those standards for concepts and skills.

Domain	Social and Emotional Development	Language and Communication	Cognition	Perceptual, Motor, and Physical Development
Standard	Child communicates needs to familiar adults by using a variety of behaviors, such as crying, looking, smiling, pointing, dropping, reaching, or banging objects.	Takes turns in nonverbal conversations by using facial expressions, sounds, gestures, or signs to initiate or respond to communication.	Engages in reciprocal imitation games, such as patting on a table or handing an object back and forth.	Coordinates hands and eyes when reaching for and holding stable or moving objects.

(Continued)

(Continued)

Concepts (Nouns)	• Needs • Familiar adults	• Conversations	• Partner (reciprocal) Games	• Hands • Eyes • Objects
Skills (Verbs)	• Communicate	• Takes turns • Initiate • Respond	• Imitate	• Coordinates • Reaching • Holding • Moving

YOUR TURN!

The green shaded box is for your original standard—the one you previously analyzed above. Look at the other standards you use through the lens of this green one. What other standards have a strong, meaningful connection? What other standards would it make sense to teach intentionally at the same time? Remember, you're looking for two to four standards total. When you've found them, list and analyze these standards for concepts and skills.

Domain				
Standard				
Concepts (Nouns)	• •	• •	• •	• •
Skills (Verbs)	• •	• •	• •	• •

When we look for closely related standards across developmental domains to intentionally teach together, we are beginning the work of integration. There are three types of integration: multidisciplinary, interdisciplinary, and transdisciplinary integration (Drake, 2012). We will brainstorm ideas for each type of integration, but then we will choose just one to implement.

Multidisciplinary Integration. We can identify a common theme that unites standards and provides a common context for working within each developmental domain. This is multidisciplinary integration.

Important Vocabulary

For example, looking across these standards (Office of Head Start, 2021), what common theme do you notice?

> **Social and Emotional Development Goal:** Communicates needs to familiar adults by using a variety of behaviors, such as crying, looking, smiling, pointing, dropping, reaching, or banging objects.

> **Language and Communication Goal:** Takes turns in nonverbal conversations by using facial expressions, sounds, gestures, or signs to initiate or respond to communication.

> **Cognition Goal:** Engages in reciprocal imitation games, such as patting on a table or handing an object back and forth.

> **Perceptual, Motor, and Physical Development Goal:** Coordinates hands and eyes when reaching for and holding stable or moving objects.

One early childhood educator identified the theme of *Peek-a-Boo* to unite the standards. By engaging infants with Peek-a-Boo books, songs, and toys, she was able to create a familiar context for interactions where she could intentionally practice goals across developmental domains.

Interdisciplinary Integration. We can also find overlapping standards or ways the developmental domains intersect through concepts (nouns) or skills (verbs). This is interdisciplinary integration.

Look back at the same four standards; what concepts (nouns) or skills (verbs) overlap or intersect? One early childhood educator noticed many of the concepts and skills overlap with nonverbal behaviors. She focused on the overarching concept of imitation—growing her infants' nonverbal behaviors through imitating gestures, facial expressions, sounds, and signs in a variety of contexts.

Transdisciplinary Integration. We can begin with the questions our learners are asking or the problems they encounter, and then we can examine the standards to find opportunities to answer their questions and solve their problems within each developmental domain. This is transdisciplinary integration.

For example, communicating needs or interests is a typical problem that infants are learning to solve. We can intentionally integrate multiple standards by imitating, pointing, and reaching for toys, books, and people to practice solving this problem in the moment. These standards could help solve many other problems too.

Here are the three types of integration possibilities that we brainstormed. We can now choose just one way to implement. Will we teach a unit on the Peek-a-Boo theme? Will we teach a unit focused on the overarching skill of imitation? Or will we teach a unit that emphasizes problem solving the question: *How do I communicate what I need or want?*

Integration Possibilities	**Multidisciplinary**	Peek-a-Boo Theme
	Interdisciplinary	Imitation
	Transdisciplinary	How do I communicate what I need or want?

YOUR TURN!

As you look at your two to four analyzed standards, what do you notice about their connections and relationships? Do you see a common theme? Or an overarching concept or skill? Do you see the answer to a question your learners have been wondering or a solution to a problem they have been encountering? Brainstorm possible integration opportunities. Then circle or highlight the one integration idea that you feel most confident and excited about implementing.

Integration Possibilities	**Multidisciplinary** A common theme that unites standards and provides a common context for working within each developmental domain	
	Interdisciplinary Intersecting or overarching concepts (nouns) or skills (verbs) from across developmental domains	
	Transdisciplinary Opportunities to answer learners' wonderings or solve their problems within each developmental domain	

Identifying the common concepts and skills in the standards helps us brainstorm integration possibilities. One is not better than another. The decision of which to implement depends on our self-efficacy to intentionally teach the standards' concepts and skills through one integration lens or another. Regardless of the degree of integration, these intentional connections enhance the unique characteristics of early childhood and positively impact children's learning (effect size of integrated curriculum = 0.40). Therefore, when we analyze standards, it is worth our time and energy to look for a way to integrate multiple standards across developmental domains.

As you identify and analyze standards, it is important to note that standards can take months or a whole school year for a child to master. As we continue in Part 2, we will look at ways to identify the chunk of the standard you are working on within a specific unit of study and within a specific day of learning.

MODELS/EXEMPLARS

Infant (Standards from *Head Start Early Learning Outcomes Framework*, Office of Head Start, 2021)

Domain	Social and Emotional Development	Language and Communication	Cognition	Perceptual, Motor, and Physical Development
Standard	Child communicates needs to familiar adults by using a variety of behaviors, such as crying, looking, smiling, pointing, dropping, reaching, or banging objects.	Takes turns in non-verbal conversations by using facial expressions, sounds, gestures, or signs to initiate or respond to communication.	Engages in reciprocal imitation games, such as patting on a table or handing an object back and forth.	Coordinates hands and eyes when reaching for and holding stable or moving objects.
Concepts (Nouns)	• Needs • Familiar adults	• Conversations	• Partner (reciprocal) Games	• Hands • Eyes • Objects
Skills (Verbs)	• Communicate	• Takes turns • Initiate • Respond	• Imitate	• Coordinates • Reaching • Holding • Moving

(Continued)

(Continued)

Considerations	Developmental Variability	Birth to 9 months			
	Opportunity, Access, & Context	Who is familiar? How many familiar adults or older children do they engage with? Am I *familiar* yet?	Who is familiar? Who does the child spend time interacting with? Am I *familiar* yet? How much time do I spend interacting with the child?	What objects are familiar, interesting? What opportunities does the child have to play imitation games? What access does the child have to objects for play?	What objects are familiar, interesting? What opportunities does the child have to reach and hold objects? What access does the child have to objects?
	Cultural, Linguistic, & Ability Diversity	Ways of communicating beyond the standard: signs, grunting. Ask families what the child already does to communicate needs and wants.	Ways of engaging in conversation beyond the standard: simultaneous/ mirrored sounds. Ask families what conversations look like and sound like in their homes and how the child participates.	What objects can they grasp? How does the child move their body confidently and comfortably? Ask families how the child already engages in imitation games or other games.	What objects can they grasp? How does the child reach, hold, or explore objects? Ask families what objects the child is particularly interested in and has access to at home. What does engaging with the objects look like and sound like?
Integration Possibilities	Multidisciplinary	Theme: Peek-a-Boo			
	Interdisciplinary	Overarching Concept and Skill: Imitation			
	Transdisciplinary	Problem: How do I communicate what I need or want?			

Toddler (Standards from *Belonging, Being, and Becoming: The Early Years Learning Framework for Australia*, Australian Government Department of Education and Training, 2019)

Standard	Outcome 5: Children are effective communicators.	Outcome 1: Children have a strong sense of identity.	Outcome 4: Children are confident and involved learners.	Outcome 5: Children are effective communicators.
	Children interact verbally and non-verbally with others for a range of purposes.	Children learn to interact in relation to others with care, empathy, and respect	Children resource their own learning through connecting with people, place, technologies, and natural and processed materials.	Children express ideas and make meaning using a range of media.
Concepts (Nouns)	• Purpose	• Care • Empathy • Respect	• Learning • People • Place • Technologies • Natural materials • Processed materials	• Ideas • Media
Skills (Verbs)	• Interact verbally & non-verbally	• Interact	• Resource • Connect	• Express • Make meaning

Considerations	**Developmental Variability**	These standards span birth through age 5 while also reflecting vertical standards that children will continue working on beyond age 5. Toddlers are focused on exposure to these standards, watching models, and imitating models with guidance and scaffolding.			
	Opportunity, Access, & Context	Who does the child spend time interacting with? Who is familiar? How does the child already interact verbally and non-verbally? Why does the child need or want to interact with peers?	Who does the child spend time interacting with? Who is familiar? How does the child already show care, empathy, or respect?	What are the child's experiences with experimenting, problem solving, trying? Is this done alone or with peers, siblings, cousins, neighbors, or adults? In what settings does the child explore and play?	How does the child express ideas verbally and non-verbally? With whom does the child express ideas? What media does the child prefer to use or have access to?

(Continued)

Considerations	Cultural, Linguistic, & Ability Diversity	Ways of interacting: imitation, gestures, facial expressions, sounds, signs, spoken words, exchanging, or sharing objects. Ask families what verbal and non-verbal interactions the child already uses or sees family members using.	Ways of showing care: offering toys or objects, hugging, moving closer, smiling, waving, saying hi, blowing kisses. Ways of showing empathy: mimicking facial expressions, body gestures, sounds, signs (crying when they hear crying). Ways of showing respect: saying or signing please and thank you. Ask families how the child already shows care, empathy, and respect. Ask families how they show care, empathy, and respect at home.	Ask families about their expectations for children resourcing their own learning and what people, places, technologies, and natural resources they do/could have access to. What specialized resources does the child need to learn to use?	Ways of expressing ideas non-verbally and verbally: music, dance, art, movement, construction, drawing, speaking, signing. Ask families how the child already expresses ideas, what media the child prefers and shows strengths in, and what media the family would like the child to try.
Integration Possibilities	Multidisciplinary	Theme: Music			
	Interdisciplinary	Overarching Concept and Skill: Learning Together			
	Transdisciplinary	Problem: How can I play *with* a friend using the same materials?			

Preschool (Standards from *California Preschool Learning Foundations*, California Department of Education, 2008)

Domain	Language and Literacy	Social Emotional Development	Language and Literacy
Standard	Demonstrate knowledge from informational text through labeling, describing, playing, or creating artwork.	Interact easily with peers in shared activities that occasionally become cooperative efforts.	Use language to construct short narratives that are real or fictional.

Concepts (Nouns)	• Informational text • Artwork	• Peers • Shared activities • Cooperative efforts	• Language • Short narratives • Real narratives
Skills (Verbs)	• Demonstrate knowledge • Labeling • Describing • Playing • Creating	• Interact	• Use language • Construct narratives

Considerations	Developmental Variability	These standards span ages 48 months to 60 months. These standards cover the growth of all children, including those with special educational needs and disabilities. While there are additional English-Language Development standards for English Learners, we will use those to make decisions about scaffolds and extensions.		
	Opportunity, Access, & Context	What experiences with informational text has the child had? What informational topics does the child show interest in?	What opportunities for peer interactions have the child had? What kinds of cooperative tasks does the child gravitate toward?	What opportunities to express a real or fictional narrative has the child had? In what ways does the child convey narratives? What does the child like to talk about?
	Cultural, Linguistic, & Ability Diversity	Partner with families to discuss any home experiences or materials children may have had with informational materials (i.e., books, shows, trips). Ways of labeling: pictures, letters/words, glued premade labels, stickers, etc.	Knowing various ways children interact with peers. Provide spaces and experiences that foster peer interactions in a way that students are familiar with.	What is the child's ability to recall and describe experiences? Know the vocabulary of common items you may see on a nature walk (i.e., bird, flower, tree, etc.) in the language of the children.
Integration Possibilities	Multidisciplinary	Nature Walks Theme		
	Interdisciplinary	Overarching Concept and Skill: Describe and label		
	Transdisciplinary	Wondering: What is in the natural habitat around my home and/or neighborhood?		

Primary (Standards from *Common Core State Standards* [for First Grade], National Governors Association Center, 2010)

Domain		Mathematics	Literacy
Standard		Distinguish between defining attributes (e.g., triangles are closed and three-sided) versus non-defining attributes (e.g., color, orientation, overall size); build and draw shapes to possess defining attributes.	• Define words by category and by one or more key attributes (e.g., a *duck* is a bird that swims; a *tiger* is a large cat with stripes).
Concepts (Nouns)		• Defining attributes • Non-defining attributes • Shapes	• Words • Category • Key attributes
Skills (Verbs)		• Distinguish • Build • Draw	• Define
Considerations	Developmental Variability	These standards are for mastery by the end of first grade. During first grade, children may be at varying points toward mastery.	
Considerations	Opportunity, Access, & Context	What shapes are children familiar with? What misconceptions around shapes do children typically hold (ex: a triangle is a triangle no matter which way it is oriented)? Where in the classroom environment or routines do children currently engage with shapes?	What experiences have children had with sorting and defining categories? Do children have experience generating labels for items? Do children have experiences describing a wide variety of objects and experiences?
Considerations	Cultural, Linguistic, & Ability Diversity	Partner with families to know the familiar shape names in the children's home languages. Think through various ways of recording shape names and similar and different attributes for the children to reference.	Partner with families to know familiar vocabulary in children's home language (i.e., shapes, colors, textures, sizes, etc.).
Integration Possibilities	Multidisciplinary	Shapes Theme	
Integration Possibilities	Interdisciplinary	Overarching Concept and Skill: Sorting	
Integration Possibilities	Transdisciplinary	Wondering: Does everything in the world have a shape?	

TEMPLATES

Planning Template

Now, it's your turn to bring this strategy to your work with your children. As you prepare to plan each unit of study, first begin by identifying the focal standard. Use this template to analyze the standard, find related standards to analyze, make sense of the standards in your context, and brainstorm integration options. This planning template is also downloadable.

Domain				
Standard				
Concepts (Nouns)		• • •	• • •	• • •
Skills (Verbs)		• • •	• • •	• • •
Considerations	Developmental Variability			
	Opportunity, Access, & Context			
	Cultural, Linguistic, & Ability Diversity			
Integration Possibilities	Multidisciplinary			
	Interdisciplinary			
	Transdisciplinary			

online resources

LEARNING INTENTION AND SUCCESS CRITERIA FOR MODULE 5

Now that you have engaged with the learning in this module, reread what we intended to learn (LI, the learning intention) and what it looks and sounds like to have mastered learning this (SC, the success criteria). Next, reread the levels, descriptions, and images of the path to mastery (the rubric). Reevaluate where you are right now for each success criteria. Use the box to reflect on the evidence you have of where you are and where you are headed next.

LI: We are learning to deeply understand standards so that we can make decisions about what to teach when. To grow this expertise, we are analyzing standards and learning foundations, making sense of them in the early childhood context, and finding connections across developmental domains.

SC: I'll know I've learned this when I can

Beginning	Emerging	Developing	Expanding	Bridging
Becoming aware	Initially trying	Deliberately practicing	Intentionally stretching	Transferring and generalizing

Icon source: istock.com/rambo182

- Analyze standards and learning foundations to identify concepts and skills.

  _____

  _____

  _____

  _____

  _____

- Analyze standards and learning foundations for considerations of developmental variability, opportunity, access, and context, and cultural, linguistic, and ability diversity.

  _____

  _____

  _____

  _____

  _____

- Identify related standards and learning foundations for meaningful integration.

_____

_____

_____

_____

_____

- Brainstorm options for multidisciplinary, interdisciplinary, and transdisciplinary integration.

_____

_____

_____

_____

_____

6

LEARNING PROGRESSIONS

We have analyzed and made sense of specific standards within the context of early childhood learning and development. Next, we will consider the experiences and interactions that build upon each other toward mastery of those standards. With this knowledge, we can create learning experiences and interactions to move learning and development intentionally forward. As you know, moving learning forward includes multiple domains: cognitive, social, emotional, behavioral, and psychomotor learning.

Big Ideas

LEARNING INTENTION AND SUCCESS CRITERIA FOR MODULE 6

Before you engage with the learning in this module, read what we intend to learn (LI, the learning intention) and what it'll look and sound like when we've learned this (SC, the success criteria). Next, read the levels, descriptions, and images of the path to mastery (the rubric). Evaluate where you are right now for each success criteria. At the end of the module, we'll return to this self-evaluation and document the ways we've intentionally grown our teaching practice over time.

LI: We are learning about the significant experiences and interactions that lead toward mastery of standards and learning foundations so that we can make decisions about how to sequence these experiences and interactions.

SC: I'll know I've learned this when I can

(Continued)

(Continued)

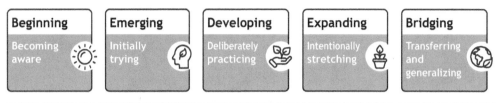

Icon source: istock.com/rambo182

- Identify significant experiences and interactions described within developmental milestones and learning trajectories.

_____

_____

_____

_____

_____

- Describe children's prior knowledge to leverage.

_____

_____

_____

_____

_____

- Rely on our partnerships to brainstorm experiences, interactions, and language that are significant to our learners and their families and that reflect the rich diversity of our learners.

_____

_____

_____

_____

_____

- Create learning progressions that sequence significant experiences and interactions.

_____

_____

_____

_____

_____

In this module, we are learning about learning progressions, which are different from developmental stages, developmental milestones, and learning trajectories. Let's examine the differences between these and the relationships among them.

DEVELOPMENTAL MILESTONES AND LEARNING TRAJECTORIES

There are well-established developmental stages and milestones in early childhood.

Developmental stages and milestones encompass large periods of time to track growth and development over the lifespan of children.

Important Vocabulary

They typically describe developmental domains such as social/emotional, motor/physical, cognitive, and language/communication. While the experiences and interactions within our classrooms influence milestones, developmental milestones describe a set of general skills or age-related tasks that most children can do at a certain age.

If developmental milestones describe a set of general skills or age-related tasks, learning trajectories provide the same description for specific content areas.

Learning trajectories describe milestones along mastery of content-specific concepts and skills.

For example, the oral counting learning trajectory describes when children typically master specific oral counting skills (i.e., counting to 5, counting to 10, counting backward, skip counting). Early word writing trajectories describe children's movement from scribbles to letter-like lines and shapes, then to strings of random letters, then to letters that represent sounds, and finally to standard spelling. In science, young learners begin with *observations* of pushes and pulls, then *predict* how pushes and pulls affect motion, and finally *plan and conduct* an investigation with pushing and pulling.

Developmental Stages and Milestones		
CDC's Developmental Milestones (bit.ly/3Bl10q3)		
Learning Trajectories		
Mathematics	Literacy	Science
• *Learning and Teaching with Learning Trajectories: Early Math—Birth to Grade 3* (bit.ly/3UkcQJJ) • *Concrete-Representational-Abstract (CRA)** (Berry & Thunder, 2017)	• *Written Composition Development*: Oral storytelling, Drawing, and Writing* (Horn & Giacobbe, 2007) • *Pictorial Imagery Development for Visual Arts** (Kindler & Darras, 1998) • *Model of Word Recognition Development* (Ehri, 1999)	• *A Framework for K-12 Science Education* (National Research Council, 2012) • *The Next Generation Science Standards* (NGSS Lead States, 2013)

*You can read more about these learning trajectories and see them in action in the anchor text *Visible Learning in Early Childhood* (Thunder et al., 2021).

Developmental stages and learning trajectories are important references for us as we make sense of standards. They help us develop vertical knowledge—knowledge of how concepts and skills build over time. They also help us develop horizontal knowledge—knowledge of how concepts and skills connect across developmental domains and content areas. We explored our horizontal knowledge in Module 5 when we found related standards and brainstormed ways to integrate multiple standards.

LEARNING PROGRESSIONS

As children grow and develop, they do not simply leap from one developmental stage or milestone to the next. There are many steps in between, many significant interactions and experiences, many attempts and missteps, that all contribute to learning and development. These significant interactions and experiences that build upon each other are learning progressions.

When we consider learning progressions, we are thinking about the sequence of learning within developmental stages, between developmental milestones, and within units of study.

Learning progressions inform our decisions about how to sequence experiences and interactions necessary for children to intentionally learn and grow.

When we create a learning progression, we are thinking about the significant experiences and interactions children need to learn and grow over long chunks of time like a unit of study, which is typically two to five weeks long. To create a learning progression, we begin with the analyzed standards and then brainstorm and reflect using a series of questions (Table 6.1) to guide our thinking. Throughout, we keep in mind the concepts and skills we identified from the standards as well as the integration option we chose.

6.1   Learning Progressions Brainstorm and Reflection

Guiding Questions	Reflections and Brainstorming
What do we know already about our learners and families that can make these experiences and interactions more meaningful?	
What concepts and skills have learners already mastered?	
How are the concepts and skills related to each other (horizontal knowledge) and how do they build upon each other (vertical knowledge)? What does typical development look like?	
What new experiences, unfamiliar contexts, and significant language do learners need the opportunity to access?	
How do we need to expand options for engaging, expressing, and representing concepts and skills to accurately represent our diverse learners?	

For example, in Module 5, we began to plan a unit of study with toddlers. We analyzed and made sense of a focal standard and three related standards. We also brainstormed three possible integration ideas and chose the transdisciplinary integration possibility: How can I play *with* a friend using the same materials? Look back at pp. 101–102 to see this work. Then, we used the five guiding questions to reflect and brainstorm ideas for our learning progression (see Table 6.2).

6.2 Toddler Unit to Solve the Problem: How can I play *with* a friend using the same materials?

Learning Progressions Brainstorm and Reflection

Guiding Questions	The Thinking Behind Our Ideas	Reflections and Brainstorming
What do we know already about our learners and families that can make these experiences and interactions more meaningful?	We add Peek-a-Boo because every family plays a version of this interactive game with their child, and this game could be played with a friend and using toys. We add vehicles, balls, dolls, and stuffed animals because these are high interest items for our learners and familiar toys from many homes. We also add singing songs because all our families have favorite songs that we can share with the whole class and that can be sung with instruments, dance moves, or actions.	• *Peek-a-Boo* • *singing songs with actions* • *their unique "favorite things": vehicles, balls, dolls, stuffed animals*
What concepts and skills have learners already mastered? What are they ready for next?	We look at the developmental milestones of 12-month-old children because all the children in the class are over one year old.	*From developmental milestones, 12-month-olds can typically play games like Pat-a-Cake, wave bye, put something in a container, look for things you hide, and pick things up with a pincer grasp.*
	Our focus in the toddler unit is on concepts and skills *across* developmental domains so we will rely on developmental stages and milestones rather than learning trajectories. We need to understand where toddlers are within the developmental stages and milestones related to these standards. In a toddler classroom, there may be children between 12 and 35 months old. We examined the developmental stages and milestones to know where toddlers may typically begin this work (at 12 months) and what it looks like to move to the	• *play games like Pat-a-Cake* • *pick things up with pincer grasp* • *body-parts games and songs* • *clap* • *waves and hugs* • *use familiar objects right way* • *put things into containers* • *stack things* • *read books and point to familiar things* • *read books and name things to find* • *walk* • *hold things in one hand and use another*

Guiding Questions	The Thinking Behind Our Ideas	Reflections and Brainstorming
	preschooler stage (at 36 months). These milestones give us an idea of starting and ending points for our learning progression. Based on our analyzed standard (p. 90), we read developmental milestones for 15-month-olds through 36-month-olds with a focus on verbal and nonverbal interactions and the purpose of learning together.	• *scribble* • *toys with knobs, switches, buttons*
What new experiences, unfamiliar contexts, and significant language do learners need the opportunity to access?	We note materials in our classroom that might be new and language that allows for turn taking and participating in songs and games.	• *puzzles* • *dollhouse* • *toys with knobs, switches, buttons* • *routines: greeting, parting, clean up* • *drawing* • *working next to or with a peer* • *reading books* • *musical instruments* • *____'s turn, my turn, your turn* • *body part names* • *action verbs: shake, tap, clap, walk, hop*
How do we need to expand options for engaging, expressing, and representing concepts and skills to accurately represent our diverse learners?	We reflect on the children in our classroom—some are communicating nonverbally and some speak multiple languages. We brainstorm options with our partners, including special educators.	• *sign language* • *pointing* • *action verbs and books in heritage languages*

CASE IN POINT

Jess Harper wants to design a learning center for children to interact with items that would be introduced in a read aloud. Her idea is to share the book *Taking a Walk: Winter in the City* (Tarsky, 2019) to help learners master one of the foundations. The learning

(Continued)

(Continued)

foundation reads as follows: "Demonstrate knowledge from informational text through labeling, describing, playing, or creating artwork" (California Department of Education, 2008, p. 68). The book is filled with images of things that you might find in the city, such as boots, fire engines, taxis, animals, and so on. She has to decide if she wants to introduce the items first, read the book first, have the children interact with the toy replicas first, or something else. She knows that there is no one right way to create the sequence of learning, and that there are probably some wrong ways.

> What advice do you have for Ms. Harper? What questions should she consider as she designs the sequence of learning experiences and interactions?

 YOUR TURN!

Now, it's your turn to reflect and brainstorm. Begin by returning to the concepts (nouns) and skills (verbs) that you identified in Module 5 (look at p. 91). Then, fill in the chart:

Learning Progressions Brainstorm and Reflection

Guiding Questions	Prompts and Scaffolds	Reflections and Brainstorming
What do we know already about our learners and families that can make these experiences and interactions more meaningful?	*To answer this question, we return to our work to build partnerships with learners and families from Module 2. We need to deeply know each learner and communicate with their families.*	
What concepts and skills have learners already mastered?	*Here, we rely on either the developmental stages and milestones, the learning trajectories, or the previous standards that children have already mastered.*	

Guiding Questions	Prompts and Scaffolds	Reflections and Brainstorming
How are the concepts and skills related to each other (horizontal knowledge) and how do they build upon each other (vertical knowledge)? What does typical development look like?	*Again, we can rely on developmental milestones, learning trajectories, or standards to describe the relationships and development of the concepts and skills. We need to be most familiar with experiences and interactions that align with the standards we will intentionally teach during this unit. To narrow what we're looking for, we can return to the concepts (nouns) and skills (verbs) that we identified and keep these in mind as we read.*	
What new experiences, unfamiliar contexts, and significant language do learners need the opportunity to access?	*To answer this question, we consider what we know about our learners and their families, what we know about the standards, and what we know about the vast experiences and contexts that our learners will encounter in life. We look for new experiences and unfamiliar contexts within the previous question's answer and we brainstorm significant language that is important across all these settings.*	
How do we need to expand options for engaging, expressing, and representing concepts and skills to accurately represent our diverse learners?	*Again, we return to our partnership work of Module 2 to answer this question. By partnering, we can identify ways to broaden ways of showing and knowing the concepts and skills.*	

Now we need to identify the significant experiences and interactions that will move children from one end of the progression to the other. In our toddler unit, we are working to move children forward in their learning and development in order to solve the problem: How can I play *with* a friend using the same materials? To identify and sequence the significant experiences and interactions, we'll use a strategy called list-group-label.

Here is the <u>list</u> of significant experiences and interactions for toddlers learning to play with a friend using the same materials. We pulled this list from the Learning Progressions Brainstorm and Reflection on p. 116:

- Peek-a-Boo
- singing songs with actions
- their unique "favorite things": vehicles, balls, dolls, stuffed animals
- play games like Pat-a-Cake
- pick things up with pincer grasp
- body-parts games and songs
- clap
- waves and hugs
- use familiar objects the "right" way
- put things into containers
- stack things
- read multilingual books and point to familiar things
- read multilingual books and name familiar things to find

- walk
- hold things in one hand and use the other hand
- scribble
- toys with knobs, switches, buttons
- puzzles
- dollhouse
- routines: greeting, parting, clean up
- working next to or with a peer
- musical instruments
- _____'s turn, my turn, your turn
- action verbs (multiple languages): shake, tap, clap, walk, hop
- sign language
- pointing

Now, we **group and label** these significant experiences and interactions based on the levels of complexity for engaging with the unit concepts and skills aligned with the integration option we chose. The groups and labels should represent levels from simple to complex. In our example, we create three groups (though we could have created more or fewer) and then label each group with a phrase that is meaningful to us. Each group of experiences and interactions helps us move closer to solving the typical toddler problem: How can I play *with* a friend using the same materials?

Our first group includes imitating, mimicking, and echoing so we label this *Simultaneous Actions* or things we do at the same time; this is the simplest way to interact. Our second group includes ways to engage in parallel play so we label this *Side-by-Side Actions*; this is more complex than simultaneous actions. Our third group includes activities where each child can have their own object to interact with one common object so we label this *Sharing One Focal Object*.

An even more complex way to interact would be cooperative play, but this is not developmentally expected until children are three-years-old; therefore, sharing one focal object is the most complex way to interact for our toddler unit.

Finally, we **sequence** these groups of significant experiences and interactions moving from simple to complex, gradually answering the question: How can I play *with* a friend using the same materials? We begin with *Simultaneous Actions* because most of these experiences and interactions are listed near the starting point of the developmental milestone range. Then we move to *Side-by-Side Actions* as the experiences and interactions become more complex. Our final label, *Sharing One Focal Object*, is the most complex solution to our problem and most closely aligns with developmental milestones near the ending point of our range.

Here is our learning progression for our toddler unit to solve the problem: How can I play *with* a friend using the same materials?

1	**Simultaneous Actions** (imitating, mimicking, echoing)
	• Play games like Peek-a-Boo and Pat-a-Cake as a trio
	• Sing songs with the same actions together—clapping, picking things up, using instruments the right way (shake, tap)
	• Play and sing body-parts games and songs
	• Greetings and Partings (waves and hugs)
2	**Side-by-Side Actions** (parallel play)
	• Each has toys with knobs, switches, buttons next to each other
	• Ask questions and label with language as each plays with own containers, stacking, reading, scribbling, cars/balls, puzzles, dolls/stuffed animals, etc. with language labels
	• Sing songs with same actions together—stomp/walk, holding in one hand and use another (triangle, drum)
	• Play and sing body-parts games and songs
	• Play and sing favorite things games and songs
	• Clean up side by side
3	**Sharing One Focal Object** (have own objects to contribute to one common object)
	• Both have things to put into one container
	• Both have things to stack together
	• Read one book together and point to familiar things as well as play seek and find
	• Scribble side by side on same paper
	• Each have cars or balls to roll down one ramp
	• Put puzzle pieces together with one puzzle
	• Put dolls in dollhouse
	• Clean up together

YOUR TURN!

1. Return to your Learning Progressions Brainstorm and Reflection chart (p. 116). Make a list below of all the experiences and interactions you included. These are the significant experiences and interactions you should include in your unit.

   List of Significant Experiences and Interactions

Our labeled groups in sequence look very clean and organized now. But when we were working to group, label, and then sequence them, our work was full of highlights, circles, lines, and other edits. As you work, remember this is *your* draft, *your* process, and *your* thinking. There are many right ways to sequence learning. Use color. Cross things out. Draw arrows. Get out more paper. Do whatever you need to do to create meaningful groups and labels.

2. Return to your list and **group** common skills, actions, and tasks together based on complexity. Think about the big buckets of concepts and skills that can be grouped together moving from simple to complex understanding of the concepts and skills and aligned with the integration option. Aim for no more than five groups.

3. When you have groups, name the groups. These are the **labels**. Use phrases that are specific and have meaning for you. You should be able to use the label as a prompt to name other skills, actions, and tasks that fit within that category.

4. Finally, look back at your labels and the developmental milestones or learning trajectories you relied on as resources. **Sequence** the labels moving from simple to complex toward mastery of the concepts and skills.

You did it! This is your learning progression!

Now, we have created learning progressions that will help us intentionally engage children in significant experiences and interactions throughout a unit of study. Learning progressions helps us make decisions about how to sequence these experiences and interactions so that all children are active participants.

Learning progressions are important to our planning process. First, and perhaps most obvious, is the idea that some content precedes other content. Learners go from the known to the new. In other words, we build on the knowledge and experiences that children have and keep extending their understanding of the world. Second, learning progressions guide the development of daily learning expectations or intentions. Each learning progression will require a number of days to ensure deep learning. We think of the learning progressions as the stepping stones that shine a light on the path to learning whereas the learning intentions are the daily milestones that children accomplish. We will explore learning intentions in the next module.

MODELS/EXEMPLARS

Infant—Imitation Unit

(Standards from *Head Start Early Learning Outcomes Framework,* Office of Head Start, 2021)

1	**Attend, Model, Narrate** (sounds, gestures, movements with toy, facial expressions)
	• Watches you as you move
	• Makes sounds other than crying
	• Smiles
	• Chuckles when you try to make laugh
	• Looks at you, moves, or makes sounds to get your attention
	• Makes sounds like ooo and ahh
	• Makes sounds back when you talk
	• Turns head toward the sound of your voice

(Continued)

(Continued)

	• Holds a toy when you put it in their hand, such as a rattle (shake, tap)
	• Uses arm to swing at toys (feet keyboard for kicking)
	• Holds head steady without support when you are holding
	• Likes to look at self in a mirror; look in mirror together
	• Echo baby
	• Lots of eye contact
	• Sing songs with shake, tap, big facial expressions, repeating sounds
	• Read books with flaps and animal sounds
2	**Take Turns** (sounds, gestures, movements with toy, facial expressions)
	• Laughs
	• Takes turns making sounds with you
	• Blows "raspberries"
	• Makes squealing noises
	• Puts things in mouth to explore
	• Reaches to grab a toy, such as a rattle (shake, tap)
	• Rolls over, leans on hands to support while sitting
	• Shows several facial expressions, like happy, sad, angry, surprised
	• Looks when you call name
	• Smiles or laughs when you play Peek-a-Boo
	• Makes a lot of different sounds
	• Lifts arms to be picked up
	• Looks for objects dropped out of sight—Peek-a-Boo with toys
	• Bangs two things together—clap, pat, tap
	• Sits
	• Moves things from one hand to the other
	• Imitate each other
	• Sing songs with actions
	• Read books with flaps, Peek-a-Boo, and animals sounds (encourage child to move flaps)

Toddler—Unit to Solve the Problem: How can I play *with* a friend using the same materials?

(Standards from *Belonging, Being, and Becoming: The Early Years Learning Framework for Australia,* Australian Government, 2011)

1	**Simultaneous Actions** (imitating, mimicking, echoing)
	• Play games like Peek-a-Boo and Pat-a-Cake as a trio
	• Sing songs with same actions together—clapping, picking things up, using instruments the right way (shake, tap)
	• Play and sing body-parts games and songs
	• Greetings and partings (waves and hugs)

2	**Side-by-Side Actions** (parallel play)
	• Each have toys with knobs, switches, buttons next to each other
	• Ask questions and label with language as play with own containers, stacking, reading, scribbling, cars/balls, puzzles, dolls/stuffed animals, etc.
	• Sing songs with same actions together—stomp/walk, holding in one hand and use another (triangle, drum)
	• Play and sing body-parts games and songs
	• Play and sing favorite things games and songs
	• Clean up side by side
3	**Sharing One Focal Object** (have own objects to contribute)
	• Both have things to put into one container
	• Both have things to stack together
	• Read one book together and point to familiar things as well as play seek and find
	• Scribble side by side on same paper
	• Each have cars or balls to roll down one ramp
	• Put puzzle pieces together with one puzzle
	• Put dolls in dollhouse
	• Clean up together

Preschool—Describe and Label Unit

(Standards from *California Preschool Learning Foundations*, California Department of Education, 2008)

1	**Exploration and Creation**
	• Exposure to different types of nonfiction texts: cereal boxes, magazines, posters, books, flyers, recipes, Lego directions
	• Create art inspired by the text: paints, play dough, paper cutting, gluing
	• Use words and/or actions from the text when playing in different environments with others: sensory table, outside play, pretend, building area
2	**Listening and Describing**
	• Listen to informational texts about various subjects: animals, space, sports, monster trucks, Legos
	• Describe what is in the text or what the text is about using four or more words
3	**Asking Questions and Conversations**
	• Have conversations about the text with others
	• Ask questions about the text, including who, what, where, when, why
	• Interact with similar items found in the selected text with others
4	**Describing, Utilizing and Collaboration**
	• Work together on a common task using an informational text: collect leaves that mirror ones found in a book about leaves or identify different insects using an insect pamphlet

Primary—Shapes Unit

(Standards from *Common Core State Standards* [for First Grade], National Governors Association, 2010)

1	**Nonverbal Playing, Building, and Comparing**
	• Play with shapes: Magna-tiles, pattern blocks, attribute blocks, wooden blocks
	• Build with shapes: Magna-tiles, pattern blocks, attribute blocks, wooden blocks
	• Create or replicate images using manipulative shapes
	• Trace shapes
	• Draw shapes
2	**Describing and Comparing Using Informal Language**
	• Play and build with shapes while describing and comparing
	• Describe shapes using familiar words that focus on size, color, and orientation
	• Name and describe categories made for shapes using familiar language
	• Sing songs about shapes
3	**Comparing Using Shape Names and Attributes**
	• Play and build with shapes while naming and comparing attributes
	• Sort shapes based on various attributes
	• Identify and explain how shapes are similar and/or different
	• Use words representing various shades of meaning, for example, tiny, small, petite
	• Compare shapes using geometric vocabulary

TEMPLATES

Learning Progressions Brainstorm and Reflection Template

Now, it's your turn to bring this strategy to your work with your children. As you plan each unit of study, create a learning progression to guide your decisions about how to sequence experiences and interactions. Remember, a unit of study is typically two to five weeks long. Use this template to reflect and brainstorm significant experiences and interactions to include in your learning progression. Then, use the list-group-label strategy to create the components of your learning progression. Finally, sequence your learning progression from simple to complex. This planning template is also downloadable.

Guiding Questions	Reflections and Brainstorming
What do we know already about our learners and families that can make these experiences and interactions more meaningful?	
What concepts and skills have learners already mastered?	
How are the concepts and skills related to each other (horizontal knowledge) and how do they build upon each other (vertical knowledge)? What does typical development look like?	
What new experiences, unfamiliar contexts, and significant language do learners need the opportunity to access?	
How do we need to expand options for engaging, expressing, and representing concepts and skills to accurately represent our diverse learners?	

LEARNING INTENTION AND SUCCESS CRITERIA FOR MODULE 6

Now that you have engaged with the learning in this module, reread what we intended to learn (LI, the learning intention) and what it looks and sounds like to have mastered learning this (SC, the success criteria). Next, reread the levels, descriptions, and images of the path to mastery (the rubric). Reevaluate where you are right now for each success criteria. Use the box to reflect on the evidence you have of where you are and where you are headed next.

LI: We are learning about the significant experiences and interactions that lead toward mastery of standards and learning foundations so that we can make decisions about how to sequence these experiences and interactions.

SC: I'll know I've learned this when I can

Icon source: istock.com/rambo182

- Identify significant experiences and interactions described within developmental milestones and learning trajectories.

_____

_____

_____

_____

_____

- Describe children's prior knowledge to leverage.

_____

_____

_____

_____

_____

- Rely on our partnerships to brainstorm experiences, interactions, and language that are significant to our learners and their families and that reflect the diversity of our learners.

_____

_____

_____

_____

_____

- Create learning progressions that sequence significant experiences and interactions.

_____

_____

_____

_____

_____

7

LEARNING INTENTIONS AND SUCCESS CRITERIA

 ## REFLECTION

Before starting this module, reflect on how your learners would respond to the following questions:

1. What are you learning today?
2. Why are you learning this?
3. How will you know that you have learned it?

Would your learners be able to answer these three questions? What would they say? If you are not sure, ask them. Use the space provided to record the responses of several of your learners.

	Learner #1: _____	Learner #2: _____	Learner #3: _____
What are you learning today?			
Why are you learning this?			
How will you know you have learned it?			

Hold on to their responses. We will come back to this information during your work in this module.

Learning and development take time and intentionality. Learning progressions provide a clear view of the significant experiences and interactions that move learning and development forward over the course of a unit. In this module, we'll spend time examining how the learning progressions can inform the experiences and interactions that children have each day. In this way, one day can contribute to intentionally propelling learning and development forward for every child.

LEARNING INTENTION AND SUCCESS CRITERIA FOR MODULE 7

Before you engage with the learning in this module, read what we intend to learn (LI, the learning intention) and what it'll look and sound like when we've learned this (SC, the success criteria). Next, read the levels, descriptions, and images of the path to mastery (the rubric). Evaluate where you are right now for each success criteria. At the end of the module, we'll return to this self-evaluation and document the ways we've intentionally grown our teaching practice over time.

LI: We are learning to intentionally plan the learning intention of one day so that, at the culmination of many days, all children have intentionally moved forward in their learning and development.

SC: I'll know I've learned this when I can

Icon source: istock.com/rambo182

- Create content, language, and social learning intentions that move learning forward through a learning progression.

_____

_____

_____

_____

_____

- Explain the relevance or purpose for the learning intention.

_____

_____

_____

_____

_____

- Create success criteria that monitor learning toward the learning intention and evaluate when learners have arrived at mastery of the learning intention.

_____

_____

_____

_____

_____

So much learning can happen in a single day with young children. Sometimes by the end of the day, when we finally sit down and reflect, it's hard to remember what happened. As educators, we need to direct this whirlwind of activity along a path toward explicit learning goals. The experiences and interactions of each day can have positive impacts on children's learning and development when they are intentional. To effectively plan for one day's experiences and interactions, we must have a clear vision of our learning goal and how we will evaluate our progress toward that goal.

Three questions and answers, stated from the perspective of children, should guide our work:

Guiding Question	Guiding Answer	What We Call It
What am I learning today?	Today, I am learning . . .	Learning Intention
Why am I learning this?	So that . . .	Relevance
How will I know when I have learned it?	I'll know I've learned it when I can . . .	Success Criteria

The learning intentions communicate the what of learning: *What am I learning today?* The relevance explains why this learning is important, needed, or interesting: *Why am I learning this?* The success criteria communicate how we'll know when learners are successful: *How will I know when I've learned it?*

First, let's consider why these guiding questions and answers matter in early childhood.

REFLECTION

Flip back to Module 1 (p. 21) and select the two big ideas you think align best with these guiding questions. Write them here.

> •
>
> •

Hopefully you recorded these:

Big Ideas

➤ Early childhood educators and learners **have high expectations for learning that communicate equity of access and opportunity to the highest level of learning possible.**

➤ Learning experiences move learning toward **explicit and inclusive success criteria.**

If you listed others, don't erase them, just make sure you add these two to your list.

The learning intentions and relevance make high expectations for learning and development actionable. The explicit success criteria provide us with ways to evaluate when children have learned what we intended for them to learn. We take aim at our shared, high expectations for learning and development and intentionally engage children in learning experiences and interactions that move every child forward.

You may wonder if this is true even for infants and toddlers. It is. These three guiding questions are important for all ages of learners, including infants and toddlers. While infants and toddlers may not be able to answer the questions, we can use these questions to guide our interactions and especially our language within the interactions. We can also share these guiding questions and their answers with families to help create continuity of context, where we are truly working in partnership with families toward a shared learning goal and we all know what successfully reaching that goal looks like and sounds like.

We also know we want to grow Visible Learners.

REFLECTION

Let's look back at the characteristics of Visible Learners. Use the space provided to respond to the following question:

What are the connections between Visible Learners and the guiding questions presented in this module? If you need some time to flip back to the Welcome Module (p. 1) and review the characteristics of Visible Learners, that is fine.

• **What am I learning today?** • **Why am I learning this?** • **How will I know when I have learned it?**	

In order for our learners to become Visible Learners, we have to be clear in our planning about the what, why, and how of learning. When we are clear about these questions and their answers, we can communicate them to our children and families. Together, we should all know the learning intentions, relevance, and success criteria so that we can intentionally interact with children to move learning and development forward. Our partnerships are central to children's learning and development.

Big Ideas

FROM LEARNING PROGRESSIONS TO LEARNING INTENTIONS

Throughout Part 2, we have engaged in a planning process to teach with intentionality. Figure 7.1 represents this process. We began in Module 5 by analyzing **standards** to create an integrated unit of study. In Module 6, we grouped and sequenced significant experiences and interactions aligned

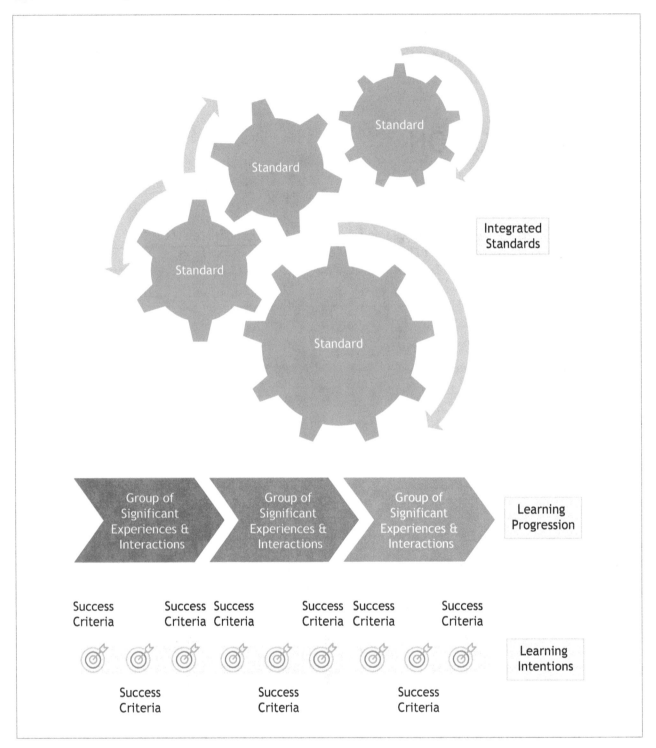

with those standards to create a **learning progression.** In this module, we will tease out the **learning intentions, relevance, and success criteria** for one day.

The learning intentions, relevance, and success criteria may be for one part of our learning day, such as mathematics or literacy, or for our youngest learners, the learning intentions, relevance, and success criteria might address learning across the day. In other words, whether we're reading aloud, playing outside, exploring centers, or gathering together to sing a song, we can rely on the same, single set of learning intentions, relevance, and success criteria. This is one of the unique aspects of early childhood, particularly when working with infants and toddlers. We can use the same learning intentions, relevance, and success criteria across the whole learning day to create continuity across contexts and multiple opportunities for interactions and experiences.

Learning intentions answer the question, *What am I learning today?* We can think of this as helping us, our learners, and families know what to focus on, what to emphasize, what to pay attention to, what to talk about, and what to interact about. High-quality learning intentions

➤ state the *what* of the learning goal,

➤ focus on the learning, not the task,

➤ are stated in child- and family-friendly language,

➤ are a bite (day)-sized chunk of the learning progression, and

➤ align with the standards. (Almarode et al., 2021)

Let's look at an example—the Imitation Unit from an infant classroom.

Recall that when we analyzed the standards for integration, we identified concepts and skills that we need to intentionally teach. Our Imitation Unit planning chart with analyzed standards is on pp. 99-100.

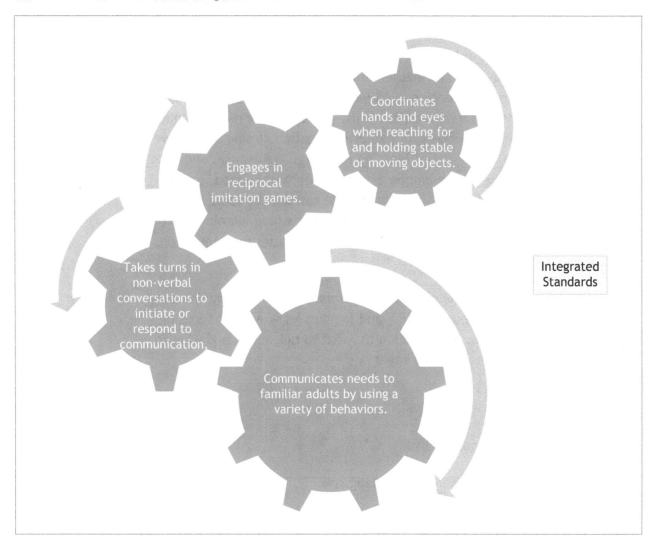

Next, we used developmental milestones and stages as well as our partnerships with learners, families, and collaborating educators to create a learning progression. The list-group-label work to create our Imitation Unit learning progression is on pp. 118-119.

7.3 Infant Imitation Unit's Learning Progression

Now, we can create learning intentions for each day of our Infant Imitation Unit. There may be more days in one part of the learning progression than in the other. The number of days depends on our context and our learners. For this infant classroom, the teacher has planned to spend one month or twenty school days on this unit with the first eight days focused on attending, modeling and narrating, and the remaining twelve days focused on taking turns. Of course, this is an estimate, and the teacher will use formative evaluation and feedback from families and collaborating educators to adjust the pace. She may also decide to integrate the same standards into future units in order to deliberately practice, extend, and transfer the concepts and skills. In other words, infants' learning about imitation does not end because the unit ends.

7.4   Imitation Unit's Learning Intentions

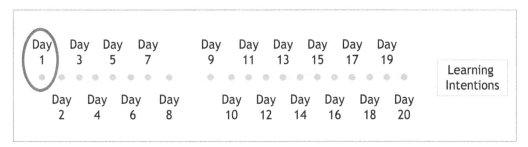

Let's start at the beginning and create a learning intention for Day 1 of the Imitation Unit. For this group of infants, the learning intention will be woven throughout the day from arrival to pick-up. The learning intention will give clarity to the teachers' decisions as they plan experiences and interact with the infants throughout the day. Recall the characteristics of high-quality learning intentions (p. 135). We want to create a simple statement that tells what infants are learning throughout the first day of the Imitation Unit:

Guiding Question	Guiding Answer	What We Call It
What am I learning today?	Today, I am learning **to notice the sounds I make.**	Learning Intention

 **YOUR TURN!**

Return to your integrated standards and learning progression. Your planning chart with analyzed standards is on p. 121. Record your standards in the gears below.

Next, look back at the learning progression you created on p. 136. Record the sequence in the arrows below.

Decide how many days your unit will be and which day you would like to focus on to create a learning intention. Circle this day in your unit.

(Continued)

(Continued)

Now for the challenging new piece—writing a learning intention. We've made space for you to *draft* four possible learning intentions. You may need more space or less. But the purpose of this draft space is to assure you that trying to write a high-quality learning intention takes multiple attempts.

Review the characteristics of high-quality learning intentions (p. 135). What bite-size chunk of the learning progression are you tackling that day? What do you want children to learn? And what language can you use so that both children and their families can make sense of the learning goal? After you've drafted several options, reread and choose the one that most closely aligns with the characteristics of high-quality learning intentions. Star, circle, or highlight this learning intention.

TEMPLATES

7.5 My Planning Process Template

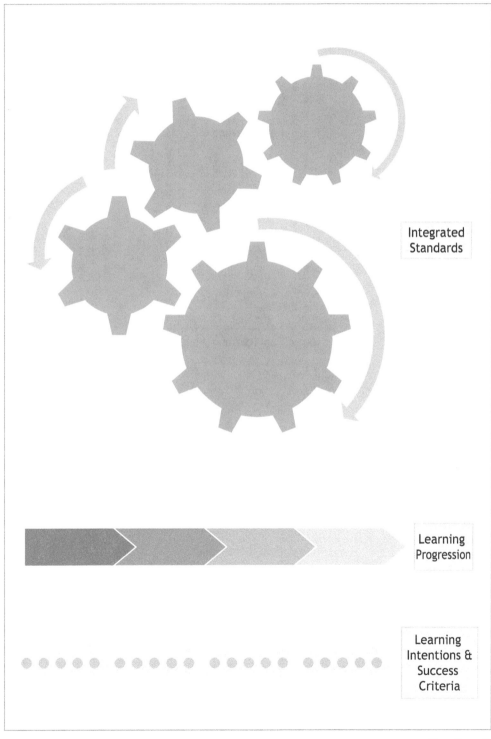

Integrated Standards

Learning Progression

Learning Intentions & Success Criteria

(Continued)

(Continued)

Guiding Question	Guiding Answer	What We Call It
What am I learning today?	Today, I am learning . . .	Learning Intention
	Today, I am learning . . .	
	Today, I am learning . . .	
	Today, I am learning . . .	

THREE TYPES OF LEARNING INTENTIONS

You only need one learning intention. But sometimes you have more than one focus for learning. Sometimes you want to be explicit about multiple learning goals within the same experiences and interactions. And sometimes naming the what of learning through different lenses creates a truly integrated learning experience. These are times when it can help to consider three types of learning intentions: content, language, and social learning intentions.

Content learning intentions communicate the what of learning related to the emotional, cognitive, and motor domains as well as content areas such as mathematics, reading, writing, science, and creative arts.

Important Vocabulary

Language learning intentions communicate the what of learning related to the communication domains as well as the vocabulary, structure, and function of language within content areas.

Social learning intentions communicates the what of learning related to the social domain as well as the practices, processes, and dispositions within content areas.

For example, on Day 3 within our Imitation Unit, we may want to emphasize a language learning intention because the goal for learning is vocabulary.

7.6   Infant Imitation Unit's Learning Intentions

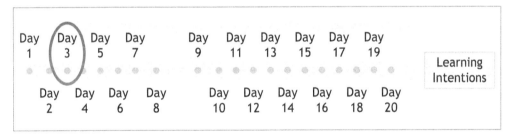

Guiding Question	Guiding Answer	What We Call It
What am I learning today?	Today, I am learning the **names of actions that make sounds.**	Language Learning Intention

Similarly, on Day 12, we may want to emphasize all three types of learning intentions because the learning goals overlap between content, language, and social learning.

7.7 Infant Imitation Unit's Learning Intentions

Guiding Question	Guiding Answer	What We Call It
What am I learning today?	Today, I am learning **facial expressions show different emotions.**	Content Learning Intention
	Today, I am learning **the names of emotions: happy, silly.**	Language Learning Intention
	Today, I am learning **to watch a face and imitate the facial expression.**	Social Learning Intention

YOUR TURN!

Look back at the learning intention you drafted on p. 141. Which kind of learning intention did you create? Finish the statement below:

I created a _____ learning intention because the learning goal is related to

_____.

Use the learning intention you created to develop the other two types of learning intentions. For example, if you created a language learning intention, what content would contextualize that language? What social development outcomes would support the language learning intention? Similarly, if you created a content learning intention, what language and social learning would enrich this particular content outcome?

Use the below chart to record your thinking and work.

Guiding Question	Guiding Answer	What We Call It
What am I learning today?	Today, I am learning . . .	Content Learning Intention

Guiding Question	Guiding Answer	What We Call It
	Today, I am learning . . .	Language Learning Intention
	Today, I am learning . . .	Social Learning Intention

Whatever type of learning intention you create, however many learning intentions you create for one day, remember the characteristics of high-quality learning intentions.

REFLECTION

Use the space below to list the characteristics of high-quality learning intentions. Flip back to page 135 for help with this task.

-
-
-
-
-

The purpose of a learning intention is to make the what of learning transparent to teachers, children, and families. When families pick up their child or meet their child at the bus stop and ask, *What did you learn today?*, what do you want the answer to be? This is the learning intention.

CASE IN POINT

Dani Cruz is learning to develop learning intentions. The learning foundation that Ms. Cruz is focused on reads as follows: "Orally blend and delete words and syllables without the support of pictures or objects" (CDOE, 2008, p. 64). On one day, Ms. Cruz has the following learning intention: *I am learning to put word parts together.* Another teacher says that the learning intention could be, *I am learning to orally combine two syllables and produce the target word.* Using the criteria for high-quality learning intentions, analyze the options.

Criteria	I am learning to put word parts together.	I am learning to orally combine two syllables and produce the target word.
States the *what* of the learning goal.		
Focuses on the learning, not the task.		
Is stated in child- and family-friendly language.		
Is a bite (day)-size chunk of the learning progression.		
Is aligned with the standards.		

RELEVANCE

One of children's favorite questions to ask is *Why?* Let's answer that question every day! *Why am I learning this?* is our guiding question for relevance. Explaining why we are working on the learning intention(s) provides the "so what" of our work.

Relevance can be a connection to something in children's world, a wondering that children want to answer, a problem that children want to solve, or a springboard to new learning. Communicating relevance to families can explain the importance of the bridge between this specific learning at school and continued learning at home.

In our Imitation Unit, we consider why it is significant for an infant to notice the sounds they make. What does this noticing allow an infant to do that they couldn't do before? This question led us right back to the standards and the concepts and skills that we unpacked from the standards: communicate. Making sounds on purpose is communication. By noticing the sounds we make, we can then make those sounds on purpose to communicate.

Guiding Question	Guiding Answer	What We Call It
What am I learning today?	Today, I am learning *to notice the sounds I make.*	Content Learning Intention
Why am I learning this?	So that *I can make sounds on purpose to communicate.*	Relevance

 # YOUR TURN!

Consider the why of your learning intention. Why is it important for your children to learn this?

Guiding Question	Guiding Answer	What We Call It
What am I learning today?	Today, I am learning . . .	Learning Intention

(Continued)

(Continued)

Guiding Question	Guiding Answer	What We Call It
Why am I learning this?	So that . . .	Relevance

SUCCESS CRITERIA

Big Ideas

Knowing the destination and the reason for the journey are important. Knowing how to evaluate if we've arrived successfully at the destination is paramount. This knowledge allows us to gauge where we are along the journey, make adjustments and refinements, and recalibrate our efforts. This knowledge also allows us to celebrate when we've arrived and set our sights on a new destination.

This is the how of learning—how we'll know when children have learned what we intended for them to learn. We call this the success criteria. Success criteria answer the question, *How will I know I've learned it?* We can think of this as helping us, our learners, and families know how to gauge where children are along the learning path toward mastery, where to go next, and when and what scaffolds to provide. High-quality success criteria

➤ provide the ingredients for meeting the learning intentions flexibly enough for children to find different ways to demonstrate learning and development,

➤ answer the question, "How will I know I have learned it?" by focusing on the learning, not the task,

➤ are actionable,

➤ are stated in child- and family-friendly language, and

➤ align with the qualities of the standards. (Almarode et al., 2021)

Looking at the image of our planning process (Figure 7.1), you may have noticed that the success criteria are targets with a bullseye. This is how we think of success criteria—the concentric rings that get closer and closer to a bullseye.

To create success criteria, we engage in cognitive task analysis, which means we break down a task into the qualities of successful mastery. We consider this question: *What would it look like and sound like when a child has mastered the learning intention?*

Sometimes we can describe success with just one statement. Sometimes we need more than one success criterion. This is where cognitive task analysis can be particularly helpful (Almarode et al., 2021):

1. Begin with a foundational idea.

2. Then, show the multiple components of learning.

3. Next, show the relational thinking across learning.

4. And finally, show application of the concept and thinking.

Thus, the success criteria gradually become more complex, and the whole set of success criteria describes what it would look like and sound like when a child has mastered the learning intention. If there are multiple learning intentions, the success criteria must embody *all* the learning intentions and may even make clear why the learning intentions are related. There is not a separate success criterion for each learning intention.

For example, in our Imitation Unit, we used cognitive task analysis to determine a foundational idea (pausing between sounds) or an initial way to create the quiet space necessary to notice a sound. Then, we identified the relational thinking of the concept and skill: Noticing can be expressed by repeating a sound or by noting the relationship between the sound and making the sound again. We only needed two success criteria to completely describe what it would look and sound like for an infant to successfully notice the sounds they make.

Guiding Question	Guiding Answer	What We Call It
What am I learning today?	Today, I am learning *to notice the sounds I make.*	Content Learning Intention
Why am I learning this?	So that *I can make sounds on purpose to communicate.*	Relevance
How will I know I've learned this?	I'll know I've learned it when • I can **pause between making sounds.** • I can **repeat a sound I just made.**	Success Criteria

REFLECTION

Use the space below to list the characteristics of high-quality success criteria. Flip back to page 146 for help with this task.

-
-
-
-
-

YOUR TURN!

Now it is your turn to develop success criteria for your learning intentions. Use the above examples and the chart below to create success criteria, the answer to the third guiding question. Then use the characteristics of high-quality success criteria to revise and refine your success criteria.

Guiding Question	Guiding Answer	What We Call It
What am I learning today?	Today, I am learning . . .	Learning Intention
Why am I learning this?	So that . . .	Relevance

Guiding Question	Guiding Answer	What We Call It
How will I know I've learned this?	I'll know I've learned this when I can . . .	Success Criteria

As early childhood educators, we see learners change at rapid paces compared to what other educators witness. It may appear that simply being present with young children contributes to their growth. But this leaves learning and development to chance. And as early childhood educators, our work is to move all children's learning and development forward by design.

We need to identify our destination or our learning intentions. And we need to be intentional in our creation of a path toward that destination or the success criteria. Each day should have a clear purpose for learning and actionable criteria to evaluate progress toward that learning goal. But it's not enough to create learning intentions and success criteria. We also need to communicate them to our learners and their families.

 # REFLECTION

Before moving on to the next module, return to the opening task of this module (p. 129). With your learning around learning intentions and success criteria, what do the responses of your learners tell you about where you are successful (your glows) and where you may need to make some tweaks (your grows) to your learning experiences and interactions?

My Glows	My Grows

MODELS/EXEMPLARS

Infant—Imitation Unit

(Standards from *Head Start Early Learning Outcomes Framework*, Office of Head Start, 2021)

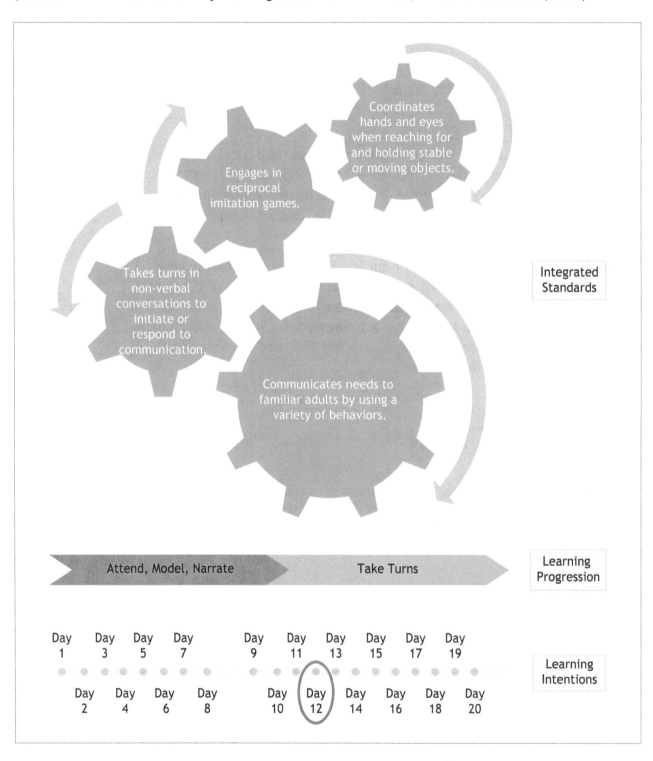

Guiding Question	Guiding Answer	What We Call It
What am I learning today?	Today, I am learning **facial expressions show different emotions.**	Content Learning Intention
	Today, I am learning **the names of emotions: happy, silly.**	Language Learning Intention
	Today, I am learning **to watch a face and imitate the facial expression.**	Social Learning Intention
Why am I learning this?	So that **I can understand how others feel by looking at their faces.**	Relevance
How will I know I've learned this?	I'll know I've learned it when • I can **imitate a smile for happy.** • I can **imitate sticking a tongue out for silly.**	Success Criteria

Toddler—Unit to Solve the Problem: How can I play *with* a friend using the same materials?

(Standards from *Belonging, Being, and Becoming: The Early Years Learning Framework for Australia*, Australian Government, 2011)

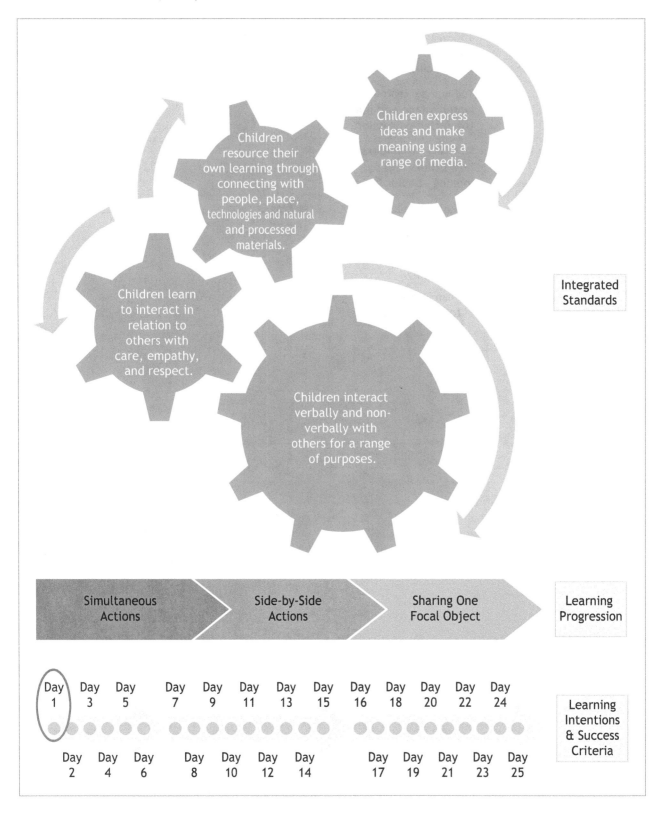

Guiding Question	Guiding Answer	What We Call It
What am I learning today?	Today, I am learning **I can say words to describe actions: clap, stomp, pat.**	Language Learning Intention
	Today, I am learning **we can sing and dance together.**	Social Learning Intention
Why am I learning this?	So that **we can sing action songs as a class and as a family.**	Relevance
How will I know I've learned this?	I'll know I've learned this when • I can **move my body to match action songs' words.**	Success Criteria

Preschool—Describe and Label Unit

(Standards from *California Preschool Learning Foundations*, California Department of Education, 2008)

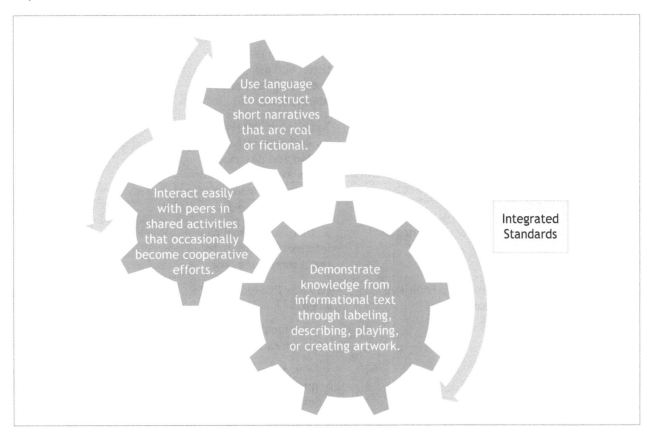

Use language to construct short narratives that are real or fictional.

Interact easily with peers in shared activities that occasionally become cooperative efforts.

Demonstrate knowledge from informational text through labeling, describing, playing, or creating artwork.

Integrated Standards

(Continued)

(Continued)

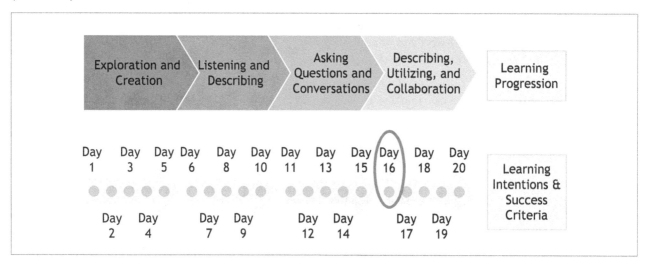

Guiding Question	Guiding Answer	What We Call It
What am I learning today?	Today, I am learning **true information from nonfiction informational (All About) texts.**	Content Learning Intention
	Today, I am learning **to listen and ask questions about informational (All About) texts.**	Language Learning Intention
	Today, I am learning **to work with others to find and describe things around me using our learning from informational texts.**	Social Learning Intention
Why am I learning this?	So that **I know how to use informational texts to learn something new.**	Relevance
How will I know I've learned this?	I'll know I've learned this when • I can **look or listen to an informational text.** • I can **ask a question about the informational text.** • I can **work together to play, create, or use information from the text.**	Success Criteria

Primary—Shapes Unit

(Standards from *Common Core State Standards* [for First Grade], National Governors Association, 2010)

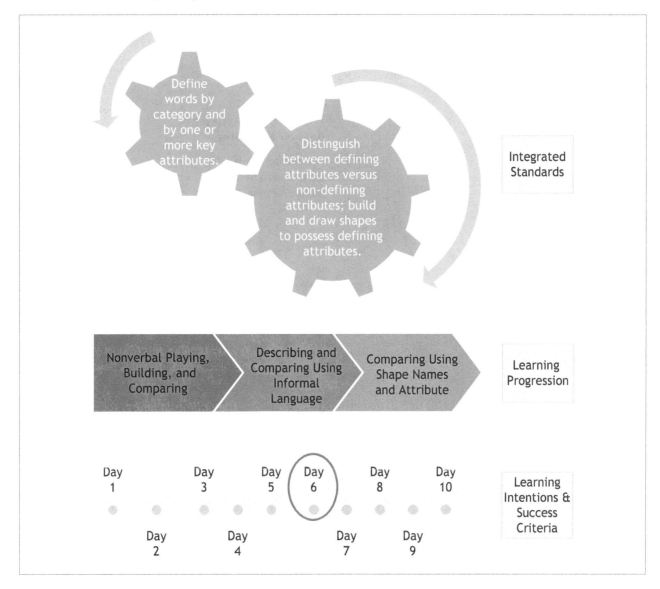

Guiding Question	Guiding Answer	What We Call It
What am I learning today?	Today, I am learning **to sort shapes based on their attributes.**	Content Learning Intention
	Today, I am learning **to describe shapes using attribute words: side, vertex.**	Language Learning Intention
	Today, I am learning **to listen to another peer's ideas.**	Social Learning Intention

(Continued)

(Continued)

Guiding Question	Guiding Answer	What We Call It
Why am I learning this?	So that **I can identify what is the same and what is different about shapes.**	Relevance
How will I know I've learned this?	I'll know I've learned this when • I can **sort shapes based on their attributes.** • I can **describe how I sorted my shapes to someone else.**	Success Criteria

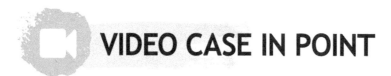

VIDEO CASE IN POINT

Let's join an infant class to see and hear the ways the teacher intentionally engages her infants in guided play as well as a playful learning read aloud. Today is Day 5 of her unit on the overarching concept imitation.

It's interesting to note that this teacher relies on the *California Infant/Toddler Learning and Development Foundations* rather than the *Office of Head Start Early Learning Outcomes Framework*, but many of the standards are the same and so imitation is the same overarching concept and skill for interdisciplinary integration. This is because both sets of standards are informed by the developmental milestones.

Learning and Development Foundations (*California Infant/Toddler Learning and Development Foundations*, California Department of Education, 2009):

• Hold small objects in one hand and sometimes use both hands together to manipulate objects. (p. 98)

• Use the information received from the senses to change the way they interact with the environment. (p. 94)

• Imitate others' actions that have more than one step and imitate simple actions that they have observed others doing at an earlier time. (p. 71)

• Experiment with sounds, practice making sounds, and use sounds or gestures to communicate needs, wants, or interests. (p. 49)

• Engage in back-and-forth interactions with others.

• Experiment with different ways of making things happen, persist in trying to do things even when faced with difficulty, and show a sense of satisfaction with what they can do. (p. 23)

> Content Learning Intention:
>
> I am learning sounds describe objects and actions.
>
> Relevance:
>
> So that I can make sounds on purpose to communicate.
>
> Success Criteria:
>
> I'll know I've learned this when
>
> - I can attend to the sounds others make when they describe objects and actions.
>
> - I can make sounds when I see or do something.

We're going to watch the teacher interact with two infants across their day while focusing on the same learning intention, relevance, and success criteria each time. In all three clips, the teacher is moving the infants toward the learning intentions and success criteria by intentionally engaging them either in guided play (Tasks 1 and 3) or a playful learning read aloud.

As you watch, pay attention to the ways the teacher enters play with respect for the children and their self-initiated play as well as the ways she enters play with intentionality around the learning intention and success criteria. During the read aloud, notice the ways the teacher creates a sense of interactive playfulness while reading aloud. Look for evidence of the three defining characteristics of guided play. Record your observations in the table below:

Defining Characteristics of Guided Play	Video Evidence
The adult has a clear learning goal in mind and makes choices about setting up the play space and the playful activity based on that goal.	
The child has opportunities to make choices and share their unique voice within the playful activity.	
The adult engages with the child intentionally and responsively as a conversational partner and/or as a language facilitator.	

Task 1: Exploring blocks and pop-up animals.

Blocks and Buttons
bit.ly/3d4t9d0

(Continued)

(Continued)

Task 2: Read aloud.

Reading Animal Name Books
bit.ly/3KZlMjH

Task 3: Exploring books.

DJ Makes a Cool Sound:
bit.ly/3B21m52

 # VIDEO CASE IN POINT

Next, let's join a preschool class to see and hear the ways the teacher intentionally engages her three-, four-, and five-year-old learners in guided play. First, the teacher analyzed standards for her unit of study on letter sounds. She created a learning progression to inform her sequencing of significant experiences and interactions. Then, she created these learning intentions and success criteria for the first day of the study during their indoor play or centers time.

Learning Foundations (*California Preschool Learning Foundations*, California Department of Education, 2008):

- Match some letter names to their printed form. (p. 178)
- Begin to recognize that letters have sounds. (p. 178)
- Enjoy learning and are confident in their abilities to make new discoveries although may not persist at solving difficult problems (p. 173).
- Understand and use accepted words for objects, actions, and attributes encountered frequently in both real and symbolic contexts. (p. 176)

Content Learning Intention:

We are learning how letter sounds are related to initial sounds of words.

Language Learning Intention:

We are learning to use what we know to name familiar and unfamiliar objects.

Social Learning Intention:

We are learning to discover and share connections.

Success Criteria:

I'll know I've learned this when

- I can name some letters and some objects.
- I can make a connection between letters, letter sounds, and objects.
- I can share my connection with words and actions.

These learning goals unite each of the centers during indoor play. The teacher has intentionally placed relevant letter and letter sound materials in each of the centers, such as letter and letter sound stamps and ink in art area, pretend food cans labeled with images and words in the pretend kitchen, and letter and letter sound blocks and train cars in the construction area. The teacher will keep these same learning intentions and success criteria over multiple days.

In the video, we'll watch as the teacher enters the play in the classroom library area. Two children have chosen to work with lacing pictures of letters and images with letter initial sounds.

As you watch, pay attention to the ways the teacher enters play with respect for the children and their self-initiated play as well as the ways she enters play with intentionality around the learning intentions and success criteria. Look for evidence of the three defining characteristics of guided play. Record your observations in the table below:

Defining Characteristics of Guided Play	Video Evidence
The adult has a clear learning goal in mind and makes choices about setting up the play space and the playful activity based on that goal.	
The child has opportunities to make choices and share their unique voice within the playful activity.	
The adult engages with the child intentionally and responsively as a conversational partner and/or as a language facilitator.	

Lacing, Identifying Letters:
bit.ly/3cWBMq9

YOUR TURN!

Now, it's your turn to bring this strategy to your work with your children. Go back to page 125 and complete the planning template there. As you plan each unit of study, create learning intentions, relevance, and success criteria to guide the what, why, and how of learning.

LEARNING INTENTION AND SUCCESS CRITERIA FOR MODULE 7

Now that you have engaged with the learning in this module, reread what we intended to learn (LI, the learning intention) and what it looks and sounds like to have mastered learning this (SC, the success criteria). Next, reread the levels, descriptions, and images of the path to mastery (the rubric). Reevaluate where you are right now for each success criteria. Use the box to reflect on the evidence you have of where you are and where you are headed next.

LI: We are learning how to intentionally plan the learning intention of one day so that, at the culmination of many days, all children have intentionally moved forward in their learning and development.

SC: I'll know I've learned it when I can

Beginning	Emerging	Developing	Expanding	Bridging
Becoming aware 	Initially trying	Deliberately practicing	Intentionally stretching	Transferring and generalizing 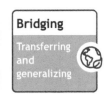

Icon source: istock.com/rambo182

- Create content, language, and social learning intentions that move learning forward through a learning progression.

_____

_____

_____

_____

_____

- Explain the relevance or purpose for the learning intention.

_____

_____

_____

_____

_____

- Create success criteria that monitor learning toward the learning intention and evaluate when learners have arrived at mastery of the learning intention.

_____

_____

_____

_____

_____

THE FOUR ESSENTIALS OF COMMUNICATING CLARITY

8

Developing our clarity about the what, why, and how of learning is only part of our work. Another critical part of clarity is communicating clarity to learners *and* families. We must communicate learning intentions and success criteria in ways that grow Visible Learners who

Big Ideas

- Know their current level of understanding; they can communicate what they do and do not yet know,

- Know where they are going next in their learning and are ready to take on the challenge,

- Select tools to move their learning and development forward,

- Seek feedback about their learning and recognize errors as opportunities to learn,

- Monitor their learning and make adjustments when necessary, and

- Recognize when they have learned something and serve as a teacher to others. (Frey et al., 2018)

Teacher clarity (effect size = 0.84) has the potential to considerably accelerate learning and development, but only if this clarity is shared with learners. The communication of clarity takes place through deliberate, intentional, and purposeful practices.

LEARNING INTENTION AND SUCCESS CRITERIA FOR MODULE 8

Before you engage with the learning in this module, read what we intend to learn (LI, the learning intention) and what it'll look and sound like when we've learned this (SC, the success criteria). Next, read the levels, descriptions, and images of the path to mastery (the rubric). Evaluate where you are right now for each success criteria. At the end of the module, we'll return to this self-evaluation and document the ways we've intentionally grown our teaching practice over time.

LI: We are learning what it looks like and sounds like to effectively communicate clarity in the early childhood classroom so that we can use our partnerships to develop Visible Learners.

SC: I'll know I've learned this when I can

Icon source: istock.com/rambo182

- Explain the four essentials of communicating clarity in the early childhood classroom.

  _____

  _____

  _____

  _____

  _____

- Describe ways to effectively communicate clarity throughout our interactions with both children and families.

  _____

  _____

  _____

  _____

  _____

In early childhood, communicating clarity is vital. In fact, in early childhood, often communicating with families about learning intentions and success criteria is equally important to communicating these with learners. Our partnerships depend upon each person (family member, classroom teacher, paraprofessional, special educator, specialist, and child) knowing and interacting deliberately based on the what, why, and how of learning.

The way we communicate clarity in early childhood is also crucial because most of our youngest learners do not read yet, many are learning English as an additional language, and all are developing language skills and understanding. We can rely on the four essentials for communicating clarity in the early childhood classroom (Figure 8.1) to make sure clarity is communicated effectively to all our partners. The four essentials for communicating clarity are

⤷ visuals with vocabulary,

⤷ model thinking,

⤷ metacognitive questioning, and

⤷ scaffold self-monitoring.

8.1 **The 4 Essentials of Communicating Clarity in the Early Childhood Classroom**

Visuals With Vocabulary	Model Thinking	Metacognitive Questioning	Scaffold Self-Monitoring
Use visuals alongside academic vocabulary in the context of learning.	Demonstrate high-order thinking skills and processes by modeling.	Explicitly teach metacognitive skills through questioning.	Provide visual rubrics, checklists, exemplars, and models to support learners as they self-monitor.

Icon source: istock.com/AlexeyBlogoodf

As we unpack each of these essentials, we will take a peek inside two classrooms to see what it looks and sounds like to make these essentials reality with our youngest learners. Valerie Jara's infant class is in the middle of an Imitation Unit. She has thoughtfully planned the what, why, and how of the whole day's interactions and experiences focused on imitation:

Guiding Question	Guiding Answer	What We Call It
What am I learning today?	Today, I am learning **facial expressions show different emotions.**	Content Learning Intention
	Today, I am learning **the names of emotions: happy, silly.**	Language Learning Intention
	Today, I am learning **to watch a face and imitate the facial expression.**	Social Learning Intention
Why am I learning this?	So that **I can understand how others feel by looking at their faces.**	Relevance
How will I know I've learned this?	I'll know I've learned it when • I can **imitate a smile for happy.** • I can **imitate sticking my tongue out for silly.**	Success Criteria

Jeremy Harrison's first-grade class is on the sixth day of their shape unit. He has planned these learning intentions, relevance, and success criteria for today's mathematics lesson:

Guiding Question	Guiding Answer	What We Call It
What am I learning today?	Today, I am learning **to sort shapes based on their attributes.**	Content Learning Intention
	Today, I am learning **to describe shapes using attribute words: side, vertex.**	Language Learning Intention
	Today, I am learning **to listen to another peer's ideas.**	Social Learning Intention
Why am I learning this?	So that **I can identify what is the same and what is different about shapes.**	Relevance
How will I know I've learned this?	I'll know I've learned this when • I can **sort shapes based on their attributes.** • I can **describe how I sorted my shapes to someone else.**	Success Criteria

VISUALS WITH VOCABULARY

The first essential of communicating clarity is to use visuals alongside academic vocabulary within the context of learning. A visual can be a picture, diagram, video, or physical objects. It can include labels such as words, phrases, or sentences in multiple languages. Visuals can be purchased, premade by teachers, families, or learners, and co-constructed with learners and families.

By looking at the visual, learners should be able to make sense of what they're learning, why, and how they'll know when they've learned it. A visual should be used alongside talk about the visual. In this way, the teacher can explicitly connect the language of the learning intention and success criteria with the visual.

Visuals paired with vocabulary help make the abstract ideas of learning intentions and success criteria concrete. They scaffold children's language for talking about the what, why, and how of learning. They grow children's independence as learners who can make sense of, read, and use visuals to self-monitor. Visuals are also accessible regardless of primary language, fluency with English, or ability to read.

 # CASE IN POINT

As you read about Valerie and Jeremy's classrooms, look for the ways they use visuals with vocabulary to make the what, why, and how of learning come to life. Refer to their learning intentions, relevance, and success criteria (p. 166). Highlight, circle, and note below where you see these communicated in their classrooms through visuals paired with vocabulary. Then reflect on each example.

Valerie Jara's Infant Classroom	Jeremy Harrison's First-Grade Class
Valerie wants to be sure her infants' families and her collaborating educators know the what, why, and how of learning each day. She also wants to be intentional about her interactions and language and to surround her infants with opportunities to encounter the learning.	Learners are spread out across the floor sorting shapes. Mr. Harrison shares, "Yesterday, when we were exploring shapes, someone in our class posed an interesting question: 'Does everything in the whole world have a shape?' What do you think about that question?" "Of course, everything has a shape!" yells Margo.

(Continued)

(Continued)

For each of the emotions they study, Valerie makes photo books. Today, she has small books with photos of each infant and adult who spends time in the classroom smiling big happy smiles and making silly faces. The photos include all five infants, Valerie, her paraprofessional, the physical therapist, and the childcare center director. There are also spaces for more photos; as families send them in, Valerie adds pictures of family members smiling and sticking tongues out.

Each page has the repeating line from the song they will sing together, "This Is a Happy/Silly Face," followed by the caption: _____ (name) smiles/ sticks their tongue out. For the infants whose families speak Spanish or Turkish at home, she has the lyrics in their heritage languages. Valerie sings the song frequently throughout the day. Sometimes she sings while reading the photo books and sometimes she sings while showing her own facial expressions and the children their own via mirrors.

"But if everything has a shape, what shape are you?" asks Charles.

"Well, I don't know the name of my shape, but I am a shape. Maybe I am a person shape?" Margo replies.

Mr. Harrison suggests, "Let's start a chart to keep track of names of shapes and what we already know about them. Then, as we continue with our sorting work, if we find new shapes, we can add them to our chart." He writes triangle, rectangle, pentagon, and hexagon.

8.2   Anchor Chart

"We are going to write down each shape's attributes. Say the word *attribute*." The children respond. "In this case, an attribute is a quality that belongs to a certain thing, like a shape. An attribute is something you can say a shape has, like the number of sides or vertices. We can describe shapes using their attributes. Let's fill in the attributes for some shapes we have already been discussing."

What do you notice about the example?	What do you notice about the example?

How does this example exemplify *visuals with vocabulary?*	How does this example exemplify *visuals with vocabulary?*
How could you use this example in your own classroom?	How could you use this example in your own classroom?

 # CASE IN POINT

Jesse Soriano is a preschool teacher who has decided to increase the focus on clarity in the classroom. Jesse has created a focus wall where children's attention is directed for each of the lessons. There are visuals and words for each lesson that will be taught for the day. Jesse returns to the focus wall on a regular basis during the lessons to ensure that the learners know what it is they are learning, why it is important, and how they will know that they have learned.

The children in the class have had several conflicts and are saying that they are not friends with other children. These are temporary spats, but it seems to have become a common interaction with children saying to others, "You are not my friend." Jesse decides to focus on "friendships" and develops a series of lessons about friends and why we need friends.

What might be some effective ways for ensuring that family members understood the what, why, and how of the learning? How might Jesse communicate clarity of these lessons with the caregivers of the children in the class?

(Continued)

(Continued)

MODEL THINKING

The second essential of communicating clarity is to demonstrate higher-order thinking skills and processes by modeling. In other words, we need to think aloud about reasoning, problem-solving, and decision-making. When we think aloud, we model asking and answering higher-order questions, such as these:

- Why?

- What if . . . ?

- Will this always work?

- What caused this?

- How are these related?

- How is this like . . . ?

- What's another way to think about this?

- What is a reasonable prediction?

- How do I know?

By listening to a think aloud, learners make sense of what they're learning, why, and how they'll know when they've learned it. Modeling our thinking is often paired with modeling the task, which can be interactive; however, the think aloud is focused on the learning, modeling the language of the learning intentions and success criteria, and emphasizing decision points. While teachers are often the modelers, family members and learners can model thinking and teach others.

By modeling our thinking, we help children become more aware of their own thinking and how it may be similar or different to others'. We connect the abstract ideas of learning intentions and success criteria with nameable decision points and highlight these moments as places for children to actively make choices and own their learning processes. We also teach children how to engage in a task while remaining focused on the learning from the task rather than simply doing the task.

CASE IN POINT

Let's step back into Valerie and Jeremy's classrooms. How are they modeling their thinking in order to highlight and make sense of the learning intentions, relevance, and success criteria? How do they model asking and answering higher-order questions to emphasize the learning taking place within the tasks? Remember to look back at their learning intentions, relevance, and success criteria (p. 155). Highlight, circle, and note below where you see these communicated in their classrooms by modeling thinking. After reading, again pause to reflect.

Valerie Jara's Infant Classroom	Jeremy Harrison's First Grade Class
Valerie is singing the song lyrics as she shows two infants the photo book of familiar faces smiling and sticking out their tongues. As she sings, Valerie holds the book so the babies can touch the pictures.	The children in Mr. Harrison's class have been working on their shape attribute chart. Mr. Harrison has noticed that some learners are confused when a triangle is oriented in an unfamiliar way. He wants to clear up this misunderstanding, "I have noticed something about this shape." Mr. Harrison holds up a triangle. "Sometimes this shape points this direction," he holds the triangle with one vertex up. "And sometimes it points this direction," he flips the triangle so the vertex is pointing down. "Other times I have even seen it this way!" he turns it on its side. "That makes me wonder: What if I change the direction or orientation of the shape, does it change into another shape?"
She pauses on the photo of the paraprofessional to ask aloud, "What is Ms. Thompson doing? She's smiling. Ms. Thompson is happy. Smile!" Valerie points to the photo of Ms. Thompson and then makes a big smile herself. The babies look at the photo and at Valerie. "Smile! We're happy!" she says again and continues singing.	
At a photo of Bianca's sister, Valerie pauses again to wonder aloud, "Kayla sonríe. ¿Por qué está sonriendo? Kayla smiles. Why is she smiling? Oh, Kayla's smiling because she's happy. She loves to sing and dance. Kayla está sonriendo porque está feliz. Le encanta cantar y bailar."	Mr. Harrison waits a few seconds and then continues thinking aloud, "What's another way I can think about this?" He points to the anchor chart of shapes they've started. "I know I can think about what I know about the attributes of this shape, the triangle. The triangle has three sides and three vertices. If I hold the shape like this, I can count three sides (1, 2, 3) and three vertices (1, 2, 3). Will there still be three sides and three vertices if I turn the triangle upside down? Let me check."
Now Bianca is smiling too. Valerie smiles, claps, and says, "Bianca también sonríe! Bianca smiles too! Bianca is happy to see her sister Kayla. Biance está felix de ver a su hermana Kayla." Valerie holds up a mirror so Bianca can see her smiling face.	

(Continued)

(Continued)

Valerie Jara's Infant Classroom	Jeremy Harrison's First Grade Class
Valerie returns to singing the lyrics while pointing to Bianca's smiling face in the mirror, "This is a happy face. Esta es una cara feliz."	Mr. Harrison turns and counts, "Will this always be true no matter how I turn the shape?" Mr. Harrison turns and counts again and keeps turning and counting. He is getting more and more excited, "I can't believe it! Every time I turn the triangle, it still has three sides and three vertices!" The children giggle at his excitement and join in.
What do you notice about the example?	What do you notice about the example?
How does this example exemplify *model thinking?*	How does this example exemplify *model thinking?*
How could you use this example in your own classroom?	How could you use this example in your own classroom?

METACOGNITIVE QUESTIONING

The third essential of communicating clarity is to explicitly teach metacognitive thinking through questioning. Metacognitive thinking is thinking about our thinking. We can engage in metacognitive thinking to self-monitor, self-reflect, and self-evaluate. These go hand in hand with learning intentions and success criteria.

Self-monitoring is observing behavior in the moment, comparing it to the success criteria, and making adjustments when necessary. To explicitly teach self-monitoring, we should ask questions ongoing throughout a task that help build awareness of the learning from the task.

Important
Vocabulary

Self-reflecting is making sense of the learning journey at multiple points. We can explicitly teach self-reflecting by asking children to think about three questions: *Where am I going? How am I going? Where do I go next?* These questions direct learners' attention to the relationship between their work and the learning intentions and success criteria. Children can reflect on what and how they learned from the task as well as identify next steps along the learning journey.

Self-evaluating involves analyzing the learning journey compared to the success criteria and determining progress toward mastering the learning intention. To explicitly teach self-evaluating, we should intentionally ask questions at the completion of a task or the culmination of multiple tasks that emphasize evaluating learning over time.

By using metacognitive questioning, we can explicitly teach learners how to use learning intentions and success criteria to self-reflect, self-monitor, and self-evaluate.

CASE IN POINT

When we are in Valerie's and Jeremy's classrooms, we'll hear them asking metacognitive questions. They know that providing opportunities to hear and make connections with these types of questions is important even if the children can't answer them *yet*. Both teachers scaffold their learners' response to these questions. As you read, highlight, circle, and note where Valerie and Jeremy are asking metacognitive questions to engage children in self-reflecting, self-monitoring, and self-evaluating about the what, why, and how of learning. Pay attention to the ways their questions align with their learning intentions, relevance, and success criteria (p. 155). Reflect after reading.

(Continued)

(Continued)

Valerie Jara's Infant Classroom	Jeremy Harrison's First Grade Class
The infants are waking up from nap in Valerie's classroom. Valerie reads a mirror book with Lincoln. On each page, she reads about an emotion and a facial expression, "Monkey feels silly. Monkey sticks out her tongue." Valerie makes the face and points to herself in the mirror. Lincoln looks at her face and looks in the mirror. Valerie asks, "Can you stick out your tongue? Can you make your face look like this? I see you moving your tongue. Can you get your tongue out? You've almost made a silly face. Stick your tongue out!" She sticks her tongue out again while Lincoln opens his mouth and moves his tongue around. Valerie says, "You can do it! That's so silly!"	While learners are working on sorting and recording their shapes, Mr. Harrison notices Mary has sorted the shapes based on color. He asks, "Mary, how did you choose to sort your shapes?" Mary responds, "I put yellow ones here, blue ones here, green ones right here, and red ones over here." Mr. Harrison affirms Mary's work and directs her to look at the anchor chart. "You are sorting by the attribute of color. Color is a great attribute for sorting. Now let's try a new sort. Today, we are trying new ways to sort shapes. We are sorting by special attributes that just shapes have. For example, we could sort by the number of sides or the number of vertices. How can you reorganize your sort so that they are sorted based on a shape attribute?" He pauses to give her thinking time. When she still doesn't respond, he points to the rectangle Mary is holding and prompts, "What do you notice about this shape?" She replies, "It has four corners." "It has four corners. Those are also called *vertices*." Mr. Harrison points to this new word on the anchor chart and then points and counts the vertices on the rectangle. He says, "Let's find all the shapes with four vertices and put them with this one."
What do you notice about the example?	What do you notice about the example?

Valerie Jara's Infant Classroom	Jeremy Harrison's First Grade Class
How does this example exemplify *metacognitive questioning*?	How does this example exemplify *metacognitive questioning*?
How could you use this example in your own classroom?	How could you use this example in your own classroom?

CASE IN POINT

Lenor Padilla's children have been working on metacognitive questioning. This is a mixed-age class with learners who are four, five, or six years old. Lenor has provided learners with visual tools that they can use to self-assess. These are essentially checklists that children use to identify what they have accomplished and what they still need to learn and/or do. The children in Lenor's class also use these tools as they interact with one another. For example, two learners were discussing their illustrations. Maria, using the visual checklist, says, "I like how you drew the bat. You wrote about the bat and you made a picture of the bat with wings and big ears. What do you like about your picture?" The conversation continues as the children reflect and monitor, in this case with peers.

How might you teach family members about self-monitoring, self-reflecting, and self-evaluating? What could you do to ensure that family members understand the importance of metacognitive questioning and can use some of these strategies with their children?

(Continued)

(Continued)

Self-Monitoring	
Self-Reflecting	
Self-Evaluating	

SCAFFOLD SELF-MONITORING

The fourth essential of communicating clarity is to provide visual rubrics, checklists, exemplars, and models to scaffold learners as they self-monitor. While this essential component certainly overlaps with the other three, the unique feature here is that we *provide* these supports rather than serve as the supports ourselves. The scaffolds must be actionable by learners and their families even when we are not present. In other words, we create scaffolds that gradually develop children's independent self-monitoring as Visible Learners who use learning intentions and success criteria to drive their own learning.

Visual rubrics, checklists, exemplars, and models are scaffolds to support self-monitoring. These may be the visuals paired with vocabulary, the think aloud, or the metacognitive questioning. But most importantly, they are tools that we explicitly teach learners and families to use in order to self-monitor and then we provide opportunities for them to deliberately practice using the tools and to receive feedback.

CASE IN POINT

During our final visit to Valerie's and Jeremy's classrooms, look for the scaffolds they provide to engage their learners, families, and collaborating educators in self-monitoring. The scaffolds empower their partners to monitor children's progress toward making sense of the learning intentions, relevance, and success criteria (p. 155). Highlight, circle, and note below where you see the what, why, and how of learning communicated in their classrooms through scaffolds for self-monitoring. Finally, reflect on each example.

Valerie Jara's Infant Classroom	Jeremy Harrison's First Grade Class
In addition to the class photo books, Valerie makes a version of the photo book for each infant to take home. When families send in their photos, she adds them to the class photo books and the infants' individual books. Valerie includes the lyrics to their song and photo captions in each child's heritage language. Valerie records a video of herself singing and reading each photo book followed by her singing and making facial expressions using a mirror. She begins and ends the videos with the same statements in English and the child's heritage language: "Today, we're learning facial expressions show different emotions so that we can understand how others feel by looking at their faces. We can imitate a smile to show we are happy. Smile! We can imitate sticking out our tongues to show we feel silly. Silly! You try! Happy! Silly! Happy! Silly!" Valerie invites families to share anecdotes, photos, and videos when they see their child imitate a smile or sticking out their tongue and she does the same.	When Mr. Harrison's class completes their shape anchor chart, he takes a picture of the chart and prints out copies. He strategically places these images in areas around the room. When children are working on their sorts, they refer to the anchor chart to check their sorts and to use the vocabulary from the chart when describing their work. Mr. Harrisons' school uses a learning management system that allows children to record themselves talking about their work. The recordings in the digital journal are shared with families. Mr. Harrison knows how important it is for children's overall language development to deepen and extend their heritage languages, so he encourages children to speak in their heritage languages as they show, describe, and record their sorts. He collaborates with families and the school EL teacher to ensure children practice shape and attribute vocabulary in each of their languages. Families use the digital journal to identify what shape vocabulary they need to teach their children *and* Mr. Harrison. Mr. Harrison can then add shape vocabulary from multiple languages to the class anchor chart and send home copies of it as well.

(Continued)

(Continued)

Valerie Jara's Infant Classroom	Jeremy Harrison's First Grade Class
What do you notice about the example?	What do you notice about the example?
How does this example exemplify *scaffold self-monitoring*?	How does this example exemplify *scaffold self-monitoring*?
How could you use this example in your own classroom?	How could you use this example in your own classroom?

COMMUNICATING CLARITY AND OUR INTERACTIONS

We've devoted substantial time and energy to creating learning intentions and success criteria. We know this work is worth our time and energy. But their potential impact on learning depends on how we implement learning intentions and success criteria. In early childhood, learners make sense of and act on what they are learning, why, and how they'll know they've learned it in concrete ways without having to read words.

After crafting learning intentions and success criteria, what do we do with them? We may post them in our classroom so that, while most of our learners do not read yet, anyone joining our class (administrators, directors, instructional coaches, paraprofessionals, special educators, specialists, and family members) can use them as a guide for intentional interactions with children. We may post them or carry them on a clipboard as reminders to ourselves as we interact with children. We may include them in lesson plans, newsletters, or daily updates.

Regardless of where they are written, we must communicate them to learners and families throughout our interactions. Clarity must be communicated to impact learning and development. At the beginning, middle, and end of lessons, tasks, and play, the language of our interactions should be informed by our learning intentions and success criteria.

 VIDEO CASE IN POINT

Let's join another preschool class to see and hear the ways the teacher communicates clarity as her three-, four-, and five-year-old learners work together in a small group. First, the teacher analyzed standards to create learning intentions and success criteria.

Learning Foundations (*California Preschool Learning Foundations*, California Department of Education, 2008):

- Demonstrate knowledge of details in a familiar story, including characters, events, and ordering of events through answering questions (particularly summarizing, predicting, and inferencing), retelling, reenacting, or creating artwork. (p. 178)

- Understand and use an increasing variety and specificity of accepted words for objects, actions, and attributes encountered in both real and symbolic contexts. (p. 176)

- Participate in group activities and are beginning to understand and cooperate with social expectations, group rules, and roles. (p. 174)

Content Learning Intention:

I am learning to retell a familiar story with details.

Language Learning Intention:

I am learning to use sequencing words: first, next, then.

Social Learning Intention:

I am learning to take turns using the same materials and sharing ideas with a small group.

(Continued)

(Continued)

> **Success Criteria:**
>
> I'll know I've learned this when
>
> - I can take turns retelling the events of a story using pictures.
> - I can answer questions about what happened in a story.

The teacher then used these goals to determine the task: retell the classic story of *The Very Hungry Caterpillar* (Carle, 1969) in a small group using images as supports.

In the video, we'll watch as the teacher introduces the task to a small group of learners and interacts with them throughout the task to communicate clarity throughout the learning. As you watch, pay attention to the ways the teacher creates a space for playful learning with intentionality. Look for evidence of the four essentials for communicating clarity. Record your observations in the table below:

The Four Essentials of Communicating Clarity	Video Evidence
Visuals With Vocabulary	
Model Thinking	
Metacognitive Questioning	
Scaffold Self-Monitoring	

Hungry Caterpillar Pictures:
bit.ly/3L36Y3s

YOUR TURN!

Return to your learning intentions, relevance, and success criteria on p. 155 of Module 7. How will you communicate these using the four essentials? Under each essential of communicating clarity in the early childhood classroom, record your ideas for implementation with your specific learners in your context and with your learning intentions, relevance, and success criteria.

8.3 Can I implement the 4 Essentials of Communicating Clarity in MY Early Childhood Classroom?

Yes, I can! ☐	Yes, I can! ☐	Yes, I can! ☐	Yes, I can! ☐
Visuals With Vocabulary	**Model Thinking**	**Metacognitive Questioning**	**Scaffold Self-Monitoring**
Use visuals alongside academic vocabulary in the context of learning.	Demonstrate high-order thinking skills and processes by modeling.	Explicitly teach metacognitive skills through questioning.	Provide visual rubrics, checklists, exemplars, and models to support learners as they self-monitor.
My Implementation Plan	My Implementation Plan	My Implementation Plan	My Implementation Plan

Icon source: istock.com/AlexeyBlogoodf

Our purpose is to grow our expertise so that we can grow Visible Learners. Our learning intentions and success criteria are our compass. We use them to guide the rest of our instructional decisions from tasks and learning strategies to formative evaluation and feedback.

LEARNING INTENTION AND SUCCESS CRITERIA FOR MODULE 8

Now that you have engaged with the learning in this module, reread what we intended to learn (LI, the learning intention) and what it looks and sounds like to have mastered learning this (SC, the success criteria). Next, reread the levels, descriptions, and images of the path to mastery (the rubric). Reevaluate where you are right now for each success criteria. Use the box to reflect on the evidence you have of where you are and where you are headed next.

LI: We are learning what it looks like and sounds like to effectively communicate clarity in the early childhood classroom so that we can use our partnerships to develop Visible Learners.

SC: I'll know I've learned this when I can

Icon source: istock.com/rambo182

- Explain the four essentials of communicating clarity in the early childhood classroom.

  _____

  _____

  _____

  _____

  _____

- Describe ways to effectively communicate clarity throughout our interactions with both children and families.

  _____

  _____

  _____

  _____

  _____

PART III

TASKS, LEARNING STRATEGIES, AND SCAFFOLDS

HIGH-QUALITY TASKS

From our work in Part 2, we know what children are learning, why, and how we and they will know when they've learned it. Next, we select the tasks, learning strategies, and tools that will be the catalysts for learning. Visible Learners select tools to move their learning and development forward, recognize errors as opportunities to learn, and are ready to take on challenge. In order to grow these and all the characteristics of Visible Learners, learners must engage in high-quality tasks that provide them with opportunities for high-quality language, interactions, and learning.

Big Ideas

LEARNING INTENTION AND SUCCESS CRITERIA FOR MODULE 9

Before you engage with the learning in this module, read what we intend to learn (LI, the learning intention) and what it'll look and sound like when we've learned this (SC, the success criteria). Next, read the levels, descriptions, and images of the path to mastery (the rubric). Evaluate where you are right now for each success criteria. At the end of the module, we'll return to this self-evaluation and document the ways we've intentionally grown our teaching practice over time.

LI: We are learning the qualities of tasks that provide all learners with opportunities for high-quality language, interactions, and learning so that we can select, revise, or create high-quality tasks.

SC: I'll know I've learned it when I can

(Continued)

(Continued)

Icon source: istock.com/rambo182

- Describe the qualities of tasks aligned with learning intentions and success criteria, of tasks that promote equity, and of rigorous and engaging tasks.

_____

_____

_____

_____

_____

- Explain the importance of these qualities for moving learning and development forward for all children.

_____

_____

_____

_____

_____

- Apply these qualities as we select, revise, or create tasks for our learners.

_____

_____

_____

_____

_____

We've all had those moments where we look around our classroom and there is a hum of activity. Children are engaged, interacting with each other, laughing, smiling, and focused on the task at hand. The learning is playful. And we've all had those other moments where signs of boredom, frustration, disinterest, and passive compliance abound. The disengagement is obvious.

REFLECTION

What makes those moments different? Using the chart below, document the nature of the learning experiences, interactions, and tasks associated with a time when your learners were fully engaged and then a time when your learners were not engaged.

Engaged	Disengaged
Features of the learning experience, interactions, and task	*Features of the learning experience, interactions, and task*

ALIGNMENT WITH LEARNING INTENTIONS AND SUCCESS CRITERIA

High-quality tasks are aligned with the learning intentions and success criteria. In other words, the goals determine the task. The task does not determine the goals.

There are countless tasks to choose from. We all have our favorites. But we should not select the task first and then identify what can be learned through the task.

Instead, we set the learning intentions and success criteria and then select the task that fits. The task must align with the verbs of the success criteria, which align with the concepts and skills of the analyzed standard. Tasks that are not aligned may be impactful, worthwhile tasks . . . for another day when the learning intentions and success criteria align with it.

YOUR TURN!

Let's try applying this first attribute of high-quality tasks: The task aligns with the learning intentions and success criteria. In the table, you'll see learning intentions and success criteria paired with two possible tasks. You decide which task aligns with the

(Continued)

(Continued)

learning intentions and success criteria. Then explain why one task aligns while the other does not.

Remember, the goals determine the task.

Infant—Imitation Unit

Learning Intentions & Success Criteria	**Content Learning Intention:** Today, I am learning facial expressions show different emotions. **Language Learning Intention:** Today, I am learning the names of emotions: happy, silly. **Social Learning Intention:** Today, I am learning to watch faces and imitate facial expressions. **Relevance:** So that I can understand how others feel by looking at their faces. **Success Criteria:** I'll know I've learned it when I can imitate a smile for happy and I can imitate sticking my tongue out for silly.	
Which task is aligned with the learning intentions and success criteria?	**Task A** Play Peek-a-Boo: Cover your eyes and name a child: "Where's happy Anna?" or "Where's silly Eli?" Then peek out and make smiling faces or stick out tongues. "Peek-a-Boo! Here's happy Anna!" or "Here's silly Eli!"	**Task B** Play Peek-a-Boo: Cover a favorite toy with a cloth. "Where's (toy name)?" Uncover toy and say, "Peek-a-Boo! Here's (toy name)!" Clap and smile together.
Explain your reasoning.		

Toddler—Unit to Solve the Problem: How can I play *with* a friend using the same materials?

Learning Intentions & Success Criteria	**Language Learning Intention:** Today, I am learning I can say words to describe actions: clap, stomp, pat. **Social Learning Intention:** Today, I am learning we can sing and dance together. **Relevance:** So that we can sing action songs as a class and as a family. **Success Criteria:** I'll know I've learned it when I can move my body to match action songs' words.

Which task is aligned with the learning intentions and success criteria?	Task A Sing and dance to *"El Twist de los Ratoncitos*/The Twist of the Little Mice" and count down from 5 to 0 mice.	Task B Sing and dance to *"Este es el baile del movimiento*/This is the Dance of Movement" with actions of *aplaudir*/clap, *pisar muy fuerte*/stomp, and *palmadita*/pat.
Explain your reasoning.		

Preschool—Describe and Label Unit

Learning Intentions & Success Criteria	**Content Learning Intention:** Today, I am learning true information from nonfiction informational texts. **Language Learning Intention:** Today, I am learning to listen and ask questions about informational texts. **Social Learning Intention:** Today, I am learning to work with others to find and describe things around me using our learning from informational texts. **Relevance:** So that I know how to use informational texts to learn something new. **Success Criteria:** I'll know I've learned this when I can look at or listen to an informational text, ask a question about the informational text, and work together to play, create, or use information from the text.	
Which task is aligned with the learning intentions and success criteria?	Task A Learners listen to the book *We're Going on a Leaf Hunt* (Metzger, 2005) and then reenact the story during the second reread.	Task B Learners listen and ask questions about the page, *Trees on the Trail*, from the book, *On the Nature Trail* (Storey Publishing, 2018). Then in small groups, children use images of leaves from the book to find and collect similar leaves outside.
Explain your reasoning.		

(Continued)

(Continued)

Learning Intentions & Success Criteria	**Content Learning Intention:** Today, I am learning to sort shapes based on their attributes.	
	Language Learning Intention: Today, I am learning to describe shapes using attribute words: side, vertex.	
	Social Learning Intention: Today, I am learning to listen to another peer's ideas.	
	Relevance: So that I can identify what is the same and what is different about shapes.	
	Success Criteria: I'll know I've learned this when I can sort shapes based on their attributes and describe how I sorted my shapes to someone else.	
Which task is aligned with the learning intentions and success criteria?	**Task A** Sort a set of attribute blocks with the peers at the table and use index cards to label each group.	**Task B** Sort a set of attribute blocks independently, label the groups, then share groups with an assigned peer.
Explain your reasoning.		

Compare your answers with the suggested answers at the end of this module in Module 9 Appendix: Your Turn Possible Answers on pp. 204-206.

The goals determine the task. This means the goals also determine the learning environment in which the task takes place. The way we set up the learning environment is a pivotal part of our intentional teaching and children's learning and development (NAEYC, 2020). From the physical space to the materials to the storage of materials, the learning environment of the task must align with the learning intentions and success criteria. The learning environment can help us communicate clarity as well as ensure every learner can experience success.

In Module 8, we examined the four essentials of communicating clarity. To scaffold self-monitoring, we must intentionally make decisions about the way the learning environment is a scaffold for self-monitoring of learners' journeys toward mastery of the learning intentions. We saw Valerie Jara create photo books for her infants and their families. The content of the books was carefully aligned to the learning intentions and success criteria of her lesson within her Imitation Unit. We also observed Jeremy Harrison co-create an anchor chart of shape attributes with his first graders. Then, he printed copies of the anchor chart and strategically placed them in work areas to scaffold his learners' self-monitoring. Both Valerie and Jeremy were intentional in their decisions to create the learning environment based on the learning goals and to use the learning environment intentionally to support children's learning and development toward the learning goals.

In Module 10, we will look closely at our decisions about multiple ways of engaging, representing, acting and expressing as well as our selection of tools as temporary scaffolds. The goals determine the task and they determine the ways we adjust the task to ensure access and opportunity for *all* learners. To maintain the quality of a task from planning to implementation, each of these decisions must align with our learning intentions and success criteria.

 CASE IN POINT

Michelle Brooks is reflecting with her paraprofessional, Camille De León, about their preschoolers' learning today. Michelle and Camille know how important it is to read aloud daily and to reread books multiple times. As a class, they read aloud four to six books each day. During read alouds, the class sits in rows on a colored carpet, and everyone is expected to remain quiet so the book can be heard by everyone. At the end of reading, the children can raise hands and two comments or questions are shared. The class books are kept on the shelves above the art area counters and a crate of books from the library is put out for the children to look at once each day for ten minutes of "reading to self," which typically involves children sitting on their colored square with a book, turning pages.

Based on the learning outcome, "Child asks and responds to questions relevant to the text read aloud" (Texas Commissioner of Education, p. 75), Michelle and Camille created the following learning intention and success criteria for today's read aloud before lunch:

- We are learning to ask and answer questions as we read nonfiction books so that we can understand what we read.
- We'll know we've learned this when we can ask questions inspired by the book and then answer our questions by rereading, talking, and reading new books.

Michelle expresses her disappointment, "I thought they'd have tons of questions about worms. They love finding them outside on the playground after it rains. That's why we chose to read aloud the book, *Wiggling Worms at Work* (Pfeffer, 2003)."

(Continued)

(Continued)

"But they didn't ask much. Arely asked where worms lived, but Zaire answered really quickly," Camille adds.

"We didn't get to reread or talk or read any new books to find answers to their questions. I thought the learning intentions and success criteria were really well aligned to the standard. I don't understand why we weren't successful," Michelle wonders with frustration.

"And you know, I heard Kia and Alejo's table talking all about the thunderstorm we had last night. They were posing all these amazing questions like why is thunder so loud and is there always lightning with thunder?"

Camille reflects. "Oh, is that why Alejo asked me for the book about weather? It wasn't time for the crate of books so I told him we'd look later and then we both forgot about it. Was he trying to answer that question?" Michelle realizes.

Michelle and Camille want to try again tomorrow. Look back at their learning intention and success criteria. Describe how the learning environment, including the physical space, the materials, the storage of materials, and the expectations for engagement, could better align to these goals. What adjustments do you recommend they make to ensure the implementation of the task takes place in a learning environment aligned with the learning intention and success criteria?

TASKS TO PROMOTE EQUITY

Big Ideas

Tasks that grow Visible Learners also promote equity. When tasks promote equity, children see what they currently know as useful and valuable within a new challenge, they identify familiar tools and make adjustments to apply these tools in new situations, and they recognize their own expertise to serve as teachers to others.

There are five qualities of tasks that promote equity (Berry & Thunder, 2012). In Module 3, we examined the ways our interactions can create equity in our classrooms. You'll see these ways mirrored in the qualities of tasks that promote equity (Figure 9.1).

9.1 **Qualities of Tasks to Promote Equity**

Situated Within Children's Prior Knowledge	To situate a task within children's prior knowledge, we apply what we know from our partnerships to identify familiar contexts, materials, or language. When tasks are situated within children's prior knowledge, children see familiar aspects within the task and can more readily access novel and challenging aspects of the task. These tasks emphasize relational understanding, scaffold children's retrieval of information, and communicate to learners' the importance of being a Visible Learner who knows their current level of understanding and where they're going next in learning.
Promote Positive Identity	Tasks can serve as mirrors that reflect to children affirming images of themselves, their families, and their experiences. Particularly in early childhood, young children are just embarking on forming their identities separately from their families as well as their identities as learners. We can select tasks that protect space for *all* children to express, represent, and engage in ways that reflect who they are. These tasks can reflect demographics, families, interests and wonderings.
Grow Agency	Tasks that grow children's agency are tasks that develop their initiative, self-regulation, and problem-solving. There is not a single or obvious path, rather there are multiple options that welcome the learner as a decision-maker. By having the developmentally appropriate or right level of challenge, the tasks communicate to children that they are ready to take on the challenge of the task and the new learning. Combined with the essentials for communicating clarity, the tasks intentionally engage children in self-monitoring and realizing when they have learned something new.
Position All Learners as Competent	Every child has valuable contributions for their learning community. Tasks can communicate this collective effort to learn by leveraging the strengths of the individuals for the collective whole. Learners can share and together learn from each other's experiences, wonderings, discoveries, explanations, and mistakes. Children realize what they know and that they can teach others when learners are able to interact about the task. When tasks have multiple entry points or ways to get started, then every learner can access and make meaning of the task. When the focus is on the learning by emphasizing the learning intentions and success criteria, rather than task completion, then all learners are positioned as competent.
Share Authority for Learning With Learners	Sometimes the hardest quality to make a reality is sharing authority for learning with learners. We have to be comfortable saying we don't know everything, that children's voices are more important than our own, and that every child deserves the right to make decisions about their own learning. When we do these things, we share authority for learning with learners and select tasks that reflect content or materials where learners are the experts, that elevate children's insights, and that require children to drive next steps.

# CASE IN POINT

Meredyth Williams' preschool class is in the midst of a unit focused on the overarching skills describe and label. She planned these goals for today:

Guiding Question	Guiding Answer	What We Call It
What am I learning today?	Today, I am learning **true information from nonfiction informational texts.**	Content Learning Intention
	Today, I am learning **to listen and ask questions about informational texts.**	Language Learning Intention
	Today, I am learning **to work with others to find and describe things around me using our learning from informational texts.**	Social Learning Intention
Why am I learning this?	So that **I know how to use informational texts to learn something new.**	Relevance
How will I know I've learned this?	I'll know I've learned this when • I can **look or listen to an informational text.** • I can **ask a question about the informational text.** • I can **work together to play, create, or use information from the text.**	Success Criteria

The class has been reading nonfiction informational, or All About, books on various topics. They have engaged in multiple reads of different read alouds by asking questions and having class discussions. Ms. Williams has chosen texts based on individual interests and outside-of-school experiences, like sports, animals, things found in nature, and people, places, and occupations found in the neighborhood. Now, Ms. Williams would like to incorporate informational texts into center time giving learners the chance to use different texts with their peers.

Prior to the lesson, Ms. Williams prepares the centers in a way that encourages peer interactions and collaboration as well as the use of informational texts. The centers are developed to mirror experiences children may have outside of school. Since she communicates with families regularly, she knows their family routines and can incorporate them. For example, the kitchen is equipped with "real" kitchen tools, such as whisks, plates, pots, and utensils. She wants children to have choice within each center. The kitchen has several family recipes as well as visual directions for setting the table and loading the dishwasher. There are books about different type of foods from countries around the world and food magazines. The construction center has visual directions for wooden block structures, Lego structures, and a marble run in addition to books about construction trucks and different kinds of treehouses.

Today, Ms. Williams wants learners to work together to complete a common goal using an informational text. At the beginning of centers, she calls everyone to the rug. "Today when you are at your center, you will see different types of informational texts, like the ones we have been reading together. When we are at centers today, you are going to use information from the books to help you create something as a group. For example, in kitchen, maybe your group would like to look through the books to help you decide what to cook or how to set the table. At the sensory table, you could use the nature book to decide how to sort the nature items in the table—like putting all the leaves together, then all the pinecones, then the rocks, and so forth. When you get to your center, talk to the friends who are with you and see which informational book you would like to use and what you would like to use it for. When you have created or made something using an informational text, call me over so you can show me and tell me about your hard work! At the end, we will share what we accomplished together"

While the children are working, Ms. Williams moves around the classroom and meets with children in each center. She encourages the children to use the classroom environment (i.e., anchor charts with pictures, labeled material bins) and each other when they have questions or are stuck. Often, children will struggle to make decisions together, but Ms. Williams is there to support children in practicing this important skill, offering support and feedback to children using purposeful language frames.

When center time is over, Ms. Williams gathers learners back to the carpet. She wants to check in with each group and see how they used an informational text today. She also wants them to hear and teach each other. "Construction group, I saw you built three structures that looked like buildings from the skyscraper book. Tell us, how did the book help you?" She gives each group an opportunity to respond and to connect with each other. Often, after one group shares, others will chime in, "We did that too!" Ms. Williams, replies, "I cannot wait to share your hard work today with your families!" Learners are aware that Ms. Williams takes pictures of their work and sends them to their families. This is echoed in their frequent requests, "Come take a picture so I can show my Daddy!"

Return to the story of Ms. Williams' lesson during centers. Do a close reading for each of the five qualities that promote equity. This means you reread about Meredyth William's planning and teaching through the lens of these five qualities. Identify evidence that her task meets each of the qualities and list the evidence in the chart below.

(Continued)

(Continued)

Quality of Tasks to Promote Equity	Evidence
Situated within children's prior knowledge	
Promote positive identity	
Grow agency	
Position all learners as competent	
Share authority for learning with learners	

REFLECTION

After your close reading of Meredyth Williams' process and teaching, reflect on these questions:

Overall, what do you notice Meredyth does to intentionally plan a task that promotes equity?

How is this similar to what you already do when you select a task and make plans to implement it?

What are some new considerations for your planning process?

ENGAGING AND RIGOROUS TASKS

Let's add another layer to our thinking about quality tasks. To grow Visible Learners, we need tasks that promote equity and these tasks must be engaging and rigorous.

When tasks are engaging and rigorous, children see their prior knowledge and their own identities as valuable for making sense of the tasks. Engaging and rigorous tasks present children with a real need to grow their agency by selecting tools to move their learning and development forward. They are all positioned as competent where making errors is a safe part of the learning

Big Ideas

process; in fact, errors are learning opportunities in engaging and rigorous tasks. Children see challenge as desirable and attainable, and they persist through challenge when tasks are engaging and rigorous. They become authorities of their new learning when they recognize that they have learned something and can teach others.

There are eight qualities of engaging and rigorous tasks (Antonetti & Garver, 2015). These deepen our understanding of high-quality tasks that promote equity. They also provide insights into specific actions we can take to select and revise tasks to share these characteristics.

9.2   **Qualities of Engaging and Rigorous Tasks**

Clear and Modeled Expectations	We accomplish this by communicating the learning intentions and success criteria, which put the focus on learning. Implementing the four essentials of communicating clarity help ensure the expectations are clear and modeled, which positions every learner as competent or capable of reaching the success criteria.
Emotional and Intellectual Safety	When we select tasks that have the developmentally appropriate level or right level of challenge, we situate tasks within children's prior knowledge and communicate that every learner is competent and ready to take on the challenge. We create opportunities for learners to take risks, just-the-right-size risks. By intentionally interacting as children engage in the task, we seek and provide feedback to scaffold and extend the task. The just-right task combined with intentional interactions establishes trust, self-regulation of the emotional process of learning, and a sense of safety so that mistakes are opportunities to learn. This also promotes children's positive identity as learners.
Social Interaction	Social interaction is where learning and development happen. We can create spaces for peers to interact about the learning and the task before, during, and after engaging in the task. We can value both verbal and nonverbal interactions to develop children's communication skills across familiar contexts (situated within prior knowledge) and unfamiliar contexts. These intentional social interactions communicate that every learner contributes significant ideas to the learning community (position all learners as competent) and share authority for learning with learners, where they provide important feedback to each other. And of course, we constantly interact with children as conversational partners and language facilitators to intentionally use our language to focus on learning.
Personal Response	Personal response is about creating space within tasks for children to share their unique voice, thus promoting their positive identity. Personal response can take place through peer or adult-child interactions and through children's decisions about the task and the learning. This decision-making role grows children's agency and shares authority for learning with them. Opportunities for personal response communicate the value of children and families' identities by valuing multiple forms of expression.

Choice	Choice within a task provides the just-right opportunities for children to develop their decision-making processes as learners (growing agency). Choice also values multiple forms of expressing, engaging, and representing so that all children are included, valued, and positioned as competent. Tasks can include choices about materials, location, collaborators, process, and product. Choice allows for and encourages children to own their learning journeys by developing Visible Learners who select tools, self-monitor, and make adjustments.
Novelty and Variety	Novelty and variety promote engagement, inquiry, exploration, risk taking, and the transfer of learning to new contexts. This newness can be presented through novel materials, locations, collaborators, process, and product. These may be brand new, newly transferred to the school context, or newly discovered after a period of time. Novelty and variety can promote positive identity by allowing children to see themselves in new roles and contexts. These characteristics also grow children's agency by providing opportunities to develop initiative, self-regulation, and problem-solving.
Authenticity	Authenticity creates a sense of purpose that is validated by what people really do or what really happens in the world. We can engage children in tasks that connect them to their school, neighborhood, and world communities, thus promoting their positive identity and situating learning within their prior knowledge or contexts of expertise. Authentic tasks can also reflect aspects of the real work of readers, writers, mathematicians, historians, scientists, artists, and athletes, which can expand their positive identities. Authentic tasks can create opportunities for children to experience and interact as community, family, and team members, where children hold authority for learning.
Sense of Audience	Another way to create a sense of purpose is by communicating the audience. Sharing with family is always a great audience, but audience can also be sharing and teaching others (sharing authority). The authenticity of the task may inform who an authentic audience is as well.

 # CASE IN POINT

Let's return to Meredyth Williams' preschool task. She thoughtfully and intentionally planned a task that aligns with the learning intentions and success criteria and promotes equity. She made specific decisions to promote equity using the eight qualities of engaging and rigorous tasks.

Reread the vignette on pp. 194-195, and this time, look for the eight qualities of rigorous and engaging tasks. This means you read about Meredyth's planning and teaching process through the lens of these qualities. Record your evidence that her task meets each of the qualities in the table below.

Remember, we already know there will be a lot overlap with the qualities you already labeled (tasks that promote equity). This overlap exists because the qualities of rigorous and engaging tasks can help activate the qualities of tasks that promote equity.

(Continued)

(Continued)

Qualities of Engaging and Rigorous Tasks	Evidence
Clear and modeled expectations	
Emotional and intellectual safety	
Social interaction	
Personal response	
Choice	
Novelty and variety	

Qualities of Engaging and Rigorous Tasks	Evidence
Authenticity	
Sense of audience	

REFLECTION

After your close reading, reflect on these questions:

Notice	Wonder	Create
What do you notice about high-quality tasks? What new insights did you gain from these close readings?	What do you wonder about high-quality tasks? What new questions do you have from these close readings?	What is one of your favorite tasks? Why is it a high-quality task? (Use the qualities we just examined to explain your evaluation.) Or explain how you could revise it to make it high quality.

We shared three sets of qualities for tasks that develop Visible Learners. Each set of qualities moves us deeper into identifying tasks that will maximize children's learning and development. Whether the work and play of young children is child or adult initiated, pretend, inquiry, exploration, or direct instruction, high-quality tasks are important to children's learning and development.

Our role is incredibly important too. We must bring our growing expertise and intentionality into each space and interaction while also valuing what our learners and their families bring to those spaces and interactions as well. We identify and create high-quality tasks, we use what we know about our learners and their families to refine high-quality tasks, and we intentionally interact with learners as they engage with high-quality tasks. The tasks we choose matter. The materials and contexts we provide for children to create their own tasks matter. In the next module, we will examine how to adjust high-quality tasks so that every learner is included and valued.

REFLECTION

What is the take-away message you want to remember from this module? Thinking about "tasks" in reference to all the different types of play and work young children engage in as playful learning, why do high-quality tasks matter for children's learning and development? We've started a statement for you.

> **High-quality tasks are important for moving learning and development forward for all children because . . .**

LEARNING INTENTION AND SUCCESS CRITERIA FOR MODULE 9

Now that you have engaged with the learning in this module, reread what we intended to learn (LI, the learning intention) and what it looks and sounds like to have mastered learning this (SC, the success criteria). Next, reread the levels, descriptions, and images of the path to mastery (the rubric). Reevaluate where you are right now for each success criteria. Use the box to reflect on the evidence you have of where you are and where you are headed next.

LI: We are learning the qualities of tasks that provide all learners with opportunities for high-quality language, interactions, and learning so that we can select, revise, or create high-quality tasks.

SC: I'll know I've learned it when I can

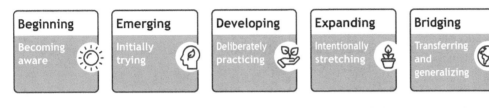

Icon source: istock.com/rambo182

- Describe the qualities of tasks aligned with learning intentions and success criteria, of tasks that promote equity, and of rigorous and engaging tasks.

  _____

  _____

  _____

  _____

  _____

- Explain the importance of these qualities for moving learning and development forward for all children.

  _____

  _____

  _____

  _____

  _____

- Apply these qualities as we select, revise, or create tasks for our learners.

  _____

  _____

  _____

  _____

  _____

MODULE 9 APPENDIX
Your Turn Possible Answers

Infant—Imitation Unit

Learning Intentions & Success Criteria	**Content Learning Intention:** Today, I am learning facial expressions show different emotions. **Language Learning Intention:** Today, I am learning the names of emotions: happy, silly. **Social Learning Intention:** Today, I am learning to watch faces and imitate facial expressions. **Relevance:** So that I can understand how others feel by looking at their faces. **Success Criteria:** I'll know I've learned it when I can imitate a smile for happy and I can imitate sticking my tongue out for silly.	
Which task is aligned with the learning intentions and success criteria?	**Task A** Play Peek-a-Boo: Cover your eyes and name a child: "Where's happy Anna?" or "Where's silly Eli?" Then peek out and make smiling faces or stick out tongues. "Peek-a-Boo! Here's happy Anna!" or "Here's silly Eli!"	**Task B** Play Peek-a-Boo: Cover a favorite toy with a cloth. "Where's (toy name)?" Uncover toy and say, "Peek-a-Boo! Here's (toy name)!" Clap and smile together.
Explain your reasoning.	*Task A is aligned with the learning intentions and success criteria because it is focused on making and imitating the facial expressions of smiling and sticking out tongues. The children are described using the emotion that is shown by their facial expression: happy or silly.*	*While Task B is a great task, it is not aligned with the learning intentions and success criteria. The learning from the task emphasizes finding the toy, naming the toy, and clapping to celebrate. This would be a great task for different learning intentions and success criteria.*

Toddler—Unit to Solve the Problem: How can I play with a friend using the same materials?

Learning Intentions & Success Criteria	**Language Learning Intention:** Today, I am learning I can say words to describe actions: clap, stomp, pat. **Social Learning Intention:** Today, I am learning we can sing and dance together. **Relevance:** So that we can sing action songs as a class and as a family. **Success Criteria:** I'll know I've learned it when I can move my body to match action songs' words.

Which task is aligned with the learning intentions and success criteria?	Task A Sing and dance to "El Twist de los Ratoncitos/The Twist of the Little Mice" and count backward from 5 to 0 mice.	Task B Sing and dance to "Este es el baile del movimiento/This is the Dance of Movement" with actions of *aplaudir*/clap, *pisar muy fuerte*/stomp, and *palmadita*/pat.
Explain your reasoning.	*Task A is a fantastic bilingual counting song with movement; however, it is not aligned with the learning intentions and success criteria. In this task, children are learning to count backward and the concept of one less.*	*Task B aligns with the learning intentions and success criteria because children are learning to move their bodies and name the actions in English and Spanish. This is an action song that can be sung as a class and as a family with everyone moving together.*

Preschool—Describe and Label Unit

Learning Intentions & Success Criteria	**Content Learning Intention:** Today, I am learning true information from nonfiction informational texts. **Language Learning Intention:** Today, I am learning to listen and ask questions about informational texts. **Social Learning Intention:** Today, I am learning to work with others to find and describe things around me using our learning from informational texts. **Relevance:** So that I know how to use informational texts to learn something new. **Success Criteria:** I'll know I've learned this when I can look or listen to an informational text, ask a question about the informational text, and work together to play, create, or use information from the text.	
Which task is aligned with the learning intentions and success criteria?	Task A Learners listen to the book *We're Going on a Leaf Hunt* (Metzger, 2005) and then reenact the story during the second reread.	Task B Learners listen and ask questions about the page, *Trees on the Trail*, from the book, *On the Nature Trail* (Storey Publishing, 2018). Then in small groups, children use images of leaves from the book to find and collect similar leaves outside.
Explain your reasoning.	*Task A utilizes an engaging book, We're Going on a Leaf Hunt, which does include nonfiction information. However, the text itself is not nonfiction and the focus on reenacting the story lends itself better to a goal of retelling.*	*Task B is aligned to the success criteria by using a section from an actual informational text, followed by children working in groups to use the text (including images from the text).*

(Continued)

(Continued)

Learning Intentions & Success Criteria	**Content Learning Intention:** Today, I am learning to sort shapes based on their attributes.	
	Language Learning Intention: Today, I am learning to describe shapes using attribute words: side, vertex.	
	Social Learning Intention: Today, I am learning to listen to another peer's ideas.	
	Relevance: So that I can identify what is the same and what is different about shapes.	
	Success Criteria: I'll know I've learned this when I can sort shapes based on their attributes and describe how I sorted my shapes to someone else.	
Which task is aligned with the learning intentions and success criteria?	**Task A** Sort a set of attribute blocks with the peers at the table and use index cards to label each group.	**Task B** Sort a set of attribute blocks independently, label the groups, then share groups with an assigned peer.
Explain your reasoning.	*Task A is a strong collaborative task focused on sorting by shape attributes. However, it leaves out part of the success criteria—describing and listening to a peer—by assuming those things would happen implicitly in the group conversation.*	*Task B is aligned to all the success criteria by ensuring children have the opportunity to sort their shapes and describe their sort to a peer.*

INTENTIONALLY INCLUSIVE TASKS

REFLECTION

Inclusion is a common term surrounding education, teaching, and learning. However, we often use the same term, but mean very different things. Before moving forward in this module, define *inclusion*. Use the space provided to write down what you mean by inclusion.

Definition of inclusion	What is the role of inclusion in early childhood learning and development?

We examined our definition of inclusion in Module 2 (p. 38). Look back at how you defined inclusion then. How has your definition of inclusion developed, changed, or stayed the same as you've worked through this Playbook?

Creating intentionally inclusive tasks is an issue of equity. We have high expectations for learning. We set the same learning intentions and success criteria for *all* learners. With success criteria focused on learning rather than a specific task, there are multiple ways of engaging, representing, and expressing learning that meet those goals. By valuing multiple ways of engaging, representing, and expressing learning, we also value our learners' identities and the "funds of knowledge" they bring to learning. When we create learning experiences that move *all* learners toward those explicit success criteria, we must also adjust tasks to have the right level of challenge for each learner. In this module, we will examine how to scaffold high-quality tasks.

Big Ideas

LEARNING INTENTION AND SUCCESS CRITERIA FOR MODULE 10

Before you engage with the learning in this module, read what we intend to learn (LI, the learning intention) and what it'll look and sound like when we've learned this (SC, the success criteria). Next, read the levels, descriptions, and images of the path to mastery (the rubric). Evaluate where you are right now for each success criteria. At the end of the module, we'll return to this self-evaluation and document the ways we've intentionally grown our teaching practice over time.

LI: We are learning ways to intentionally create inclusive tasks so that *all* children have opportunity and access to engage in high-quality learning experiences as contributing members of their community of learners.

SC: I'll know I've learned it when I can

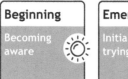 

Icon source: istock.com/rambo182

- Describe the role of teacher clarity in creating inclusive learning experiences and tasks.

_____

_____

_____

_____

_____

- Explain how a task can be adjusted to provide learners with multiple means of engagement, representation, and action and expression so that all children are included, valued, and successful learners.

_____

_____

_____

_____

_____

- Make decisions about which questions, prompts, cues, and tools are the "just right", temporary scaffolds to ensure access and opportunity for *all* learners.

_____

_____

_____

_____

_____

- Identify partnerships that contribute to our collective efficacy for creating inclusive early childhood communities.

_____

_____

_____

_____

A high-quality task provides children with the opportunity to respond in ways that show what they know, what they don't know yet, and the sense-making that is in progress. While a high-quality task is the right work for all learners, there is not a singular, optimal way for all learners to engage, represent, and express their learning within that task. In other words, no size fits all. To truly position *all* learners as competent, we need to adjust tasks so that every child can access, make sense of, and communicate their learning. At the core of this work is teacher clarity.

Big Ideas

TEACHER CLARITY

We began our work in this Playbook by defining our goals: Implement the big ideas for teaching, learning, and development in early childhood and grow the characteristics of Visible Early Childhood Learners in all children. As we work through each module, we are gaining a clearer vision of what it looks and sounds like to intentionally implement these big ideas and to grow Visible Learners.

Big Ideas

In Part 2, we began our work to plan units of study. From analyzed standards to high-quality tasks, we have clarity about what our children are learning, why, and how we'll know they are successful. Our clarity of goals informs each decision we make:

- How should we sequence learning experiences and interactions?
- How should we organize our learning environment and time?
- Which examples and guided practice should we include?
- What language should we use in our explanations?
- How should we facilitate self-monitoring, self-reflection, and self-evaluation?

Each answer is powered by our clear vision of the what, why, and how of learning. This is teacher clarity.

 **REFLECTION**

Finish the following sentences:

Teacher clarity informs my sequencing of learning experiences and interactions by . . .

Teacher clarity guides me in how I organize our learning environment and time by . . .

Teacher clarity helps me select examples and provide guided practice by . . .

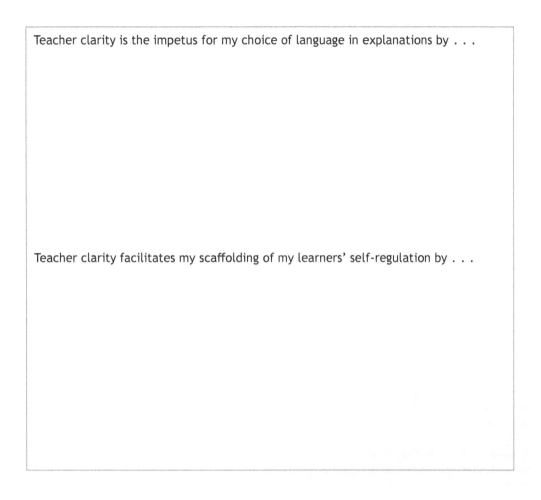

Teacher clarity is the impetus for my choice of language in explanations by . . .

Teacher clarity facilitates my scaffolding of my learners' self-regulation by . . .

We have clarity about the aims of our instruction. We communicate that clarity to our learners and their families. And we use that clarity like a compass, guiding each decision we make. Teacher clarity helps us hold high expectations for all our learners by helping us define the what, why, and how of learning for all children.

Teacher clarity also helps us identify scaffolds and extensions that align with these goals to ensure high-quality tasks have the developmentally appropriate level or right level of challenge for every child in our class. By keeping our eyes focused on the *learning* rather than the doing, we can see which scaffolds and extensions provide access and opportunity to the learning as well as when scaffolds and extensions remove, reduce, distract, or stray from the learning. Teacher clarity helps us create equity of opportunity and access to the learning goals.

Teacher clarity is the compass that guides the creation of intentionally inclusive tasks. Universal Design for Learning (UDL) are the trail markers that point out the decision points for creating intentionally inclusive tasks.

ADAPTING TASKS WITH UNIVERSAL DESIGN FOR LEARNING

Universal Design for Learning (UDL) is a framework to scaffold and extend tasks so that all learners have the access and opportunity to participate meaningfully in high-quality tasks and so that every learner moves toward explicit success criteria and high expectations (CAST, 2018; NAEYC, 2019). The success criteria are aligned to the standards and define the learning. The success criteria are also open to multiple ways of engaging, representing, and expressing learning that meet those goals.

To make an inclusive task, we must begin with a high-quality task. Then, we can adapt three aspects of the task:

1. the ways learners can **engage** in the task,

2. the ways the task is **represented** to the learner, and

3. the ways learners can take **action** and **express** their learning through the task.

Table 10.1 highlights the decision points for intentionally adapting tasks for multiple ways of engaging, representing, and acting and expressing. At each of these decision points, our motto of *who before do* is critical. We must know our learners well to decide what is the "just right" adjustment to welcome a child into a high-quality task and to meet a child within a high-quality task.

10.1 Decision Points for Inclusive Tasks

Multiple Ways of Engaging	Multiple Ways of Representing	Multiple Ways of Acting and Expressing
• Number of and types of choices • Level of novelty or familiarity • Options for collaborative and individual work	• Multiple genres, formats, and media • Multiple languages with explicit links to heritage languages • Multiple contexts and representations • Flexible materials • Chunks of information • Spaced practice • Gradual release of responsibility	• Pace • Variety of strategies and tools for problem-solving • Options for responding • Options for self-monitoring, self-reflecting, and self-evaluating

YOUR TURN!

Engage in a review of your own learning environment, the learning experiences and tasks, and the interactions in your classroom. List specific examples of each of the three aspects of UDL.

Multiple Ways of Engaging	Multiple Ways of Representing	Multiple Ways of Acting and Expressing

CASE IN POINT

Anisa Lopez's class is focused on plants and how they grow. The children have sprouted seeds and they have potatoes in water, watching the roots and leaves grow. They are learning vocabulary terms associated with plants: seeds, roots, stems, leaves, flowers. Anisa knows that it is important for children to practice using labels (words) for concepts in the context of learning and exploring as part of their vocabulary instruction, not just in isolation.

Given their current understanding of these plant-part names, Anisa wants to know if her learners can consistently identify the parts of a plant and apply their vocabulary knowledge to a variety of plants as they encounter plant images in books.

She shares several pictures of different plants and gives one to each child. She asks each learner to point to the stem, and then the roots, and finally the leaves. Some of the plants have flowers and others do not. Some have seeds, others do not. The children are not very successful in applying their vocabulary knowledge to these unfamiliar plants.

Return to the table of Decisions Points for Inclusive Tasks (p. 212). How might Anisa make decisions to increase all learners' access and opportunity to successfully learn in this task?

(Continued)

(Continued)

Multiple Ways of Engaging	
Multiple Ways of Representing	
Multiple Ways of Acting and Expressing	

SCAFFOLDS

These decision points also provide us with the opportunity to anticipate and plan for varying scaffolds. Scaffolds are supports that provide access and opportunity to every learner by adjusting tasks to the "just right" level of challenge for everyone. Scaffolds can be

- adjustments to allow for multiple ways of engaging, representing, and expressing learning,

- tools embedded within the task, and

- questions, prompts, and cues provided by adults.

Let's look more closely at each type of scaffold and how we can intentionally select and implement scaffolds to ensure every child moves toward the success criteria.

Adaptations for Multiple Ways of Engaging, Representing, and Expressing Learning. To promote equity and inclusion, we must make decisions about adaptations with intentionality. We value *who before do*, which means we must know who our learners and their families are in order to make decisions that will welcome, include, and value every learner. We must also rely on our goals, our high expectations for all learners, to determine the adaptations of our high-quality tasks. First, let's examine closely four high-quality tasks and the intentional plans to adapt each for inclusivity.

REFLECTION

Look for examples of adaptations that allow for multiple ways of engaging, representing, and acting and expressing. As you examine the examples, make note of what we need to know about our learners in order to make each decision "just right." Then reflect on each example.

Infant—Imitation Unit

Learning Intentions & Success Criteria

Content Learning Intention: Today, I am learning facial expressions show different emotions.

Language Learning Intention: Today, I am learning the names of emotions: happy, silly.

Social Learning Intention: Today, I am learning to watch faces and imitate facial expressions.

Relevance: So that I can understand how others feel by looking at their faces.

Success Criteria: I'll know I've learned it when I can imitate a smile for happy and I can imitate sticking my tongue out for silly.

High-Quality Task

Play Peek-a-Boo: Cover your eyes and name a child: "Where's happy Anna?" or "Where's silly Eli?" Then peek out looking at the child and make smiling faces or stick out tongues. "Peek-a-Boo! Here's happy Anna!" or "Here's silly Eli!"

(Continued)

(Continued)

Adapting Task With UDL	What do we need to know about our learners and their families?
• **Use hands to cover eyes or blanket to cover face.** This can adjust the task to be either *familiar or more novel* depending on which material infants have played Peek-a-Boo with previously. Hands and blankets allow for *flexibility of materials* so that infants use the material that is easily available or that they can manipulate. • **Cover and reveal adult or child.** This can also create varying *levels of familiarity and novelty* as well as provide *options for responding*. The infant may choose to respond by hiding the adult. This can also lead to the transfer of covering and revealing with *multiple contexts and representations*, such as stuffed animals, toys, and book characters. • **Sing a song after the reveal for additional practice of language and imitating action:** "Happy Anna, happy Anna, I see you, I see you. Anna is happy. Anna is happy. Let's smile too. Let's smile too." Repeating a simple song allows for *spaced practice* and adjustments to *pace* by singing as many times as the child requests or engages. The song is a *different* format than the Peek-a-Boo game that also *chunks information* into a manageable size, matching emotion (happy) with facial expression (smile). • **Use heritage languages.** The whole Peek-a-Boo game could be played in children's *heritage languages* or just certain words from heritage languages could be used in tandem with the English words, such as emotion words (happy/*feliz*) and facial expressions (smile/*sonríe*).	

• **Model smiling (I do). Encourage everyone to smile (We do). Encourage all children to smile (You all do). Encourage individual children to smile as they are named in the game (You do).** This is *gradual release*: I do, We do, You all do, You do (Fisher & Frey, 2021). It provides gradual release of modeling by the adult and peers in a group setting.
• **Use a mirror to reflect back children's smiling faces.** The mirror is a *tool* that can support problem solving and *self-monitoring*.
• **Play one on one or in group of two or three children.** This provides *opportunities for individual and collaborative play.* With each child or group, adaptations can also be selected based on common "just right" adjustments.

What do you notice about the example?

How does this example exemplify *Adaptations for Multiple Ways of Engaging, Representing, and Expressing Learning*?

How could you use this example in your own classroom?

(Continued)

(Continued)

Toddler—Unit to Solve the Problem: How can I play *with* a friend using the same materials?

Learning Intentions & Success Criteria
Language Learning Intention: Today, I am learning I can say words to describe actions: clap, stomp, pat.
Social Learning Intention: Today, I am learning we can sing and dance together.
Relevance: So that we can sing action songs as a class and as a family.
Success Criteria: I'll know I've learned it when I can move my body to match action songs' words.

High-Quality Task
Sing and dance to *"Este es el baile del movimiento/*This is the Dance of Movement" with actions of *aplaudir*/clap, *pisar muy fuerte*/stomp, and *palmadita*/pat.

Adjusting Task with UDL	What do we need to know about our learners and their families?
• **Children can dance and listen or sing and watch.** This allows for *options for responding*. • **Sing and dance one on one, with a partner, in small groups, or as a whole class.** These variations allow for *individual and collaborative options*. With each child or group, adaptations can also be selected based on common "just right" adjustments. • **Allow children to choose the sequence of actions, what to *palmadita*/pat, and additional actions.** Learners can have *varying number and types of choices*—choosing the next action, choosing what body part to pat, and even choosing novel actions. • **Model the action (I do). Encourage everyone to do the action together (We do). Encourage all children to do the action together (You all do). Encourage individual children to do the action (You do).** This is *gradual release*: I do, We do, You all do, You do (Fisher & Frey, 2021). It provides gradual release of modeling by the adult and peers in a group setting.	

- **Show pictures for each action and post them in sequence.** Images provide an additional *genre or representation* of the actions as well as a *tool* for *self-monitoring*. Sequencing the images helps to *chunk information* into manageable actions to remember.
- **Practice actions and words before singing the song or before each verse.** This provides *spaced practice* so that children can practice just the action in isolation and then practice the action again within the song.

What do you notice about the example?

How does this example exemplify *Adaptations for Multiple Ways of Engaging, Representing, and Expressing Learning?*

How could you use this example in your own classroom?

(Continued)

(Continued)

Learning Intentions & Success Criteria

Content Learning Intention: Today, I am learning true information from nonfiction informational texts.

Language Learning Intention: Today, I am learning to listen and ask questions about informational texts.

Social Learning Intention: Today, I am learning to work with others to find and describe things around me using our learning from informational texts.

Relevance: So that I know how to use informational texts to learn something new.

Success Criteria: I'll know I've learned this when I can look or listen to an informational text, ask a question about the informational text, and work together to play, create, or use information from the text.

High-Quality Task

Learners listen and ask questions about the page, *Trees on the Trail*, from the book, *On the Nature Trail* (Storey Publishing, 2018). Then in small groups, children use images of leaves from the book to find and collect similar leaves outside.

Adjusting Task with UDL	What do we need to know about our learners and their families?
• **Provide question frames for children to use while engaging with the book.** This provides children with a *tool* and *multiple options when responding*.	
• **Reread the book multiple times.** This provides learners with text *familiarity* and allows for vocabulary in the book to be used with *spaced practice*.	
• **Enlarge images of leaves from the book for children to hold and examine and later to reference while outside.** This provides *multiple representations* for engaging with the content across contents and becomes a *tool for problem-solving* and *self-monitoring*.	
• **Use small groups, pairs, and individual structures.** Allows for options of *collaborative* or *individual* work.	

• **Collect leaves from different areas over multiple days.** This can provide a *level of familiarity or novelty* depending on the chosen area. It also provides an opportunity to demonstrate the skill in *multiple contexts* with *spaced practice*.	

What do you notice about the example?

How does this example exemplify *Adaptations for Multiple Ways of Engaging, Representing, and Expressing Learning*?

How could you use this example in your own classroom?

(Continued)

(Continued)

Learning Intentions & Success Criteria

Content Learning Intention: Today, I am learning to sort shapes based on their attributes.

Language Learning Intention: Today, I am learning to describe shapes using attribute words: side, vertex.

Social Learning Intention: Today, I am learning to listen to another peer's ideas.

Relevance: So that I can identify what is the same and what is different about shapes.

Success Criteria: I'll know I've learned this when I can sort shapes based on their attributes and describe how I sorted my shapes to someone else.

High-Quality Task

Sort a set of attribute blocks independently, label the groups, then share groups with an assigned peer.

Adjusting Task with UDL	**What do we need to know about our learners and their families?**
• **Vary the number and variety of shapes available for sorting.** This provides *flexibility in material* for children as well as experience making sense of *multiple representations*. The variety of shapes can also provide varying levels of *familiarity or novelty*. • **Provide predetermined labels on index cards for learners to use as descriptors of shape attributes.** These index cards serve as a *tool* for children to use when describing their work. • **Provide language frames (in multiple languages) for use when describing and responding to peer work.** These language frames can be linked to children's' *heritage language* and provide an *option for responding* to their peers. Language frames are also a *tool* for expressing learning. • **Provide copies of the class anchor chart depicting shape names and attributes for reference.** This *tool* can be used to help children *self-monitor* and problem solve during the task by providing a visual reference connected to vocabulary and examples.	

• Provide sorting trays, bowls, and large paper with markers for creating piles of similar shapes. Each of these are *tools for problem solving* and supporting organization of groups. Children could *choose* among the tools based on what is *familiar* to them or based on their *self-monitoring*.	

What do you notice about the example?

How does this example exemplify *Adaptations for Multiple Ways of Engaging, Representing, and Expressing Learning*?

How could you use this example in your own classroom?

Tools. We would like to highlight one decision point for adapting tasks—selecting and providing tools for problem-solving. Tools allow for multiple means of acting and expressing children's learning. We must intentionally select tools that support sense making of the concepts and skills in our learning intentions and success criteria. To promote equity and inclusion, we must select the "just right" tools that provide all learners with access and opportunity to participate and successfully learn.

Big Ideas

Tools with vertical significance (useful in early learning and beyond) are most impactful. For example, language frames, manipulatives, and images are powerful tools for scaffolding language-based interactions. Maps, number lines, alphabet charts, and diagrams are powerful tools for scaffolding problem solving about specific content. Tools can also scaffold children's self-monitoring, self-reflecting, and self-evaluating. Over time, we empower our learners to select tools appropriate to their needs. This is one of the characteristics of a Visible Learner.

REFLECTION

Return to the four examples above of adaptations to high-quality tasks (Table 10.1). Make a list of the tools intentionally selected to scaffold and extend children's sense-making within each task. Then add to the list by brainstorming other tools that you use and have available in your classroom or center. We've started the list for you.

Tools as Scaffolds

anchor charts
mirror
language frames
shape manipulatives

In Module 9, we unpacked the statement "the goals determine the task." We examined how the goals also determine the learning environment in which the task takes place. The learning environment includes the physical space, the materials, and the storage of materials. What is available in the learning environment and how children access the materials, including tools, should be aligned with the learning intentions and success criteria. When you are planning and implementing instruction, you might look back at the tools in the chart above to select the "just right" scaffolds for your learners. The tools are part of the learning environment. The "just right" learning environment should communicate clarity and ensure every learner has access, participates actively, and is appropriately supported and challenged (NAEYC, 2022).

CASE IN POINT

McKinley Sandoval is new to teaching two- and three-year-olds, but her collaborating educator, Lara Piazza, has been a paraprofessional at the preschool center for two decades. When this year began, McKinley often felt like her new ideas were squashed by Lara saying statements beginning, "But we've always . . ."

McKinley invited the occupational therapist, Brian Kyn, to plan with Lara and herself in an effort to collaborate and learn from each other. Brian introduced a series of questions to support their planning whenever anyone says, "But we've always . . ." First, they ask why and then they analyze their learning and development standards and the aligned learning intentions and success criteria to see if their reasoning reflects those. This framework of analyzing why "we've always" done something has already helped them make important changes.

For example, "we've always" had the playground rules for the slide: up the steps, down the slide, and "we've always" had the playground rules for the swings: on your bottom, forward, back. Brian shared his expertise that the gross motor movements (like using shoulder and arm strength to climb up the slide) support fine motor movements (like pencil grip) and the gross motor movements (like swinging on your stomach) support other complex coordination (like pumping your legs on a swing). After analyzing the standards, the team of three agree they will expand the playground rules to support more motor development and they will create learning intentions and success criteria to intentionally teach safety, turning taking, and self-regulation.

Another "we've always" has come up today in their planning. McKinley has developed the following learning intentions and success criteria:

(Continued)

(Continued)

> **Content Learning Intention:** We are learning to notice what happens when we mix or put materials together.
>
> **Social Learning Intention:** We are learning to listen to and to try two different ideas.
>
> **Relevance:** So that we can choose the best tools for our purpose.
>
> **Success Criteria:** We'll know we've learned it when we can ask, "What if . . ." and then try the new idea and when we can describe what we see, hear, and feel.

McKinley wants to use these learning intentions and success criteria during centers time for the children's work across all the centers, including art area, blocks, and kitchen. And she plans to communicate the learning intentions and success criteria by modeling two scenarios: "What if we mix red *and* yellow paint?" and "What if we build with both Magna-tiles *and* wooden blocks?"

"But we've always told the kids to keep the colors separate," Lara explains about the paints in art area. "And they can only take out one tub of toys at a time. Otherwise, we end up with a huge mess—toys mixed up, paints all over or just a glob of brownish grey paint."

"So, our why for the rules of one paint color and one toy tub at a time is to prevent a mess and ruining the paints, right?" Brian connects. Lara nods. "Let's look at the learning and development standards to see if we need to change these rules or the learning intentions and success criteria." McKinley shares the standards she analyzed to create the learning intentions and success criteria:

- Explores a variety of media including paper, tape, glue, clay, watercolor
- Notices differences among materials such as sand and water
- Reacts to and comments on changes when mixing or manipulating materials
- Interacts with a few children on shared activities and understands simple social interaction rules (e.g., "your turn" or "my turn")
- Begins to initiate interactions with other children in shared play activities (Virginia Department of Education, 2021).

> Based on your analysis of the standards above, what do you recommend takes place so that the learning environment aligns with the standards and the learning intentions and success criteria?

Questions, Prompts, and Cues. One way to find the "just right" scaffold is to think of questions, prompts, and cues along a spectrum from the least level of support to the greatest, also known as the least to most prompt hierarchy (Libby et al., 2008). Start with the independent level of support and gradually increase the level of support in response to children's needs in the moment. Be sure to use wait time at each level so children can process and respond. And remember: All scaffolds are *temporary* and should be gradually removed or faded as learners develop their understanding and skills.

Table 10.2 shows this spectrum from least to greatest supports as well as examples of what each level would look like for scaffolding the high-quality tasks described above.

10.2 Levels of Support: Questions, Prompts, and Cues

	Levels of Support: Questions, Prompts, and Cues	What is it?	Infant High-Quality Task: Play Peek-a-Boo: Cover your eyes and name a child: "Where's happy Anna?" Then peek out looking at the child and make smiling faces. "Peek-a-Boo! Here's happy Anna!"	Toddler High-Quality Task: Sing and dance to "This is the Dance of Movement" with actions of clap, stomp, and pat.	Preschool High-Quality Task: Learners listen and ask questions about the page, *Trees on the Trail*, from the book, *On the Nature Trail* (Storey Publishing, 2018). Then in small groups, children use images of leaves from the book to find and collect similar leaves outside.	Primary High-Quality Task: Sort a set of attribute blocks independently, label the groups, then share groups with an assigned peer.
Least	Independent	The child completes the task or the step without help or hints of any kind. Always begin here, allowing every child the opportunity to experience success independently.	The child makes a smiling face when you peek out.	The child claps, stomps, and pats the correct body part to match the lyrics of the song.	The child uses part of an informational text independently to collect leaves from the book.	The child accurately sorts a pile of shapes according to number of sides or vertices.
	Visual	Provide image, chart, diagram, or other visual cue that the child can refer to as a reminder about the next step or to make sense of the task.	Show the child a picture of themselves smiling as you say, "Peek-a-Boo! Here's happy Anna!"	Show the child a picture of the action to match the lyrics of the song.	Provide the child an enlarged copy of a reference page from the book to use when collecting leaves.	Provide an individual copy of a shape anchor chart for the child to use.

(Continued)

(Continued)

Indirect Verbal	Ask a question that makes the child think metacognitively about the task or step, such as, "What are you trying to do?" or "What strategy might work?"	Ask, "How do you make a happy face?"	Ask, "How should we move our bodies right now?"	Point to the reference page in the book and ask, "How can you check to see if the leaf you have found matches the leaf on the page?"	Point to the anchor chart and ask, "What is one way you can sort the shapes?"
Gesture	Use a gesture, pointing, or facial expression to communicate the item they need to complete the step or start the task.	Point to your own smiling face.	Point to the corresponding body part named in the song lyrics.	Point to the reference page in the book.	Point to the sorting tray.
Direct Verbal	Tell the child exactly what to do next: "You need to . . ."	Tell, "Move your cheeks like me! We're happy!"	Tell, "Put your hand on your belly and pat, pat, pat!"	Tell, "Look at the leaf in your hand and the picture in the book. Check to see if they match by looking at the shape and color."	Tell, "Sort the shapes by the number of sides they have."
Model	Complete the task or step yourself or have another child model the task or step.	Model smiling and point out another child who is smiling, "I'm happy and smiling! Look at Lincoln—he's happy and smiling too!"	Point out another child patting their belly and narrate, "Abril is patting her belly!"	Model holding the leaf up to the page in the book and systematically checking it to see if it matches.	Model sorting the pile of shapes by the number of sides.
Partial Physical	Touch or move the child's hand to begin the task or step. Briefly use hand-over-hand assistance to elicit an initial response.	Lightly touch the child's cheeks and then touch your own.	Lightly touch the child's hand and then belly.	Help the child find a single leaf and put it next to the leaf image on the reference page.	Move the child's hand to trace and count the sides of one shape and put it in the sorting tray.
Full Physical	Place your hand over the child's hand or wrist to complete the entire task or step. Use hand-over-hand assistance the whole time.	Lightly tickle the child.	Place your hand over the child's hand and lightly move their hand to pat their belly.	Hold onto the child's hand while they find leaves, lay them out and compare them one by one to the reference page.	Place your hand over the child's hand as you trace and count the sides of the shapes and sort them all into the sorting tray.

Greatest

CASE IN POINT

Let's return to McKinley, Lara, and Brian's planning meeting. Their learning intentions and success criteria are

> **Content Learning Intention:** We are learning to notice what happens when we mix or put materials together.
>
> **Social Learning Intention:** We are learning to listen to and to try two different ideas.
>
> **Relevance:** So that we can choose the best tools for our purpose.
>
> **Success Criteria:** We'll know we've learned it when we can ask, "What if . . ." and then try the new idea and when we can describe what we see, hear, and feel.

The high-quality tasks will be different in each of the centers where guided play takes place, but the team has made sure every center has several choices of materials ready and available for meaningful mixtures or combinations.

As conversational partners and language facilitators, McKinley, Lara, and Brian will join the children's play and intentionally interact with them to support their learning and development toward the learning intentions and success criteria. While planning for these intentional interactions, the team knows they want to enter children's play in ways that value the children's ideas, wonderings, and imaginings. They also want to intentionally support the children to experience success through their questions, prompts, and cues, as needed.

Lara anticipates that Raheem will go to the kitchen, dump each of the pretend food tubs into the sink, stir, and then leave. What possible supports moving from least to most supportive can the team anticipate in order to help Raheem experience success with the learning intentions and success criteria? Complete the table below with your anticipated questions, prompts, and cues.

Level of Support: Questions, Prompts, and Cues	Anticipated Supports
Independent	
Visual	
Indirect Verbal	
Gesture	
Direct Verbal	
Model	
Partial Physical	
Full Physical	

LEVERAGING OUR PARTNERSHIPS

Developing our teacher clarity and adapting tasks for inclusion is cognitively demanding work. It is heavy lifting! We can tackle this challenge when we leverage the individual strengths of our partners to support all of us. In other words, we need to identify our partners with expertise in ways to adapt tasks for inclusion. Together, we can do more for our learners.

Special educators are often experts in UDL and adapting tasks with vast knowledge of varying levels of scaffolds that can be gradually removed. Specialists are experts in their content areas with a deep and wide knowledge of powerful tools, significant language, and a range of options for engaging, representing, and acting and expressing learning about concepts and skills. Paraprofessionals can provide invaluable feedback about learners' preferences for engaging, representing, and acting and expressing learning as well as feedback about scaffolds that worked or did not work for individuals.

Families and learners remain critical partners for developing our teacher clarity and adapting tasks. Families are experts about their children with critical historical knowledge of their learning and development over time. With our eyes on the goal of growing Visible Learners, we should always consider the voice of the learner. Child-initiated play is an incredible invitation into their understandings, connections, wonderings, and creativity, an invitation that we should accept and join with the intentionality to learn from them. And across all playful learning, children's preferences, perspectives, and feedback are vital.

 # REFLECTION

Think about your daily work in your early childhood learning environment.

> What part of that work is the "heaviest lift" for you? Where could you use some help problem solving, generating ideas, and making sense of this work?

Who can help? Whose expertise could you leverage? Whose partnership could help you with this heavy lift?

Make a list of partners that could support your work in the early childhood learning environment.

LEARNING INTENTION AND SUCCESS CRITERIA FOR MODULE 10

Now that you have engaged with the learning in this module, reread what we intended to learn (LI, the learning intention) and what it looks and sounds like to have mastered learning this (SC, the success criteria). Next, reread the levels, descriptions, and images of the path to mastery (the rubric). Reevaluate where you are right now for each success criteria. Use the box to reflect on the evidence you have of where you are and where you are headed next.

LI: We are learning ways to intentionally create inclusive tasks so that all children have opportunity and access to engage in high-quality learning experiences as contributing members of their community of learners.

SC: I'll know I've learned it when I can

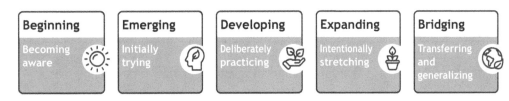

Beginning	Emerging	Developing	Expanding	Bridging
Becoming aware	Initially trying	Deliberately practicing	Intentionally stretching	Transferring and generalizing

Icon source: istock.com/rambo182

(Continued)

(Continued)

- Describe the role of teacher clarity in creating inclusive learning experiences and tasks.

  _____

  _____

  _____

  _____

  _____

- Explain how a task can be adjusted to provide learners with multiple means of engagement, representation, and action and expression so that all children are included, valued, and successful learners.

  _____

  _____

  _____

  _____

  _____

- Make decisions about which questions, prompts, cues, and tools are the "just right" temporary scaffolds to ensure access and opportunity for *all* learners.

  _____

  _____

  _____

  _____

  _____

- Identify partnerships that contribute to our collective efficacy for creating inclusive early childhood communities.

  _____

  _____

  _____

  _____

  _____

PHASES OF LEARNING

After selecting high-quality, inclusive tasks for learning and development, we make decisions about how we will implement the tasks. We select the instructional strategies that facilitate children's engagement in the tasks and focus their thinking on the learning.

When tasks have the developmentally appropriate level or right level of challenge and strike the right balance of surface and deep learning, we can maximize our impact on learning and development. We must select the right instructional strategy at the right time. And we do this by recognizing and supporting learners' movement through the three phases of learning: surface, deep, and transfer learning.

Big Ideas

LEARNING INTENTION AND SUCCESS CRITERIA FOR MODULE 11

Before you engage with the learning in this module, read what we intend to learn (LI, the learning intention) and what it'll look and sound like when we've learned this (SC, the success criteria). Next, read the levels, descriptions, and images of the path to mastery (the rubric). Evaluate where you are right now for each success criteria. At the end of the module, we'll return to this self-evaluation and document the ways we've intentionally grown our teaching practice over time.

LI: We are learning about the three phases of learning so that we can select the right instructional strategy at the right time for each of our learners.

SC: I'll know I've learned this when I can

(Continued)

233

(Continued)

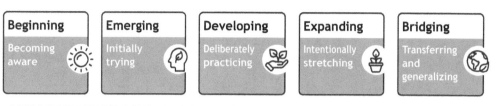

- Explain the importance of each of the three phases of learning and how to achieve the right balance of surface and deep learning.

_____

_____

_____

_____

_____

- Expand my toolbox of instructional strategies and my knowledge of when, why, and how the instructional strategies should be implemented to make their potential impact reality.

_____

_____

_____

_____

_____

- Select and implement the right instructional strategy at the right time to make sure children engage in the developmentally appropriate level or right level of challenge.

_____

_____

_____

_____

_____

Learning occurs in phases. Those phases are often identified as surface learning, deep learning, and transfer learning. The learning phases are not linear; as learners move through the learning progression around a particular topic, they will move in and out of surface, deep, and transfer learning.

REFLECTION

What do you believe are the similarities and differences between learning progressions and phases of learning? You might want to flip back to the module discussion on learning progressions to get started (see Module 6). Use the Venn diagram below to record your thinking.

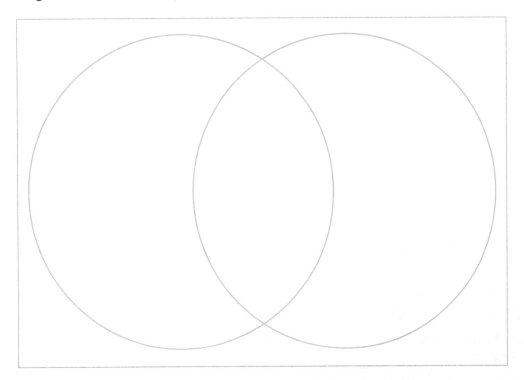

Learning Progressions map out the general pathway learners will take in moving toward the learning intentions. Learning progressions answer the question, what is the pathway toward proficiency or mastery of the concepts and skills within a specific topic?

The phases of learning describe the nature of each part of the pathway. For example, some parts of the learning progression involve the acquisition and consolidation of surface learning. Other parts of the learning progression might involve deep or transfer learning.

Depending on the topic and the concepts and skills, children will develop and learn at different paces. Particularly in early childhood, children experience spurts of growth, demonstrate wide developmental variability, have different access and opportunity to experiences and contexts, and represent exceptional cultural, linguistic, and ability diversity. At any given moment within one class on one day, different learners can be working within different phases of the learning process. We must devote time and attention to identifying where learners are relative to the learning intentions and success criteria for a particular center, experience, or lesson. Then, we need to move them forward by selecting the right instructional strategy at the right time.

The table on the next two pages has three columns of instructional strategies. When children are in the surface learning phase, the instructional strategies in the first column are most impactful. Instructional strategies in the middle column benefit children most when they are in the deep learning phase. And, the final column includes instructional strategies that meet the needs of learners in the transfer learning phase.

You will see both the effect size or potential impact of each instructional strategy when it is implemented at the right time in the right way.

]].] High-Impact Approaches to Each Phase of Learning

Surface Learning		Deep Learning		Transfer Learning	
Strategy	Effect Size	Strategy	Effect Size	Strategy	Effect Size
Wide reading (exposure to reading)	0.43	Elaborative interrogation	0.66	Problem-solving teaching	0.67
Phonics instruction	0.57	Concept mapping	0.64	Summarizing	0.74
Direct instruction	0.59	Self-questioning	0.59	Peer tutoring/ Peer learning	0.51
Vocabulary instruction	0.63	Inquiry-based teaching	0.46	Collaborative learning	0.39
Repeated reading	0.84	Metacognitive strategy instruction	0.60	Self-Reflection	0.75
Spaced practice	0.65	Class discussion	0.82	Writing programs	0.57
Imagery	0.51	Cooperative learning	0.45		
Rehearsal and memorization (songs with actions)	0.73				
Questioning	0.48				
Manipulatives	0.39				
Integrating prior knowledge	0.93				

YOUR TURN!

There may be instructional strategies in the previous chart that you are not familiar with or not completely clear on what the particular strategy would look like in your classroom. Take a moment and select a few strategies from each column. Then, visit the Visible Learning database found at www.**visiblelearningmetax.com.** Using the description found in the database, summarize what this instructional strategy is and how you would use the strategy in your classroom or center. The following table is for recording your thinking.

Surface Learning Instructional Strategies	Description of the Instructional Strategy	How I Would Use the Strategy in My Classroom or Center
Deep Learning Instructional Strategies	Description of the Instructional Strategy	How I Would Use the Strategy in My Classroom or Center

(Continued)

(Continued)

Deep Learning Instructional Strategies	Description of the Instructional Strategy	How I Would Use the Strategy in My Classroom or Center

Transfer Instructional Strategies	Description of the Instructional Strategy	How I Would Use the Strategy in My Classroom or Center

SURFACE LEARNING

When children are first making sense of a new concept or skill, this is the surface phase of learning. This is not superficial or insignificant learning. Rather, it is very important as children initially use their prior knowledge to navigate new ideas, contexts, materials, and language. In other words, it is foundational or introductory learning that is necessary for deeper learning to occur.

The surface learning phase is the "knowing that" part of learning. In early childhood, this can often look like exploration and examination. Children may communicate nonverbally or use sounds and familiar words to describe and label. While some of these labels may not be accurate (because the new vocabulary or language is not yet known), children are making important and meaningful connections. As they explore, they situate the new knowledge, action, or object within the words and sounds they are familiar with.

We can discover when individual children are in the surface learning phase by using the *Learning About Learners Protocol* (p. 30) to observe what learners are doing and saying. We can also ask open questions to notice children's thinking and familiarity with the ideas, contexts, materials, and language, such as the following:

- What does this remind you of?
- Where have you seen or used this before?
- What are you working on?
- What are you thinking about?
- What do you notice?
- What do you wonder?
- What could you create?
- What could you try?

When children are in the surface learning phase, we can meet them where they are and help move their learning and development forward by selecting the right strategy at the right time. Learners in the surface learning phase benefit the most from specific instructional strategies, shown in Table 11.1.

DEEP LEARNING

When learners are making conceptual connections and relations among ideas, they are in the deep learning phase. They use their initial understandings from surface learning to dive deeper into making meaning and forming connections among concepts.

Deep learning is the "knowing how" phase. This is a time when children have sorted through the familiar aspects of new learning and are primed to examine its unique components. Children in the deep phase of learning are ready to engage with the vast connections of overarching concepts and skills, such as systems, change, perspective, relationships, pattern, communities, and conflict. In fact, young children are often already wondering about these big ideas and making important connections, but they are also still learning the language to express their questions, hypotheses, noticings, or connections. To problem-solve, young children frequently engage in trial and error, but with scaffolds, they can develop a variety of strategies and tools.

In early childhood, we often spend too much time in surface learning and then mistakenly reduce our interactions with learners when they are ready for deep learning. Unfortunately, we allow this to become a time when we are "hands off" and emphasize "free exploration" and "free play" where we exit the learning and do not interact. Or, we make the mistake of not shifting our instructional strategies to align with their learning growth and so we engage with them using the exact same instructional strategies as when they were making initial sense of the new concept or skill in the surface learning phase.

Instead, we need to facilitate our learners' movement along the phases of learning and we need to respond to their learning and growth with our instructional strategies. To strike the right balance between surface and deep learning, we must intentionally interact with every learner in every phase. And, we must shift our instructional strategies to match the phase of learning each learner is in. Learners in the deep learning phase benefit the most from specific instructional strategies, shown in Table 11.1, which are unique from the surface learning phase strategies.

 **CASE IN POINT**

Of the nineteen children in the transitional kindergarten class, seventeen have yet to learn all the letters of the alphabet. Two of the children know all the letters, upper and lower case. Annie Huáng administered a letter recognition assessment to all of her learners and identified trends in her class. Rather than take a "letter of the week" approach in which one letter is the focus of instruction for all learners, Annie noted the letters that were problematic for every child and focused whole class instruction on those letters. She also associated sounds with the letters as she introduced them and had her learners practice. Annie used a direct instruction approach, telling children the names of the letters and having them practice recognizing them. Children also participated in singing songs with actions for each letter. Annie grouped learners based on letters that some children knew and others did not, rather than provide whole class instruction for all children. The other learners in the class were provided opportunities to practice onset and rimes with peers, play letter matching games, and use manipulatives to engage with letters and sounds.

Which surface and deep learning strategies did Annie use and how might you expect the lessons to look?

Strategy	Surface or Deep Phase	What It Might Look Like

VIDEO CASE IN POINT

Let's return to the preschool class to see and hear the ways the teacher's interactions are informed by the phases of learning as her three-, four-, and five-year-old learners work together in a small group. From formative evaluation, the teacher knows some of her learners are in the surface phase of making sense of a fiction story and its many parts (main characters, settings, events) while others are in the deep phase. She also knows all of her learners are in the surface phase of learning to work as a team to learn. With this in mind, the teacher analyzed standards to create learning intentions and success criteria.

Learning Foundations (*California Preschool Learning Foundations*, California Department of Education, 2008):

- Demonstrate knowledge of details in a familiar story, including characters, events, and ordering of events through answering questions (particularly summarizing, predicting and inferencing), retelling, reenacting, or creating artwork. (p. 178)

- Understand and use an increasing variety and specificity of accepted words for objects, actions, and attributes encountered in both real and symbolic contexts. (p. 176)

- Participate in group activities and are beginning to understand and cooperate with social expectations, group rules, and roles. (p. 174)

Content Learning Intention:

I am learning to describe details of familiar stories.

Language Learning Intention:

I am learning to use new words from books we read.

Social Learning Intention:

I am learning to use the same materials and share ideas with a small group.

Success Criteria:

I'll know I've learned this when:

- I can describe the events of a story using objects.

- I can answer questions about what happened in a story.

- I can talk and explore with friends who are also talking and exploring the same materials.

You may notice that these standards are the same as the teacher in the Video Case in Point from Module 8 (p. 179). That's because this is the same class working within the same unit of study. But this lesson actually took place *before* the lesson in the Video Case in Point from Module 8. The goals determined this task: explore a sandbox full of images and objects from *The Very Hungry Caterpillar* (Carle, 1969) and use the objects to retell, reenact, and answer questions in a small group.

In the video, we'll watch as the teacher introduces the task to a small group of learners and interacts with them throughout learning in order to select the right strategy at the right time for each learner. As you watch, pay attention to the ways the teacher creates a space for playful learning with intentionality. Look for examples of surface and deep learning strategies used by the teacher to move *all* learners forward toward the learning intentions and success criteria. Record your observations in the table below:

Strategy	Surface or Deep Phase	What It Looked/ Sounded Like

Hungry Caterpillar Tub:
bit.ly/3RMuLqq

TRANSFER LEARNING

When children are applying their understanding to new contexts, they are in the transfer phase of learning. This is when they can apply or generalize their learning to new situations. They use their conceptual connections from deep learning to make sense of and make adjustments in a novel context.

The transfer phase of learning is essential to learning and development so that learning becomes actionable regardless of who is in the context, where the situation is, and when the new context arises in the future. Language is a powerful tool in the transfer phase of learning because it allows children to recall mastered concepts and skills by name and enact them in an unfamiliar situation. Language helps make strategies and ideas generalizable.

By selecting strategies that match children's needs in the transfer phase of learning, we facilitate this generalizability. Learners in the transfer learning phase benefit the most from specific instructional strategies shown in Table 11.1. The transfer phase of learning can be quick. It can also spark entry into a new surface learning phase.

 # CASE IN POINT

Emily Morello is teaching a series of lessons about germs. She asked her learners about the staff who came into the classroom to clean, and they discussed the idea that the tables looked clean but the staff still sprayed them and then washed them off. Later, Emily shared *What Are Germs?* (Daynes, 2017) with her children and focused on key terminology, appropriate for their ages (three- and four-year olds). The next day, they read a book called, *Germs Are Not for Sharing* (Verdick, 2006) about germs that make people sick and how to reduce the chances of being sick, such as covering your nose when you sneeze, washing hands, and cleaning toys. The children were asked to find pictures in magazines that would help them remember to do these things and they made collages for the protective actions. Over several days, they engaged in class discussions about germs and responded to targeted questions that Emily asked. Some of the questions required that learners consider information from more than one text (or image). And children recorded a message to their family members about germs.

Over the course of these several days, Emily moved her learners between surface, deep, and transfer learning as they demonstrated readiness for the next phase. In the table below, identify the instructional moves that Emily used.

Strategy	Surface, Deep, or Transfer Phase	What It Might Look Like

As we transition into Part 4 of this Playbook, the instructional strategies we select should make children's thinking and learning visible. This provides visible evidence of their progress toward the learning intentions and which phase of learning they are working on. We must ensure that we use this visible evidence to know, document and adjust our teaching in response to their learning. Let's dive into Part 4.

LEARNING INTENTION AND SUCCESS CRITERIA FOR MODULE 11

Now that you have engaged with the learning in this module, reread what we intended to learn (LI, the learning intention) and what it looks and sounds like to have mastered learning this (SC, the success criteria). Next, reread the levels, descriptions, and images of the path to mastery (the rubric). Reevaluate where you are right now for each success criteria. Use the box to reflect on the evidence you have of where you are and where you are headed next.

LI: We are learning about the three phases of learning so that we can select the right instructional strategy at the right time for each of our learners.

SC: I'll know I've learned this when I can

Beginning	Emerging	Developing	Expanding	Bridging
Becoming aware	Initially trying	Deliberately practicing	Intentionally stretching	Transferring and generalizing

Icon source: istock.com/rambo182

> • Explain the importance of each of the three phases of learning and how to achieve the right balance of surface and deep learning.
>
> _____
>
> _____
>
> _____
>
> _____
>
> _____

- Expand my toolbox of instructional strategies and my knowledge of when, why, and how the instructional strategies should be implemented to make their potential impact reality.

_____

_____

_____

_____

_____

- Select and implement the right instructional strategy at the right time to make sure children engage in the developmentally appropriate level or right level of challenge.

_____

_____

_____

_____

_____

PART IV

FORMATIVE EVALUATION AND FEEDBACK

FORMATIVE EVALUATION

Our intentional work to place who before do, to plan and communicate clarity, and to select and adapt high-quality tasks has the potential to positively impact children's learning and development. Now, we must convert that potential into effective implementation through formative evaluation and feedback.

REFLECTION

Consider the two most common terms associated with evaluation: *formative evaluation* and *summative evaluation*. Using all available resources (e.g., books, internet), compare and contrast these two terms from the perspective of an early childhood educator. Use the Venn diagram to record your thinking.

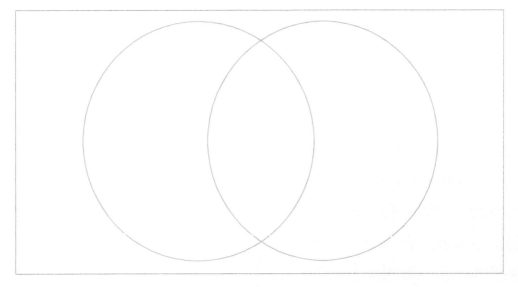

This module focuses on formative evaluation, the type of evaluation that occurs during learning experiences and interactions.

There are five key elements of formative evaluation that define its scope (Leahy et al., 2005):

> Clarify, communicate, and make sense of learning intentions and success criteria.

> Orchestrate discussions and tasks to elicit evidence of learning.

> Provide feedback to move learning forward.

> Activate learners as resources for each other.

> Activate learners as owners of their own learning.

Throughout Part 4, we explore these key elements of formative evaluation. Our implementation of formative evaluation is where the big ideas of early childhood and the characteristics of Visible Learners come to life through educator actions and interactions.

Big Ideas

In this module, we focus on formative evaluation that activates learners and orchestrates discussions in ways that also communicate clarity and elicit evidence of learning. We interact with learners as co-evaluators of learning growth and develop their understanding of where they are, how they're going, and where they're headed next in relation to the learning intentions and success criteria. Formative evaluation is our tool for making the characteristics of Visible Learners actionable and achievable by learners.

LEARNING INTENTION AND SUCCESS CRITERIA FOR MODULE 12

Before you engage with the learning in this module, read what we intend to learn (LI, the learning intention) and what it'll look and sound like when we've learned this (SC, the success criteria). Next, read the levels, descriptions, and images of the path to mastery (the rubric). Evaluate where you are right now for each success criteria. At the end of the module, we'll return to this self-evaluation and document the ways we've intentionally grown our teaching practice over time.

LI: We are learning ways to intentionally use formative evaluation so that we can plan and implement impactful interactions and discourse.

SC: I'll know I've learned it when I can

Icon source: istock.com/rambo182

- Identify and ask effective teacher questions and language based on anticipated learner strategies and interactions.

_____

_____

_____

_____

- Create and implement a plan to elicit and document evidence of learning.

_____

_____

_____

_____

- Apply the strategies for communicating clarity, selecting the right instructional strategy at the right time, and adapting tasks for the developmentally appropriate level of challenge.

_____

_____

_____

_____

- Prepare and orchestrate discussion by selecting and sequencing learners' strategies and asking connecting questions.

_____

_____

_____

_____

MODULE 12 • FORMATIVE EVALUATION   253

There are five practices for planning and implementing formative evaluation (Smith & Stein, 2018):

1. Anticipate

2. Monitor

3. Select

4. Sequence

5. Connect

Let's look at each practice and examine the ways formative evaluation can facilitate intentional interactions and discourse.

ACTIVATING LEARNERS

Practice 1: Anticipate. After selecting, revising, or creating a high-quality task, we should take time to anticipate how learners will engage in the task. We can anticipate the following:

- What might learners say? How might learners communicate about the task?

- What might learners do? What strategies might they try?

- How might learners engage with materials?

- What tools might learners need or seek?

- How might learners interact with each other?

- What mistakes or errors would make sense?

Anticipating allows us to intentionally implement the planning we examined in previous modules:

The Focus of Modules 5–11	Actions Based on Anticipations
Communicating Clarity (Modules 5–8)	When we anticipate, we notice important moments and junctures to communicate the learning intentions and success criteria. We identify language to intentionally use as conversational partners and language facilitators. This language aligns with our learning intentions and success criteria and can be communicated with visuals alongside vocabulary. We select higher-order questions to model and to ask to help children become aware of the connections between the task and the learning. We plan metacognitive questions to engage children in self-monitoring, self-reflecting, and self-evaluating. And we notice, create, and test our scaffolds for self-monitoring.

The Focus of Modules 5-11	Actions Based on Anticipations
High-Quality Tasks (Module 9)	We can use our anticipated strategies and language to note things we might do or say to maintain the qualities that promote equity, engagement, and rigor as well as things we should not do or say that would counter these qualities. We can also anticipate social interactions where learners are resources for each other as well as the ways the learning environment will support or hinder children's access and opportunity to successfully learn.
Intentionally Inclusive Tasks (Module 10)	Our anticipation works in tandem with our efforts to adapt tasks for inclusivity. When we anticipate communication and problem-solving strategies, specific language and tools, mistakes and interactions, we can more efficiently and effectively adapt the task to reflect multiple ways of engaging, representing, and acting and expressing. We can also strategically fade scaffolds so that they are truly temporary and so that our learners grow their independent mastery of learning.
Phases of Learning (Module 11)	As we anticipate, we predict how learners in each of the phases of learning may engage in the task. We can then identify instructional strategies that match those phases. This prepares us to respond to each learner with the right strategy at the right time.

Anticipating is most effective when we actually engage in the task ourselves, as though we are the learners. It's also more effective to engage in the task with colleagues so that we can talk through our anticipations and share what we know about our learners. We can even think of how individual learners would engage in the task.

Let's join Lily Swanson's planning time as she anticipates how her toddlers will engage in the action song, "Este es el baile del movimiento/This is the Dance of Movement."

 # CASE IN POINT

It's naptime and Lily is sitting with the paraprofessional, Tyree, and the speech/language pathologist, Huma. They have already developed the learning intentions, success criteria, and high-quality task for tomorrow's learning. With toddlers, the learning intentions, success criteria, and even the task span the whole day of learning in order to provide multiple opportunities to engage in the learning and to create a cohesive focus for all their interactions. The task is a new action song that they will sing and dance to many times throughout the day.

(Continued)

(Continued)

Learning Intentions & Success Criteria	**Language Learning Intention**: *Today, I am learning words describe actions: clap, stomp, pat.*
	Social Learning Intention: *Today, I am learning we can sing and dance together.*
	Relevance: *So that we can sing action songs as a class and as a family.*
	Success Criteria: *I'll know I've learned it when I can move my body to match action songs' words in a group.*
High-Quality Task	*Sing and dance to "Este es el baile del movimiento/This is the Dance of Movement" with actions of* aplaudir/*clap*, pisar muy fuerte/*stomp, and* palmadita/*pat.*

While they have danced to other action songs together, the focus for tomorrow is on doing the actions as a team and saying the action words in the song. They know the song will become a favorite.

Right now, they are making their formative evaluation plans, beginning with the first step: anticipating. The educators have just sung and danced to the song together, laughing and having fun.

Lily begins, "I think they're going to love this song! They love music! Mario and Abril are getting close to clapping so they'll probably flap their arms or move them when we clap. Stomping will be a challenge—they might look at their feet, move their feet, lift a foot, swing their arms, or keep clapping. And everyone loves to pat their head, just like when we sign 'hat.'"

"I'm curious how Thiago and Emma will join in the song. Thiago takes a while to warm up to whole group activities and Emma may not like the noise," Tyree wonders.

"Let's allow them to join as they feel ready in the way they feel ready during morning circle. Maybe they dance but don't make any sounds. Maybe they watch and listen," Lily continues. "We can also sing the song throughout the day so that Thiago and everyone can have multiple opportunities to hear it and move to it. We can each sing and dance with individuals, pairs, and small groups. That'll be a great chance for us to model how we play with friends by dancing together. Then we can sing and dance again as a whole class at the end of the day during pick-up time."

"Maybe some family members will join us!" Tyree adds. "Thiago loves to pat his belly. Maybe we could pat our heads and our bellies."

"Love it! We can ask the kids what to pat when we repeat the song in our smaller groupings," Lily connects.

Huma suggests, "I think we should also have images to show each action and word. We could start with patting our heads like signing 'hat' and show them a picture so everyone can practice that move and feel confident. Then we can do some clapping while showing a picture. We can position ourselves close to Mario and Abril to model and scaffold their clapping."

"Abril loves to hold my hands while I clap. I'll be near her and she can clap my hands and then I'll clap her hands," Lily plans.

"Great! And I'll be near Mario so he can watch me clapping closely. He'll also like looking at D'Anthony clapping. D'Anthony may even clap Mario's hands for him," Tyree says.

"For the stomping picture, we should think aloud, Where are my feet? What do my feet do when I stomp? I walk very loudly! Watch me pick up my foot and put it down again. Listen for the sound. Stomp! Stomp!" Lily models as she speaks.

"And I'll make sure Emma has her quiet headphones. I'll sit next to her and model doing the actions and saying the words so she can see my mouth and body. When it's just the two of us, I'll sing quietly without her headphones and cue the action paired with each word," Huma replies.

Lily, Tyree, and Huma use their deep knowledge of their learners to anticipate how the children will engage with this task. Their anticipating conversation takes just a few minutes. Notice how anticipating connects directly with identifying opportunities to communicate clarity, to promote equity, engagement and rigor, and to identify adaptations and phases of learning.

YOUR TURN!

Grab a high-quality task that you use in your learning experiences and interactions. Use the first chart below to document the clarity of the task and a brief description. If you do not have clarity around the specific task, now would be a good time to establish the learning intentions, relevance, and success criteria. You can also return to your clarity work in Part 2.

Learning Intentions & Success Criteria	Content Learning Intention: *Today, I am learning . . .*
	Language Learning Intention: *Today, I am learning . . .*

(Continued)

(Continued)

	Social Learning Intention: *Today, I am learning . . .* **Relevance:** *So that we can . . .* **Success Criteria:** *I'll know I've learned it when I can . . .*
High-Quality Task	

Next, anticipate how your learners will engage in this task.

What might learners say? How might learners communicate about the task?

What might learners do? What strategies might they try?

How might learners engage with materials?

What tools might learners need or seek?

How might learners interact with each other?

What mistakes or errors would make sense?

Practice 2: Monitor. We use our anticipated strategies to develop our plan for monitoring. To develop a monitoring plan, we consider ways to elicit and document evidence of learning. Often in early childhood, our primary monitoring strategy is an observation or conference chart where we note what we observe as well as what takes place within our intentional interactions (or conferences) within playful learning. We can pair the documentation of observations and conferences with other evidence, such as photos, videos, or children's work.

To make these decisions, we need to rely on our learning intentions and success criteria. Our monitoring plan must help us monitor how they are progressing toward mastery of the learning intention and which success criteria children have met.

Our plan should work for us as well as our partners—general educators, special educators, specialists, and paraprofessionals. And, our monitoring plan should empower us to communicate effectively with our other partners—learners and their families.

Let's return to the toddler team's planning meeting as they move from anticipating to monitoring.

 **CASE IN POINT**

"Our success criteria is this: I'll know I've learned it when I can move my body to match action songs' words in a group. So we're focused on receptive language comprehension," Huma notes.

"And participating in a group song," Tyree includes.

"So how do we want to monitor the kids' progress with this success criteria?" Lily poses. "As usual, I think we should all be taking notes so let's create a monitoring chart."

"The kids and their families loved seeing photos and videos of their progress. We should do that again," Tyree suggests.

"And then we can use those photos and videos to practice clapping, stomping, and patting. I can pair a photo with each of the action images," Huma adds.

Lily sketches a monitoring chart for the three of them to use. She includes the success criteria and they agree to make notes about expressive language since that is an extension that aligns with the learning intentions. Together, they brainstorm the specific language to model as conversational partners and language facilitators. They also brainstorm higher-order and metacognitive questions to communicate clarity.

	I can move my body to match action songs' words in a group. Note pairs of words and movements.	I can move my body to match action songs' words in a group. Note settings and with whom.	Action songs' words What words or sounds do they attempt?	Notes
Abril				
D'Anthony				
Emma				
Lena				
Levi				
Mario				
Thiago				

(Continued)

(Continued)

Language	Questions & Prompts
clap your hands—*aplaude tus manos* stomp your feet—*pisotea tus pies* pat your—*acaricia tu*: • head—*cabeza* • belly—*vientre* • knees—*rodillas* • shoulders—*hombros*	Can you _____? ¿*Puedes _____*? Look at _____. *Mira _____.* What do you want to pat? ¿*Que quieres acariciar?* Who can we dance with? ¿*Con quien podemos bailer?* How did you know to _____? We said _____!— ¿*Como supiste _____? Dijimos _____!* What if we say _____? What should we do?— ¿*Que tal si decimos _____? ¿Que debemos hacer?*

TEMPLATES

Monitoring Template

Learners	*Success Criteria #1*	*Success Criteria #2*	*Success Criteria #3*	Notes

CASE IN POINT

Arturo Salazar collected data about learners' performance on one of the early learning progressions: Speak clearly enough to be understood by both familiar and unfamiliar adults. Arturo recorded children speaking with staff members and noted the areas in which children struggled. He planned a field trip to a children's museum and collected additional data about learners' interactions with unfamiliar adults. During a team meeting, Arturo told the others that his learners "really struggled with communication. They are not easily understood and they all mispronounce words. They can't even ask about the bathroom or for a drink of water. The language skills in my class are so low. I think we need remediation and some referrals to special ed."

Here are some questions to consider:

Did you notice that assessment data can trigger deficit thinking? Where do you see deficit thinking?	
What advice could you offer Arturo and the team to focus on strengths?	
How could you support the team to take responsibility for children's learning?	
What types of interventions might the team try before making referrals to special education?	
What data would be required to request formal assessments for special education services?	

ORCHESTRATING DISCUSSION

Practice 3: Select. To orchestrate a classroom discussion about the learning within the task, we must intentionally select children to share their ideas, creations, interactions, and experiences. Too often, we simply call on sharers who volunteer, which results in the same children's voices dominating classroom discourse. Instead, by intentionally selecting children to share based on our interactions with them, we can position every learner as a competent and valuable member of the learning community, we can communicate the importance of diverse voices and choices, and we can activate learners as resources for each other's learning.

When we create our monitoring plan, we monitor for the characteristics of learning that we would like to select to share. Who shares and what they share depends upon our learning intentions and success criteria. We create "look fors" so that we are looking and listening for specific learning as we monitor. This gives us an even clearer vision for monitoring and documenting evidence of learning and supports our intentional interactions. Selecting children to share is another rich opportunity to communicate clarity using children's thinking as the models. In this way, we share authority with our learners.

At the same time, we should always be looking to be surprised by our learners, which means our plan to select for sharing can and should be adjusted based on the surprises our learners present. This is playful learning.

Back at the toddler team's meeting, they brainstorm interactions and learning they want to select to share based on their learning intentions and success criteria.

 # CASE IN POINT

"How do we want to use sharing to move learning forward?" Lily poses.

"We could use sharing to celebrate trying something new. It takes initiative and it's a risk to try a new movement," Tyree suggests.

"So true. And we also want to celebrate the together part of this since that's the focus of our whole unit. We're trying to learn how to play with a friend and dancing together is one way," Huma adds.

"In our monitoring chart, we are noting who kids dance with. We could have kids share who learned something from a friend or who tried something a friend showed them," Lily says.

Tyree adds, "Or who tried something new together."

"Yes! Let's star the interactions that could be great to highlight and share at closing circle. We can compare notes at nap and select three."

Practice 4: Sequence. The sequence or order that children share should also be intentional. We may move from simple to complex or from most common to less common. We may also sequence sharers to connect prior knowledge to today's learning and bridge to tomorrow's learning.

Our monitoring plan includes our "look fors" to select sharers as well as our intended sequence for sharing. Both may be revised based on the actual learning experiences and interactions of children within the task, but our plan will be a guide to help us make the decision of who to share and in what order intentional and efficient.

The educators on Lily's team move directly from the conversation about selecting into a conversation about sequencing.

CASE IN POINT

"Let's start the share with our phrase 'Just like _____'. We've used that a lot to emphasize that we can learn from each other. We can begin with a kid who watched another kid before trying an action. We can also narrate the share: 'I noticed _____ watched _____ clap their hands. Then _____ clapped their hands! _____ clapped their hands just like _____.' Then we can have those two kids take turns clapping," Lily explains.

"I'm sure one of our kids will help another clap by putting hands over hands. Many of them love to do that to me. That can be our second share: 'I noticed _____ taught _____ how to clap their hands. Now _____ can clap just like _____.' Then we can have those two kids show the hand-over-hand clapping together," Tyree extends.

"And the last one can be a pair or team that all tried something new together. Maybe a new body part to pat. Or someone will try stomping. 'I noticed _____ and _____ tried something new together. They tried to _____.' Then we can have them show us what they tried and then we can all try it with them," Huma continues.

"I like that we'll end sharing with all of us trying something new together with the kids teaching us," Tyree reflects.

Practice 5: Connect. The final step is connecting the learning of children who are selected to share. This means we need to prepare questions that create discourse among children, activate them as resources to each other, and connect their sharing to the learning intentions and success criteria.

Lily, Tyree, and Huma have already planned how they will narrate as their kids share. Now they need to plan questions to engage the children in talking, thinking, and interacting with each other because of the sharing.

CASE IN POINT

"I'd like to ask some metacognitive questions so they all have the opportunity to think about the question even if we don't answer it. I think we could ask a metacognitive question after each share: After the first share ask, 'Did you watch a friend and try to do what they did?'; after the second share ask, 'Did a friend help you clap or pat or stomp?'; and after the third share ask, 'Did you try a new move today?' Maybe one of the kids will point to a friend or do an action or remember something or maybe we'll just all hear the question. But that's OK. I want to emphasize that when we play together, we also learn together. So I'll say that after a brief think time," Lily plans.

"We use a lot of 'I notice' language. We could also ask, 'What do you notice _____ doing?' The first share is about watching and mimicking. So we could describe that and then all try it. The second share is about helping with gentle hands. We could describe and then do it. And then the last share is about trying even when you don't know how. We could describe that and then we could all try it together," Tyree describes.

Lily adds their select, sequence, and connect pieces to the end of their chart:

1. A kid who watched another kid before trying an action: 'I noticed _____ watched _____ clap their hands. Then _____ clapped their hands! _____ clapped their hands just like _____.' Then sharers take turns clapping.

   'What do you notice _____ doing? _____ is watching _____ and then _____ mimics. He does the same thing. Let's try watching and then mimicking _____.'

   'Did you watch a friend and try to do what they did today?'

2. A kid helps another clap by putting hands over hands: 'I noticed _____ taught _____ how to clap their hands. Now _____ can clap just like _____.' Kids show the hand-over-hand clapping together.

   'What do you notice _____ doing? _____ uses gentle hands to help _____ clap. Let's try using gentle hands to help each other clap.'

   'Did a friend help you clap or pat or stomp today?'

3. A pair or team that all tried something new together: 'I noticed _____ and _____ tried something new together. They tried to _____.' Sharers show us what they tried.

   'What do you notice _____ doing? _____ are trying a new move. Let's try it with them.'

   'Did you try a new move today?'

This whole planning conversation from anticipation through connecting takes about fifteen minutes. At the end, the whole toddler team has a shared plan for formative evaluation that activates learners and orchestrates discussion in ways that also communicate clarity and elicit evidence of learning. This plan addresses learning across the whole day for this toddler classroom. In an infant classroom, this process may also address the whole learning day, while in a preschool or primary classroom, the educators may need to engage in this planning process for multiple tasks over the course of the day. The more often the team engages in these five practices to make intentional formative evaluation plans, the more efficient this conversation becomes. Over time, it becomes a habit of their collaborative teaching practice.

Now, the formative evaluation plan must be implemented. Carrying a clipboard with the monitoring chart and a pen as well as a recording device is an established routine. By carrying around the tools for documenting evidence throughout the day, educators can jot notes and capture photos and videos in the moment. During nap or at the conclusion of each day, they gather for a quick fifteen minutes to look across their charts and images for patterns and trends that inform the next day's instruction. This debriefing conversation also becomes a habit. We will join Lily's toddler team for their debriefing conversation in Module 15.

REFLECTION

Here are four additional monitoring templates that early educators have developed and used to monitor learning and development as they interact with children. Look at each example and reflect on what you notice, how it allows for monitoring and documenting evidence of learning, and how you might use a similar monitoring chart in your classroom.

Monitoring Template Example #1

Learner	Outdoor Space	Connections Made	Language Used	Questions Posed	Notes

What do you notice about the example?

How does this example allow monitoring of children's growth and learning?

How could you use this example in your own classroom?

Monitoring Template Example #2

Learner:	Learner:	Learner:	Learner:
Center:	Center:	Center:	Center:
Learner:	Learner:	Learner:	Learner:
Center:	Center:	Center:	Center:
Learner:	Learner:	Learner:	Learner:
Center:	Center:	Center:	Center:

(Continued)

(Continued)

What do you notice about the example?
How does this example allow monitoring of children's growth and learning?
How could you use this example in your own classroom?

Monitoring Template Example #3

Teams of Learners	New Challenges Set (Goal-Setting)	Tools Used (Especially combining tools/ materials multiple spaces)	Areas of Expertise (How do children rely on each other as experts and of what?)	Notes

What do you notice about the example?

How does this example allow monitoring of children's growth and learning?

How could you use this example in your own classroom?

Monitoring Template Example #4

Learner	Narration (Child's description of game, creation, drawing, writing)	Inspiration (Connection to songs, books, experiences)

(Continued)

(Continued)

What do you notice about the example?

How does this example allow monitoring of children's growth and learning?

How could you use this example in your own classroom?

Monitoring charts should reflect the learning evidence needed to make visible children's progress toward the success criteria. Recording observations and noticings is a powerful way to document both learners' processes and their products in the moment. Photos and videos as well as children's creations and drawings are easily shared with family and make learning and development *over time* visible. Using multiple ways to document learning can help make learning and development visible in multiple contexts and from multiple perspectives. We'll examine ways to partner with families and learners to co-evaluate in Module 14. Most importantly, formative evaluation plans should align with the learning intentions and success criteria.

YOUR TURN!

Now, it's your turn to bring this strategy to your work with your children. Return to your anticipation of a high-quality task (pp. 258-259). Continue developing your formative evaluation plan to document evidence of children's learning and growth by planning to monitor, select, sequence, and connect.

Decide the ways you will document learning: monitoring chart, photos, videos, children's creations and drawings, or other ways. You can use one of the above templates or create your own monitoring chart.

Monitor	
Select	
Sequence	
Connect	

Remember: As we know from Module 3, our role is not simply to observe and document. We must intentionally interact by taking on the roles of conversational partners and language facilitators. These intentional interactions are where we value who before do, communicate clarity, formatively evaluate, *and* engage in feedback.

LEARNING INTENTION AND SUCCESS CRITERIA FOR MODULE 12

Now that you have engaged with the learning in this module, reread what we intended to learn (the learning intention) and what it looks and sounds like to have mastered learning this (the success criteria). Next, reread the levels, descriptions, and images of the path to mastery (the rubric). Reevaluate where you are right now for each success criteria. Use the box to reflect on the evidence you have of where you are and where you are headed next.

LI: We are learning ways to intentionally use formative evaluation so that we can plan and implement impactful interactions and discourse.

SC: I'll know I've learned it when I can

Beginning	Emerging	Developing	Expanding	Bridging
Becoming aware 	Initially trying	Deliberately practicing 	Intentionally stretching	Transferring and generalizing 

Icon source: istock.com/rambo182

- Identify and ask effective teacher questions and language based on anticipated learner strategies and interactions.

_____

_____

_____

_____

_____

- Create and implement a plan to elicit and document evidence of learning.

_____

_____

_____

_____

_____

- Apply the strategies for communicating clarity, selecting the right instructional strategy at the right time, and adapting tasks for the developmentally appropriate level of challenge.

_____

_____

_____

_____

_____

- Prepare and orchestrate discussion by selecting and sequencing learners' strategies and asking connecting questions.

_____

_____

_____

_____

_____

EFFECTIVE FEEDBACK

Interactions are the heart of early childhood. Feedback is the content of our interactions. Every interaction is feedback for children, and so we must strive to make every interaction, every moment of feedback as intentional, humane, and growth-producing as possible.

Our interactions or feedback establish our teacher–learner relationships. Feedback also closes the gap between where learners are and where they are going by aligning the language and content of the interaction with the learning intentions and success criteria.

Visible Learners are aware of the space between what they do and do not yet know. Visible Learners negotiate this space by seeking and using feedback as scaffolds to select tools, make adjustments, and recognize when they've learned something so they can teach others. They rely on the trust established by effective feedback to take on the challenge of moving their learning forward.

Big Ideas

In the previous module, we began our deep work with formative evaluation. Formative evaluation drives feedback. In this module, we dive into effective feedback.

LEARNING INTENTION AND SUCCESS CRITERIA FOR MODULE 13

Before you engage with the learning in this module, read what we intend to learn (LI, the learning intention) and what it'll look and sound like when we've learned this (SC, the success criteria). Next, read the levels, descriptions, and images of the path to mastery (the rubric). Evaluate where you are right now for each success criteria. At the end of the module, we'll return to this self-evaluation and document the ways we've intentionally grown our teaching practice over time.

LI: We are learning about the role of effective feedback in growing Visible Early Childhood Learners so that we can use our formative evaluation to drive effective feedback.

SC: I'll know I've learned it when I can

Beginning	Emerging	Developing	Expanding	Bridging
Becoming aware 	Initially trying	Deliberately practicing 	Intentionally stretching	Transferring and generalizing 

Icon source: istock.com/rambo182

- Describe the characteristics of effective feedback.

_____

_____

_____

_____

_____

- Explain the relationship between feedback and our roles as conversational partner and language facilitator.

_____

_____

_____

_____

_____

Let's start with a definition of feedback: *Feedback* is the exchange of evaluative or corrective information about an action, event, or process and is the basis for improvement (Merriam-Webster, 1999). The interaction between us and our young learners are the basis for supporting their growth and development into Visible Learners. However, feedback only supports improvement when the interaction is developmentally appropriate; this means our learners not only engage in the interaction but also effectively integrate the content of the interaction into the next steps of their learning. There is a difference in impact between feedback that is sent and feedback that is received. To increase the likelihood that feedback is received and has an impact on increasing growth and development, feedback must address three very important questions for both us and our young learners (Hattie, 2012):

1. Where are we going?

2. How are we going?

3. Where do we go next?

REFLECTION

Take a moment and brainstorm about the nature of your interactions with your young learners. How do you communicate each of the three questions associated with effective feedback?

(Continued)

(Continued)

Feedback Questions	What this looks and sounds like in my classroom
Where are we going?	
How are we going?	
Where do we go next?	

DECIDING WHAT FEEDBACK TO GIVE AND RECEIVE

Feedback has a powerful impact on learning. For feedback to work, we must have a clear understanding of the following:

- Learners' expected level of performance across all domains of learning
- Learners' current level of performance
- Instructional strategies selected to close the gap (see Module 11)

 **REFLECTION**

Take a moment and reflect on the three above-mentioned bulleted items. Flipping back through the previous modules of this Playbook, what are specific ways you can develop your understanding of each item? Use the chart below to document your ideas and thinking.

Key Understandings	How do I develop my understanding?
Learners' expected level of performance across all domains of learning	
Learners' current level of performance	
Instructional strategies selected to close the gap	

You'll see our motto *who before do* continues here. We must know our learners to meet them where they are and move them forward in learning and development. Our intentional interactions with learners should close the gap between learners' current location in the learning progression and the next level or place in the progression. With this information, our young learners can begin to support their own self-monitoring, self-reflection, and self-evaluation of their learning to meet the learning intention, thus growing into Visible Learners as well.

For our feedback to effectively move learning and development forward, we must consider feedback from the perspective of our children. What is effective feedback and how do we implement it through our intentional interactions? Let's dive in together.

 # REFLECTION

Our intentional interactions and our effective feedback are linked. Let's review what we mean by intentional interactions and the two roles we can take on within those interactions. Complete the skeleton notes in the table below using what you remember.

(Continued)

(Continued)

Then look back at Module 3 p. 62 to compare your notes with our examination of the roles.

A conversational partner is a p _____ in the task and elicits use of specific language through c _____.	A language facilitator ex _____ supports the use of specific language through language pr _____ and tr _____.
A conversational partner uses three strategies to intentionally interact with children and elicit their language use: • M _____ language • A _____ questions • Engages in b _____ exchanges.	A language facilitator uses three strategies to intentionally interact with children and support their language use: • N _____ actions • Th _____ aloud • Pr _____ language • Sc _____ language

Just-in-Time. Effective feedback is "just in time." The timing of feedback depends on where the learner is within the phases of learning. If the child is in the surface phase of learning—making initial sense of a task, content, vocabulary, or factual information—or engaging in deliberate practice, immediate feedback is effective. If the child is in the deep phase of learning—making sense of mistakes or sorting out connections—slightly delayed feedback is more effective. In either case, just-in-time feedback allows children time to act on the feedback.

In early childhood, just-in-time feedback takes place when we take on the roles of conversational partner and language facilitator. We can provide feedback by modeling, asking questions, engaging in back-and-forth exchanges, narrating action, thinking aloud, and prompting and scaffolding. These feedback-rich interactions are "just in time" during playful learning.

 # CASE IN POINT

Take a moment and consider the example of **Just-in-Time** feedback. Use the space below to write down your "noticings" about the example. What do you notice about the example? How does this example exemplify effective feedback? How could you use this example in your own classroom?

Example	Reflections
The child is playing at the pretend kitchen and the teacher asks, "What is for dinner tonight?" The child responds, "baghetti!" The teacher replies, "I love /SSS/paghetti! Let's say that fun word together. Look at my mouth and make your mouth look like mine. We are going to sound like snakes. Ready? /SSSSSS/paghetti!"	What do you notice about the example? How does this example exemplify effective feedback? How could you use this example in your own classroom?

Just-for-Me. Effective feedback is "just for me." It is specific and individualized. It is a developmentally appropriate or just right, bite-size, consumable chunk of information that moves learning forward. We can communicate just-for-me feedback because we are interacting with learners and engaging in formative evaluation. Formative evaluation *informs* the feedback we provide to learners, which illuminates for each individual where they are along the path toward the success criteria, how they're going, and where they're going next.

In early childhood, we make decisions about the content of our modeling, asking questions, engaging in back-and-forth exchanges, narrating action, thinking aloud, and prompting and scaffolding. The content of just-for-me feedback is specific to the individual child in a way that the child can access and act upon it.

Sometimes, we notice trends and patterns in our formative evaluation that the same feedback would move multiple children forward in their learning. This becomes feedback to us about our teaching and informs our next steps for instruction. We will examine this more in Module 15.

CASE IN POINT

Take a moment and consider the example of **Just-for-Me** feedback. Use the space below to write down your "noticings" about the example. What do you notice about the example? How does this example exemplify effective feedback? How could you use this example in your own classroom?

Example	Reflections
The infants are waking up from nap in Valerie's classroom. Valerie reads a mirror book with Lincoln. On each page, she reads about an emotion and a facial expression, "Monkey feels silly. Monkey sticks out her tongue." Valerie makes the face and points to herself in the mirror. Lincoln looks at her face and looks in the mirror. Valerie asks, "Can you stick out your tongue? Can you make your face look like this? I see you moving your tongue. Can you get your tongue out? You've almost made a silly face. Stick your tongue out!" She sticks her tongue out again while Lincoln opens his mouth and moves his tongue around. Valerie says, "You can do it! That's so silly!"	What do you notice about the example? How does this example exemplify effective feedback? How could you use this example in your own classroom?

Actionable. Effective feedback is actionable or constructive. It aligns with the learning intentions and success criteria and provides actionable ways to move closer to the success criteria. Actionable feedback is about the learning, not the learner. It can address the learning within the task, the learning within the more generalizable process of the task, or, the most generalizable topic, the learners' learning process overall, also known as self-regulation. Regardless, children must receive the feedback and be able to use the feedback to act in ways that move their learning about the task, process, or self-regulation forward.

CASE IN POINT

Take a moment and consider the example of **Actionable** feedback. Use the space below to write down your "noticings" about the example. What do you notice about the example? How does this example exemplify effective feedback? How could you use this example in your own classroom?

Example	Reflections
The child is outside standing, pointing to the slide and grunting. The teacher says and signs, "Slide. Do you want to go on the slide?" The child calms down and reaches for the teacher's hand. The teacher says and signs, "Slide. Slide. Slide. Your turn." The child moves their hands like the sign as the teacher repeats, "Slide," and then celebrates, "Yes! That's how you say slide. Let's walk to the slide!"	What do you notice about the example? How does this example exemplify effective feedback? How could you use this example in your own classroom?

CASE IN POINT

Skyler is a learner in Gisselle Lopez's preschool class. Skyler has been learning to count to 10, along with the other children in the class. Like many of the other learners in the class, Skyler often skips a number in the middle range, such as 5, 6, or 7, but generally gets the other numbers correct. Following their counting one day, Giselle said to the class, "You missed some numbers. Let's try this again." Gisselle then asked her learners to listen as she said the numbers aloud, slowly counting from 1 to 10.

She then asked children to repeat the numbers as a group, in unison. Gisselle corrected several of the learners as she listened. For example, she told Skyler, "You forgot some numbers." She repeated that phrase to several other children before asking them to try again to count the numbers. Their performance did not change.

Gisselle then got out some blocks and counted aloud as she touched each block. "See, there are ten. One, two, three, four, five, six, seven, eight, nine, ten. See there are ten. Let's count together while I point to the blocks."

The children started counting. Again, several learners skipped numbers as the teacher pointed to different blocks. Seemingly frustrated, Gisselle said, "Say one number each time that I touch a block." Not much changed.

How might Gisselle use the principles of feedback to change this lesson?

Principles of Feedback	Suggested Changes to This Lesson
Just-in-Time	
Just-for-Me	
Actionable	

DIFFERENT TYPES OF FEEDBACK

There are three types of feedback that are supportive of learning and development in young children: *task, process,* and *self-regulation* (Hattie & Timperley, 2007). The timing of each type of feedback is dependent on the learning intentions, success criteria, and where learners are in the phases of learning.

Task Feedback. As our young learners initially engage in the learning experience or task, *task feedback* develops learners' understanding of specific content, ideas, and terms. This interaction between us and our learners is corrective, precise, and focused on the accuracy of the new idea, concept, or task. Our learners rely on task feedback to add structure to their conceptual understanding, which comes from us providing examples and nonexamples as well as explanations of procedural steps, key features, and context.

CASE IN POINT

Take a moment and consider the example of **task** feedback. Use the space below to write down your "noticings" about the example. What do you notice about the example? How does this example exemplify effective feedback? How could you use this example in your own classroom?

Example	Reflections
While learners are working on sorting and recording their shapes, Mr. Harrison notices Mary has sorted the shapes based on color. He asks, "Mary, how did you choose to sort your shapes?" Mary responds, "I put yellow ones here, blue ones here, green ones right here, and red ones over here." Mr. Harrison affirms Mary's work and directs her to look at the anchor chart. "You are sorting by the attribute of color. Color is a great attribute for sorting. Now let's try a new sort. Today, we are trying new ways to sort shapes. We are sorting by special attributes that just shapes have.	What do you notice about the example? How does this example exemplify effective feedback?

(Continued)

(Continued)

Example	Reflections
For example, we could sort by the number of sides, the number of vertices, the kind of sides—curved or straight sides. How can you reorganize your sort so that they are sorted based on a shape attribute?" He pauses to give her thinking time. When she still doesn't respond, he points to the rectangle Mary is holding and prompts, "What do you notice about this shape?" She replies, "It has four corners." "Those are also called *vertices*," Mr. Harrison replies and points to this new word on the anchor chart and then points and counts the vertices on the rectangle. He says, "Let's find all the shapes with four vertices and put them with this one."	How could you use this example in your own classroom?

Process feedback is critical as learners explore the why and the how of specific content knowledge. Our young learners have likely identified clear boundaries between concepts and have developed awareness of examples and nonexamples associated with a specific concept. In their initial or surface learning, children assimilate task feedback into their work to develop an initial understanding of content, terms, and ideas. To move learners beyond what is simply right or wrong, or what is an example or a nonexample, they must receive and incorporate feedback that focuses on the process or strategies associated with accomplishing a specific task.

As learners begin to develop proficiency with specific content, ideas, and terms, they enter the deep learning phase and the feedback should increasingly shift to process feedback. Process feedback supports making connections, use of multiple strategies, self-explanation, self-monitoring, self-questioning, and critical thinking.

CASE IN POINT

Take a moment and consider the example of **process** feedback. Use the space below to write down your "noticings" about the example. What do you notice about the example? How does this example exemplify effective feedback? How could you use this example in your own classroom?

Example	Reflections
The child has written a letter to grandma and reads it to the teacher. The teacher says, "I can see spaces between your words!" The child explains, "That's so Grandma can read my words." The teacher confirms, "Yes, those spaces help us read your writing. What are you working on next?" The child responds, "I am going to make sure I have big letters at the starts." The teacher replies, "Capital letters will help your grandma know when a new sentence begins. While you check the beginnings, also check for end marks."	What do you notice about the example? How does this example exemplify effective feedback? How could you use this example in your own classroom?

Self-regulation feedback refers to young learners' ability to know what to do when they approach a new and different problem, are stuck, or need to apply their understanding in a new way. Learners who have reached a deep level of conceptual understanding and are armed with multiple strategies are equipped to self-regulate, as they transfer their learning to more rigorous tasks. Highly-proficient learners benefit from self-regulation feedback, although self-regulation feedback is not the only type of feedback that is important to these learners. When we detect a misconception, or when a gap arises in foundational or background learning, learners benefit from both task and process feedback. However, a majority of the feedback at this part of the learning process should be self-regulation through metacognition. The teacher's role in the feedback at this level is to ask questions to prompt further metacognition.

CASE IN POINT

Take a moment and consider the example of **self-regulation** feedback. Use the space below to write down your "noticings" about the example. What do you notice about the example? How does this example exemplify effective feedback? How could you use this example in your own classroom?

Example	Reflections
At the counting jar center, the teacher says, "I can't see all the marbles in the jar so I'm trying to estimate how many there are. How many marbles do you estimate are in the jar? The child responds, "Maybe 15?" The teacher replies, "You estimate 15 marbles. How did you think of that?" The child replies, "I can see 10 but I can't see some."	What do you notice about the example? How does this example exemplify effective feedback?

Example	Reflections
	How could you use this example in your own classroom?

Eventually, learners practice metacognition independently through self-verbalization, self-questioning, and self-reflection. Knowing the right type of feedback (task, process, self-regulation) and providing just-in-time, just-for-me, and actionable feedback is possible because we are consistently and constantly engaged in intentional interactions with our learners. This is also possible because we have clarity about the what, why, and how of learning.

An important note about praise: Praise should absolutely be part of every relationship, including teacher-student relationships. Meaningful, genuine praise comes from a place of knowing our learners and welcoming, valuing, and including who they are. Praise is about the learner not the learning. When praise and feedback are mixed, praise can dilute the power of feedback. So please praise your children. But do not mix praise and feedback.

 # VIDEO CASE IN POINT

Let's return once more to a preschool class to see and hear the ways the teacher provides effective feedback as her three-, four-, and five-year-old learners work together in a small group. In this social-emotional learning focused lesson, the teacher analyzed standards to create learning intentions and success criteria.

Learning Foundations (*California Preschool Learning Foundations*, California Department of Education, 2008):

- Understand and use simple words that describe the relations between objects. (p. 189)

- Interact easily with peers in shared activities that occasionally become cooperative efforts. (p. 174)

- Seek assistance in resolving peer conflict. (p. 174)

(Continued)

(Continued)

Content Learning Intention:

We are learning to take turns with tools.

Language Learning Intention:

We are learning to say and listen to words as we take turns.

Social Learning Intention:

We are learning to collaborate as a team.

Success Criteria:

I'll know I've learned this when

- I can use tools and then pass tools when my turn is over.
- I can say kind words to tell a friend it's my turn or which tool I need.
- I can listen and respond to a friend's words about taking turns.

Many tasks could align with these learning goals. The teacher chose a task and materials to maximize the sense of playful learning based on what she knows about her learners' interests and wonderings: work as a team to crack open geodes by taking turns sharing an anvil and rock pick.

In the video, we'll watch as the teacher enters the group's playful learning and interacts with them throughout learning in order to provide effective feedback. As you watch, pay attention to the ways the teacher creates a space for playful learning with intentionality and positions *every* learner as competent through her interactions.

Look for examples of the qualities of effective feedback and the different types of feedback. Remember, her feedback will be focused on the learning intentions and success criteria, which are social-emotional learning focused, *not* on the actual success of using an anvil and rock pick individually. Record your observations in the table below:

Feedback (Quotes or actions from the video)	What Type of Feedback Is This? (task, process, or self-regulation feedback)	What Qualities of Effective Feedback Are Evident? (just-for-me, just-in-time, actionable)	Explain Your Reasoning.

Feedback (Quotes or actions from the video)	What Type of Feedback Is This? (task, process, or self-regulation feedback)	What Qualities of Effective Feedback Are Evident? (just-for-me, just-in-time, actionable)	Explain Your Reasoning.

Geodes & Taking Turns:
bit.ly/3AW2ZB6

Our feedback can close the gap between where learners are currently and where they're going—the learning intentions and success criteria. When we implement effective feedback, we can accelerate this movement forward. As we model effective feedback, we teach children how to engage in self-feedback and peer feedback, which also have a significant impact on their learning and development.

LEARNING INTENTION AND SUCCESS CRITERIA FOR MODULE 13

Now that you have engaged with the learning in this module, reread what we intended to learn (LI, the learning intention) and what it looks and sounds like to have mastered learning this (SC, the success criteria). Next, reread the levels, descriptions, and images of the path to mastery (the rubric). Reevaluate where you are right now for each success criteria. Use the box to reflect on the evidence you have of where you are and where you are headed next.

LI: We are learning about the role of effective feedback in growing Visible Early Childhood Learners so that we can use our formative evaluation to drive effective feedback.

SC: I'll know I've learned it when I can

Icon source: istock.com/rambo182

- Describe the characteristics of effective feedback.

_____

_____

_____

_____

_____

- Explain the relationship between feedback and our roles as conversational partner and language facilitator.

_____

_____

_____

_____

_____

- Make connections among clarity, formative evaluation, and feedback.

_____

_____

_____

_____

_____

SCAFFOLDING CO-EVALUATORS

When we partner with learners and families, we have the opportunity to tap into their rich expertise and to create inclusive, anti-racist, and anti-bias learning communities. When we partner with learners and families as co-evaluators, we activate them as resources for each other and as owners of their own learning. And, when we intentionally scaffold our co-evaluators, we support their growth as Visible Learners, not just in early childhood settings but reaching over time along their journeys as lifelong learners.

Big Ideas

LEARNING INTENTION AND SUCCESS CRITERIA FOR MODULE 14

Before you engage with the learning in this module, read what we intend to learn (LI, the learning intention) and what it'll look and sound like when we've learned this (SC, the success criteria). Next, read the levels, descriptions, and images of the path to mastery (the rubric). Evaluate where you are right now for each success criteria. At the end of the module, we'll return to this self-evaluation and document the ways we've intentionally grown our teaching practice over time.

LI: We are learning ways to intentionally scaffold the formative evaluation and feedback practices of our co-evaluators so that we intentionally grow Visible Learners.

SC: I'll know I've learned it when I can

(Continued)

(Continued)

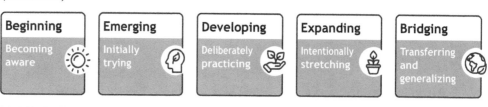

Icon source: istock.com/rambo182

- Model effective feedback to scaffold self-, peer, and family feedback.

_____

_____

_____

_____

_____

- Identify the learning environments and routines that can scaffold the evaluation and feedback practices of our co-evaluators.

_____

_____

_____

_____

_____

- Make connections among the teaching and learning of social skills and emotional development and the teaching and learning of evaluation and feedback practices as co-evaluators.

_____

_____

_____

_____

_____

In Modules 12 and 13, we examined effective formative evaluation and feedback. Becoming intentional in our formative evaluation and feedback practices is essential to scaffolding our co-evaluators because we serve as their living exemplars. When we leverage *all* learners' rich prior knowledge and intentionally promote equity and inclusivity, we invite co-evaluators to join our strengths-based stance that welcomes, values, and includes *all* learners. When we provide opportunities to consider higher-order and meta-cognitive questions, our co-evaluators access this rigorous and engaging thinking. When we model thinking aloud about self-monitoring, self-reflecting, and self-evaluating, we make visible our learning journeys. When we communicate clarity in our language and actions, we exemplify the characteristics of Visible Learners. When we intentionally teach self-evaluation and feedback practices, we are simultaneously teaching critical aspects of social emotional learning.

REFLECTION

Before moving forward in this module, take a moment and review the big ideas of formative evaluation and feedback (e.g., Modules 12 and 13).

What are three takeaways that you are going to implement in your own classroom regarding formative evaluation?

-
-
-

What are three takeaways that you are going implement in your own classroom regarding feedback?

-
-
-

What supports or partnerships will help implement these six takeaways?

As we make progress improving our formative evaluation and feedback practices, we also need to collaborate with co-evaluators. Within our partnerships, we can provide scaffolds to support their practices. Our learning environment can intentionally support co-evaluation and feedback. Routines can scaffold these practices and provide opportunities for deliberate practice. Together with families and learners, we can engage in transparent, intentional, and ongoing formative evaluation and feedback that moves learning and development forward for *every* child.

SELF-FEEDBACK

For our youngest learners, our feedback through modeling, narrating, and prompting grows their awareness. They begin to see their own capabilities in self-care, attachment and relationships, initiative, and self-regulation. Our language-based interactions provide children with opportunities to realize they can *think* about their thinking and *learn* from their learning processes. Our ongoing, intentional feedback can shift this awareness into action over time. Often nonverbally and nonexplicitly at first, children begin to self-monitor, self-reflect, and self-evaluate, which develops metacognition and self-regulation. With continued deliberate practice and modeling, children begin to verbally provide self-feedback; we call this *self-talk*. And gradually, this practice shifts back to being internalized initiative and self-regulation. The quality of self-feedback depends on the scaffolds provided to learners.

The teaching process is iterative—meaning we continually return to our foundations of interactions, clarity, and partnerships in order to move forward with greater impact on learning and development. When we intentionally assume the roles of conversational partner and language facilitator, we scaffold self-feedback by modeling, narrating, asking questions, engaging in back-and-forth exchanges, and prompting. When we implement the four essentials for communicating clarity, we intentionally scaffold children's engagement with three questions that drive self-feedback: *What am I learning? Why am I learning this? How will I know when I've learned it?* and we provide visual models to scaffold self-monitoring. When we partner with learners to collect evidence of their learning, they deliberately practice self-feedback by identifying concrete examples of their own process and progress as learners.

Beyond this foundation, we can provide scaffolds for self-feedback through the learning environment and our routines. Here are some ideas to serve as your springboard for identifying intentional ways to set up your *learning environment as scaffolds for self-feedback.*

The Learning Environment as a Scaffold for Self-Feedback

Learning Environment to Scaffold Self-Feedback	What It Looks Like and Sounds Like	My Learning Environment Audit
Visual Labels	Label supplies, materials, toys, and books with images and multiple languages. Store labeled supplies so that children can access and make decisions about what they need for their tasks. Model, practice, and gradually increase learners' responsibility for clean-up, including sorting toys and books into labeled categories.	
Clear Visual Boundaries and Paths	Define clear, visual boundaries between spaces so that children must intentionally enter and exit a space. From children's eye level, there should be a visible boundary around a space and an obvious entrance to the space while allowing adults to monitor within the space and children to see other options. Between spaces, there should be a clear path for movement.	
Choices/Centers	When you intentionally provide choice, create enough choices to engage children in meaningful decision-making. For centers, allow for 1.5 options per child to ensure choice and variety (VanHoorn et al., 2015). When working with a small group, pair, or individual, providing two choices can be enough to begin, as long as both choices are viable options for follow through.	

(Continued)

(Continued)

Learning Environment to Scaffold Self-Feedback	What It Looks Like and Sounds Like	My Learning Environment Audit
Work Display	Set aside a space to display children's work, both on paper and three-dimensional creations. Meet with children one on one to select work to display for the whole class or for the whole school. Ask each child why they selected the work. Use your formative evaluation and feedback practices to ask questions and share noticings that deepen their reflections.	
Finished and Unfinished Work	Set aside space for children to save unfinished work to continue and deepen their process another day. Have children sort and store work in folders, in trays, or on shelves labeled "Finished Work" and "Still Working." Periodically, have children review the "Still Working" items and move some to "Finished Work." During and after sorting, have children explain their decision-making process. Use this language to prompt the decision of whether work is finished or not during clean-up. If space is limited, consider ways to sketch or take a photo of a product for fast reconstruction the next day, use a hula hoop to designate and protect "Still Working" products, or use an old computer cart's shelves for "Still Working" storage.	

YOUR TURN!

My Learning Environment Audit: Self-Feedback Scaffolds

An audit is an inspection or examination. You're going to conduct an audit of your learning environment for self-feedback scaffolds.

1. Take photos of **your indoor and outdoor spaces** or go sit in your spaces.

2. Return to the chart above and inspect or examine your spaces for each of the learning environment features that scaffold self-feedback.

3. Summarize your audit in the table below.

4. Make an action plan to intentionally use the learning environment to scaffold self-feedback.

My Strengths	My Opportunities	My Action Steps

Here are some ideas to serve as your springboard for identifying intentional ways to establish your *routines as scaffolds for self-feedback*.

Routines as Scaffolds for Self-Feedback

Routine to Scaffold Self-Feedback	What It Looks Like and Sounds Like	My Routine Audit
Plan Do Review	At the start of a chunk of time, such as centers, outdoor play, or mathematics, make a plan together as a class or ask each child to make a plan. This plan should reflect the learning intentions and success criteria. Then move into actually doing the plan, but it's OK to make changes to the plan, to do different things, and to try new things. At the end of the	

(Continued)

(Continued)

Routine to Scaffold Self-Feedback	What It Looks Like and Sounds Like	My Routine Audit
	time, review what you did as a class and how it was similar and different to the plan you made or ask each child to share what they did. This review should connect with the learning intentions and success criteria.	
Language Frames	Model and use language frames to explicitly scaffold the structure of language and the use of new vocabulary in context. Provide a visual cue by pointing to dots under each word in the frame as you model saying the statement or question. Prompt children to also use the language frame as one or both of you point to the dots under the words. Language frames can emphasize metacognitive language for self-monitoring, self-reflecting, and self-assessing. Language frames can also explicitly model the characteristics of Visible Learners, such as selecting tools, making adjustments to processes, learning from mistakes, and recognizing when something new is learned.	
Just-Right Hard, Too Hard, Too Easy	Learning tasks should not be too easy or too hard. Learning happens when the task is just-right hard. This is the Goldilocks Principle. After working on a task, ask children to evaluate whether the task was just-right hard, too hard, or too easy and have them explain why. Use your formative evaluation and feedback practices to engage in conversation to help them accurately evaluate.	

Routine to Scaffold Self-Feedback	What It Looks Like and Sounds Like	My Routine Audit
Cave Time	Provide children individual think time before engaging in a conversation, answering a question, making a selection, or beginning their independent work. This individual reflection time allows them to gather their thoughts and to evaluate where they're going, how they're going, and where they're going next prior to interacting with others.	
Anchor Charts	Create charts that capture thinking and learning visually with the whole community of learners. Use children's ideas, language, examples, and nonlinguistic representations. Model and practice relying on anchor charts to support self-monitoring. Choose a consistent space to display "right now" anchor charts—one or two charts that directly pertain to the current learning intentions. Choose another consistent space to store anchor charts related to prior learning intentions for reference as needed. If space is an issue, take photos of anchor charts and put them in a class book. Send photos of anchor charts to families as well.	
Family Share	Similar to Work Display, meet with children one on one to select work or favorite tasks to share with their families. Record each child telling about the work or their favorite task and why they selected it. Ask children to explain what they learned, why,	

(Continued)

(Continued)

Routine to Scaffold Self-Feedback	What It Looks Like and Sounds Like	My Routine Audit
	and how they know they learned it or where they're going, how they're going, and where they're going next. Share recordings with families.	
Visual and Auditory Cue	Choose a visual and auditory cue to initiate transitions, including cleaning up and freezing to hear directions. Cues can be songs with actions, chimes with hand motions, calls and responses, and more. Intentionally teach and practice responding to the cues using social learning intentions and success criteria.	
Visual Schedule	Display a visual schedule with images and labels in multiple languages. Manipulate the schedule with children while thinking aloud. Refer to the schedule frequently, especially prior to or right after a transition. Visual schedules can show the whole day or part of a day for the whole community of learners or for an individual. First/Then Charts reduce the number of events to visually and cognitively process down to two.	

YOUR TURN!

My Routine Audit: Self-Feedback Scaffolds

Now, let's conduct an audit of your routines as scaffolds for self-feedback.

1. Return to your photos of **your indoor and outdoor spaces** or sit in your spaces again.

2. Return to the chart above and inspect or examine your spaces for each of the routines that scaffold self-feedback. You're looking for evidence of the routine in your learning spaces.

3. Use the chart above to examine **your plans** as well as **your schedule** for further evidence of routines that scaffold self-feedback.

4. Summarize your audit in the table below.

5. Make an action plan to intentionally use routines to scaffold self-feedback.

My Strengths	My Opportunities	My Action Steps

PEER FEEDBACK

Developing learners' capabilities with self-feedback can contribute to their effectiveness in providing peer feedback. This is because they become fluent with how to talk kindly and specifically about learning to themselves first. While self-feedback bolsters peer feedback, we can and should intentionally scaffold both simultaneously. Peer interactions fill children's days. Rather than hoping children learn intrapersonal skills, such as empathizing and forming relationships, we should intentionally teach these skills and activate learners as resources for each other. We should scaffold these interactions to increase their positive impact on learning and development.

When we create and implement social learning intentions, we make the learning of intrapersonal skills transparent, explicit, and integrated with the playful learning of content and language. Social emotional learning standards guide our creation of social learning intentions. This is also a space for developing peer feedback skills. As with self-feedback, we rely on our foundation of interactions, clarity, and partnerships to scaffold peer feedback.

We can also use the intentional ways we create the learning environment and establish routines to engage children in deliberately practicing their roles as resources for each other. Here are some ideas to serve as your springboard for identifying intentional ways to set up your *learning environment as scaffolds for peer feedback*.

The Learning Environment as a Scaffold for Peer Feedback

Learning Environment to Scaffold Peer Feedback	What It Looks Like and Sounds Like	My Learning Environment Audit
Independent, Collaborative, and Parallel Work Spaces	Create intentional spaces that reflect different types of groupings for work. One space should allow children to gather as a whole community of learners with adults. Other spaces should allow for children to work independently, collaboratively in partners or small groups, and in parallel with peers and adults.	
Visual Capacity Limits	Visually display the number of children who can work in one space at a time. Consider the size of the space when making this decision as well as the purpose of the space; when spaces are less than 25 square feet per child, aggressive and unfocused behavior increases (VanHoorn et al., 2015).	
Quiet and Loud Spaces	Both indoors and outdoors, be sure to have quiet, soft spaces as well as loud, rough and tumble spaces. Separate	

Learning Environment to Scaffold Peer Feedback	What It Looks Like and Sounds Like	My Learning Environment Audit
	the quiet spaces from the loud spaces. For example, if you have a space that is cozy for quiet reading, be sure it is on the opposite side of the room from a space that welcomes crashing vehicles and large motor movement, like dancing.	

YOUR TURN!

My Learning Environment Audit: Peer Feedback Scaffolds

Our next audit is examining your learning environment for peer feedback scaffolds.

1. Return to the photos of **your indoor and outdoor spaces** or go sit in your spaces.

2. Review the chart above and inspect or examine your spaces for each of the learning environment features that scaffold peer feedback.

3. Summarize your audit in the table below.

4. Make an action plan to intentionally use your learning environment to scaffold peer feedback.

My Strengths	My Opportunities	My Action Steps

Here are some ideas to serve as your springboard for identifying intentional ways to establish your *routines as scaffolds for peer feedback*.

Routines as Scaffolds for Peer Feedback

Routine to Scaffold Peer Feedback	What It Looks Like and Sounds Like	My Routines Audit
Talking Partners	Model and practice turning knee to knee and eye to eye with a peer to take turns talking and actively listening. Children can turn and talk to share their ideas.	
Language Frames	Model and use language frames to explicitly scaffold the structure of language and the use of new vocabulary in context. Provide a visual cue by pointing to dots under each word in the frame as you model saying the statement or question. Prompt children to also use the language frame as one or both of you point to the dots under the words. Language frames can emphasize giving and receiving feedback. Language frames can also explicitly model the characteristics of Visible Learners, such as asking for help and teaching others.	
Working Partners	When children are working on a task independently, strategically have children work near each other (children who are working on the same task or a child who has already completed the task). This way, they can help each other if they get stuck or have a question.	
Team Roles	When children are working in a team collaboratively, teach and assign roles for each team member. Some roles can be Materials Manager, Recorder, Reporter, and Questioner.	

Routine to Scaffold Peer Feedback	What It Looks Like and Sounds Like	My Routines Audit
Kid Teacher	Invite children to be the teacher by modeling for the whole community of learners or for an individual. Coach the child beforehand by practicing one on one how to model. Be sure every child is the teacher at least once.	

YOUR TURN!

My Routine Audit: Peer Feedback Scaffolds

Now, let's conduct an audit of your routines as scaffolds for peer feedback.

1. Return to the photos of **your indoor and outdoor spaces** or sit in your spaces again.

2. Return to the chart above and inspect or examine your spaces for each of the routines that scaffold peer feedback. You're looking for evidence of the routine in your learning spaces.

3. Use the chart above to examine **your plans** as well as **your schedule** for further evidence of routines that scaffold peer feedback.

4. Summarize your audit in the table below.

5. Make an action plan to intentionally use routines to scaffold peer feedback.

My Strengths	My Opportunities	My Action Steps

FAMILIES

Children are constantly learning at school and home. To maximize learning and development, we need to create continuity across these contexts and teach in culturally responsive ways. Our partnerships with families are paramount, which means we need to invite families to be our co-evaluators and we need to intentionally scaffold their formative evaluation and feedback practices. When we collect evidence of learning together, we can see a more complete picture of the whole child and their transfer of ideas and skills to new contexts. Our youngest learners are just learning about being learners. But their families are lifelong learners whose expertise we can leverage for the benefit of our whole learning community.

Like self-feedback and peer feedback, our scaffolds for family feedback are built upon the foundations of interactions, clarity, and partnerships. We can model and explain the roles of conversational partner and language facilitator as well as emphasize the importance of engaging in these roles in families' heritage languages and within their routines and familiar contexts. We can use the four essentials for communicating clarity to communicate learning intentions and success criteria to families and to partner with them by talking *and* listening.

Many of the routines that scaffold family feedback also scaffold children's deliberate practice of self-feedback and peer feedback by providing them with additional opportunities to hear and see effective feedback at home. Here is a starting point for establishing *routines to scaffold family feedback*.

Routines as Scaffolds for Family Feedback

Routine to Scaffold Family Feedback	What It Looks Like and Sounds Like	My Routines Audit
Mini-Books	Make and send home mini-books for families to read together at home. Include photos from school, home, and the neighborhood to communicate learning intentions and success criteria. The books can be song lyrics with actions depicted in images as well as stories or informational text.	
Digital Portfolio	Create a digital portfolio for each child using a learning or media management system. Communicate learning intentions and success criteria using the	

Routine to Scaffold Family Feedback	What It Looks Like and Sounds Like	My Routines Audit
	four essentials, just like we examined in Module 8 (p. 180) with children. Upload photos and videos each day that align with the learning intentions and success criteria and ask families to do the same.	
Open Classroom	At significant junctures of learning, collaborate with children to welcome their families into the classroom. During open classroom, the children are the teachers and family members are the learners. Each child makes a plan for what to teach their family when they come to the classroom (or the outdoor space). Open classroom is an intentional time to position the children as the experts of their learning journeys and to deliberately practice communicating this to their families; families should be welcomed into the classroom at other times as well.	
Student-Led Conferences	At significant junctures of learning, partner with children to select work that shows growth to share with their families. This can be two visual checklists of concepts and skills—one before and one now to show growth. This can also be photos, videos, or children's artwork from before and now. For example, an infant's family could celebrate growth around ways they can now move their body to reach toys—twist, bend, roll over, belly crawl. A preschooler may show how they	

(Continued)

(Continued)

Routine to Scaffold Family Feedback	What It Looks Like and Sounds Like	My Routines Audit
	used to draw themselves and how they now draw themselves with shapes and body parts.	
Family Readers, Experts, and Teachers	Listen to families to learn about their favorite books, songs, areas of expertise, and much more. Invite family members to join the class to read aloud, teach a song or dance, or teach about their area of expertise. You can have a regular day and time for family readers, experts, and teachers so that family members can sign up. You can also survey families based on the topics within your units of study.	
Newsletters and Family Homework	Regularly communicate clarity with families so they know what their children are learning, why, and how they'll know when they've learned it. Listen to families to learn the best ways to communicate this with them; families may prefer paper newsletters, digital newsletters shared on learning management platforms, brief videos of teachers sharing news updates (with closed captioning in multiple languages), or individualized notes about their child's daily progress. Whatever the mode or format, you can also communicate family homework—how each family can continue, extend, and support learning at home within their existing routines and with their home supplies. Also, be sure to ask families for their insights and feedback—your homework assigned by families.	

YOUR TURN!

My Routine Audit: Family Feedback Scaffolds

Now, let's conduct our final audit of your routines as scaffolds for family feedback.

1. Return to the photos of **your indoor and outdoor spaces** or sit in your spaces again.

2. Return to the chart above and inspect or examine your spaces for each of the routines that scaffold family feedback. You're looking for evidence of the routine in your learning spaces.

3. Use the chart above to examine **your plans** as well as **your schedule** for further evidence of routines that scaffold family feedback.

4. Summarize your audit in the table below.

5. Make an action plan to intentionally use routines to scaffold family feedback.

My Strengths	My Opportunities	My Action Steps

CASE IN POINT

Jeremy Harrison is the first-grade teacher we met in Module 8. In previous years, he sent home a weekly, paper newsletter to families. He would find copies of the newsletter on the floor and balled up in the bottom of backpacks. At conferences, some families would say they would love to know more about what their children are learning each day. Jeremy always replied, "Read my newsletter. I send it home every Thursday." He even showed them an example so they knew what to look for, but the same pattern continued.

(Continued)

(Continued)

This year, he is sending individualized messages on the school's learning management system. Here is a message he sent today to Gabe's family.

When families respond with photos and recordings (and they all do!), he adds them to the children's digital portfolios.

There are so many strategies Jeremy could try next to bolster his scaffolding of self-, peer, and family feedback. He has identified Family Share (p. 305) as his next step to scaffold self-feedback. He also wants to use language frames (p. 304 and p. 310) to scaffold self- and peer feedback. Eventually, Jeremy wants his learners to lead conferences with their families (p. 313). He has a vision and he's energized by the active, regular communication with families, but this also feels like a lot to do.

Attach Note

Good Afternoon!
Gabe did an amazing job sorting shapes today! He carefully counted the number of sides and vertices before making any decisions. He is working on remembering the word PENTAGON when talking about shapes with five sides and five vertices. Gabe can look for different shapes at home and in his neighborhood. After he finds some shapes, send me a picture back or an audio file of him describing the shapes he found!

Help Jeremy sequence his action steps. What order should he implement these plans? How can he build on the successful communication strategy he started with the individualized "newsletter" messages in a manageable way?

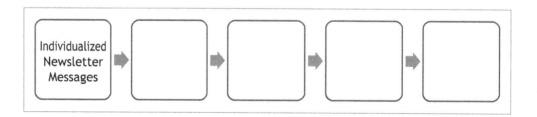

Individualized Newsletter Messages

Explain your reasoning for the sequence of action steps that you recommend.

What relationships are you noticing among these scaffolds for self-, peer, and family feedback?

 YOUR TURN!

As you completed your learning environment and routine audits, you also identified several action steps for yourself in order to scaffold self-, peer, and family feedback. Look back at each of your audits and action plans (p. 307, p. 309, p. 311, and p. 316). What relationships do you notice among your action steps? Which scaffolds need to be in place in order to implement the others? Prioritize and sequence your action steps. (If the chart below doesn't work for you, please adjust it or create one that will help you develop an action plan.)

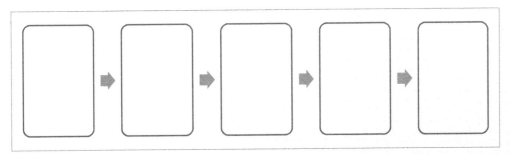

SOCIAL EMOTIONAL LEARNING IS VISIBLE LEARNING

In early childhood, we must explicitly teach social and emotional skills. Social and emotional skills are composed of the following:

➤ regulating and managing emotions,

➤ setting and working toward goals,

➤ empathizing,

➤ forming relationships, and

➤ decision-making.

These skills are both intrapersonal and interpersonal processes that rely on language skills.

 **REFLECTION**

Return to the sections above on self-feedback (p. 306) and on peer feedback (p. 308). Reread the explanation of what each type of feedback is, why it is important, and how we intentionally teach and scaffold this. Circle, underline, highlight, or note every time you see a connection to the social and emotional skills listed above. From your notes, make a list of words and phrases below. We've started each list for you.

Self-Feedback & Social and Emotional Skills	Peer Feedback & Social and Emotional Skills
• *Self-care*	• *Empathizing*
• *Self-monitoring*	• *Social learning intentions*
•	•
•	•
•	•
•	•
•	•

What are you noticing about the relationship between feedback and social emotional learning?

This module focuses on scaffolding our learners so they can become co-evaluators who give and receive effective self- and peer feedback. This work is essential to growing Visible Learners. When we intentionally grow learners who can give themselves feedback and who can give peers feedback, then we simultaneously teach and practice social and emotional skills.

REFLECTION

Flip back to the six characteristics of a Visible Learner (p. 5). Where do you see these characteristics reflected in social and emotional skills?

Use the language you gathered above, the list of social and emotional skills, and the characteristics of Visible Learners to create a concept map that illustrates the relationships among social emotional learning and being a Visible Early Childhood Learner.

Social emotional learning and Visible Learning go hand-in-hand. When we are intentional in our interactions, clarity, and partnerships, we develop our young learners' social and emotional skills while growing Visible Learners. Children and families are invaluable co-evaluators. We must invite them to partner with us. And we must seek feedback from them about our impact.

LEARNING INTENTION AND SUCCESS CRITERIA FOR MODULE 14

Now that you have engaged with the learning in this module, reread what we intended to learn (LI, the learning intention) and what it looks and sounds like to have mastered learning this (SC, the success criteria). Next, reread the levels, descriptions, and images of the path to mastery (the rubric). Reevaluate where you are right now for each success criteria. Use the box to reflect on the evidence you have of where you are and where you are headed next.

LI: We are learning ways to intentionally scaffold the formative evaluation and feedback practices of our co-evaluators so that we intentionally grow Visible Learners.

SC: I'll know I've learned it when I can

Icon source: istock.com/rambo182

> • Model effective feedback to scaffold self-, peer-, and family feedback.
>
> _____
>
> _____
>
> _____
>
> _____
>
> _____

- Identify the learning environments and routines that can scaffold the evaluation and feedback practices of our co-evaluators.

  _____

  _____

  _____

  _____

  _____

- Make connections among the teaching and learning of social skills and emotional development and the teaching and learning of evaluation and feedback practices as co-evaluators.

  _____

  _____

  _____

  _____

  _____

KNOW THY IMPACT

Effective feedback is critical for learners *and* for educators. We are continually seeking feedback about our impact on children's learning. When we partner with children and families as co-evaluators of learning growth, we can see and hear feedback from learners and families that informs our next instructional steps. We can see and hear feedback about the effectiveness of our decisions. Learning becomes visible to our learners, families, and ourselves. And when learning is visible, learners become teachers and teachers become learners.

Big Ideas

LEARNING INTENTION AND SUCCESS CRITERIA FOR MODULE 15

Before you engage with the learning in this module, read what we intend to learn (LI, the learning intention) and what it'll look and sound like when we've learned this (SC, the success criteria). Next, read the levels, descriptions, and images of the path to mastery (the rubric). Evaluate where you are right now for each success criteria. At the end of the module, we'll return to this self-evaluation and document the ways we've intentionally grown our teaching practice over time.

LI: We are learning to make sense of formative evaluation as feedback from learners so that we can ensure that *every* learner benefits from our teaching.

SC: I'll know I've learned it when I can

(Continued)

(Continued)

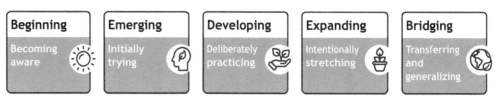

icon source: istock.com/rambo182

- Explain ways formative evaluation is feedback about the effectiveness of our selection of the right strategy at the right time for each learner, our adaptations of tasks, our interactions, and our communication of clarity.

_____

_____

_____

_____

_____

- Describe ways formative evaluation can be analyzed to determine if our instructional decisions had our intended impact for every learner.

_____

_____

_____

_____

_____

- Understand the value of feedback from learners for developing our collective teacher efficacy and equity.

_____

_____

_____

_____

_____

Throughout Part 4, we've examined ways formative evaluation drives feedback. Now, the feedback is _for_ us _from_ learners.

EFFECTIVE FEEDBACK FROM LEARNERS

Effective feedback is just-in-time, just-for-me, and actionable. This is true whether the feedback is *for* learners or *from* learners. The difference is that we must be open to receiving their feedback and we must actively seek it.

To be **just-in-time**, we must implement our formative evaluation plans from Module 12 and then immediately take time to make sense of this as feedback *from* our learners. Time is something we have very little of as educators. Therefore, our formative evaluation data should be organized and documented in a way that is efficient for our consumption. We should be able to quickly and meaningfully interpret patterns and trends in our documentation that will inform our next instructional steps.

Just-for-me feedback is bite-size, consumable, and specific chunks of information. This means we analyze formative evaluation to determine where our learners are right now relative to the learning intentions and success criteria. We also look for the following:

➤ In what phase of learning is each child currently?

➤ How did the tasks promote equity, engagement, and rigor in real time?

➤ What adaptations of tasks successfully allowed for multiple ways of engaging, representing, and acting and expressing learning?

Then, we determine what this means for moving *all* learners forward along the learning progression.

Effective feedback is **actionable**, which means we take action. We must respond to this feedback from learners in ways that communicate respect and an asset-focused stance. We may need to adjust our pace, our selection of instructional strategies and tasks, our set up of the learning environment, or our adaptations of tasks. Our next day instruction should be responsive. We can even begin our planning with, "I've noticed that . . ." and then use this noticing to create our next day's learning intentions and success criteria.

We're going to return to Lily Swanson's toddler class as the educators examine their just-for-me, just-in-time, and actionable feedback from learners. If you'd like to refresh your memory about the toddler teams' planning session, look back at Module 12 (p. 255).

CASE IN POINT

Lily Swanson's toddler class learned a new song today, *"Este es el baile del movimiento/This is the Dance of Movement."* Here were the learning intentions and success criteria:

Learning Intentions & Success Criteria	*Language Learning Intention*: Today, I am learning words describe actions: clap, stomp, pat.
	Social Learning Intention: Today, I am learning we can sing and dance together.
	Relevance: So that we can sing action songs as a class and as a family.
	Success Criteria: I'll know I've learned it when I can move my body to match action songs' words in a group.

Together, Lily (lead teacher), Tyree (paraprofessional), and Huma (speech/language pathologist) gathered formative evaluation data while interacting with children, using their monitoring charts. Below is a compilation of the three educators' monitoring charts:

	I can move my body to match action songs' words in a group. Note pairs of words and movements.	I can move my body to match action songs' words in a group. Note settings and with whom.	Action songs' words [What words or sounds do they attempt?]	Notes
Abril	Shakes arms for clap or claps others' hands. Pat belly, Pat head, Pat knees*	Pats lots of body parts with Lena, Levi, and Abril.		
D'Anthony	Clap, Pat belly, Pat head Squats to touch feet for stomp Imitates Dad stomping	Teaches Mario to clap* Participates in whole group and small group.		Dad danced during pick-up and said "big steps" and picked up his feet high during stomp. D'Anthony imitated.
Emma	Clap, Pat belly, Pat head Touches feet in image during stomp	Does actions 1-1 and with Abril Watches when other children join		

Lena	Clap, Pat belly, Pat head, Pat knees* Stand on one leg for stomp*	Pats lots of body parts with Abril, Levi, and Thiago	/p/ sound for pat	
Levi	Clap, Stomp, Pat belly, Pat head, Pat knees*	Pats lots of body parts with Abril, Lena, and Thiago		Stomped feet to walk outside
Mario	Claps for first time! Then many times! Pat head, Pat belly	Claps with D'Anthony* Then in whole group		Stomped feet on mat to come inside and get mulch off shoes
Thiago	Clap, Pat belly, Pat head, Pat knees* Looks at image and then own feet during stomp	Pats lots of body parts with Abril, Lena, and Levi Joined whole group dance at end of day with Mom!	/k/ sound for clap	

It is the end of the day, and the toddler team's time together is just ten minutes before they are pulled in separate directions for various meetings and responsibilities. They know this formative evaluation is important feedback *for* them *from* their young learners.

Huma looks across their three monitoring charts and notes where the children are now relative to the success criteria, "Levi and D'Anthony have met all of the success criteria. Emma, Lena, and Thiago are close—they have some initial strategies for stomping. And everyone has patting down!"

"Nearly everyone participated whole group and small group! Did you see D'Anthony's dad give the prompt 'big steps'? I'm so glad we danced with families during pick-up. I wonder what other strategies families have for describing and modeling actions," Lily comments.

"Yes! That was the first time I saw D'Anthony stomp! And, Mario learned to clap because D'Anthony kept clapping with him! Thiago really warmed up to dancing with his small group and then he was ready to dance with the whole group at the end of the day!" Huma celebrates growth.

"The modeling and images supported several kids. Emma kept touching the feet in the stomp image. She's making sense of what body part should be moving," Tyree notes.

"Abril is still clapping other people's hands but not her own. And I didn't see Abril or Mario try to stomp or move their feet," Huma points out.

(Continued)

(Continued)

"I saw Mario stomp his feet to get mulch off his shoes when we came inside. He just wasn't stomping when we were singing about stomping," Tyree shares.

"And Emma would dance with me or with Abril but stopped when other kids joined," Huma adds.

Lily shifts the conversation to what this means for the next day, "Tomorrow, we continue our learning about simultaneous actions. Let's continue work with clap and stomp in the same song. Let's add shake also. Then we can show Abril the difference between shaking her hands and clapping her hands, and we can show everyone the difference between shaking feet and stomping feet. Lena was standing on one foot so she's ready for both."

"We noted two kids are starting to make sounds for action words. Let's really emphasize expressive language tomorrow and see how many more kids can produce sounds when we focus on the opportunity to practice making them. We can model, show the images, and make the initial sounds," Huma extends.

The team creates these learning intentions and success criteria for the next day and plans to use the same monitoring chart:

Learning Intentions & Success Criteria	*Language Learning Intention:* Today, I am learning I can say words to describe actions: clap, stomp, pat, shake.
	Social Learning Intention: Today, I am learning we can sing and dance together.
	Relevance: So that we can sing action songs as a class and as a family.
	Success Criteria: I'll know I've learned it when
	• I can move my body to match action songs' words in a group and
	• I can make a sound for an action word.

"I'll get images ready for shake. We could add dancing to 'If You're Happy and You Know It' with all our action words," Tyree suggests.

"Good idea—we all know that song so that'll be a good way to practice matching the words with the actions in a familiar context. I'm going to point out when Levi is stomping to walk outside again. He can teach everyone how he stomps," Lily adds.

"I'll name for Mario what he's doing to get the mulch off—stomping. Then I'll remind him again when we sing and dance," Tyree continues.

"I'll be sure to dance with Emma and Abril again. I'll talk with Emma's family to see if she's singing and dancing with them at home and what they notice helps her feel comfortable in a group," Huma says.

"I'll share the photos and videos we took today with families along with the song so they can practice together. I'll also ask what actions they have been practicing, like D'Anthony and his dad with 'big steps,'" Lily plans.

What do you notice about the team's process for analyzing formative evaluation data?

How does this example exemplify the idea of feedback *from* learners?

How could you use this example in your own classroom?

COLLECTIVE TEACHER EFFICACY

The Visible Learning research points us to strategies that have the potential for high, positive impact on learning and development. Throughout this Playbook, we've worked to direct our time, energy, and effort to plan and implement what works best. Formative evaluation has the potential to accelerate learning—*if* we analyze it to determine whether our instructional decisions had the intended impact for *all* our learners *and if* we take action based on our analysis. This work is pivotal to growing our efficacy as educators.

When we see our impact, we build our teacher efficacy. We must collect and analyze evidence to make visible the impact our decisions have on children's learning and development. Seeing the proof grows our belief that we can move *all* learners forward. And when we believe we can, we are more likely to.

While we can collect and analyze evidence of learning by ourselves, a powerful way to engage in this work is as a team of educators. In this collaborative work, we activate our collective teacher efficacy—our belief that as a team of educators, we can positively impact our children's learning and development. Each member of the team brings their formative evaluation data, their perspectives and insights, and their expertise to the table for analysis and reflection. Our collective work as educators allows us to see evidence of learning in multiple contexts through multiple perspectives and to lean on each other as we move from making sense of data to taking action driven by data.

 CASE IN POINT

Return to the vignette about Lily Swanson's toddler team. Where did you see each member of the team contribute their individual perspectives and strengths for the benefit of the whole team and for the benefit of *all* learners?

Educator	Perspectives and Strengths That Benefited the Whole Team and *All* Learners
Lily (lead teacher)	
Tyree (paraprofessional)	
Huma (speech/language pathologist)	

It is worth our time and effort to build our collective expertise. Collective teacher efficacy has the potential to considerably accelerate learners' development. We invite you to again consider your partnerships and the ways you can work collaboratively and intentionally with your team.

REFLECTION

In Module 2 (p. 38), you reflected on your current and future partnerships with fellow educators. We encouraged you to consider ways to invite your partners into the work of this Playbook. Look back at your ideas and opportunities.

What partnerships have you strengthened? What partners have joined you in this work?	With whom is there space to grow your partnership for the benefit of all your learners?

When we work collaboratively with a center-based team, a grade-level team, or a PLC+, our partnerships with educators deepen and we leverage our individual strengths for the benefit of the whole team. These partnerships take an asset-focused, action-oriented stance. The work of this Playbook is an essential component of our partnerships in a PLC+. Five guiding questions led us throughout this Playbook:

- Where are we going?
- Where are we now?
- How do we move learning forward?
- What did we learn today?
- Who benefited and who did not benefit?

PLC+ Guiding Question	Early Childhood Playbook Modules	Description
Where are we going?	Part 2: Modules 5-8	In Part 2, we analyzed standards to drive our decisions about what children are learning, why, and how we'll know when they've learned it.
Where are we now?	Part 1: Modules 1-4	In Part 1, we reflected on our partnerships in early learning and the importance of "who before do." Using the *Learning About Learners Protocol*, we take time to notice the current reality of learners and the incredible strengths they bring with their families to early education spaces. We also considered intentional ways to enter children's play so that we can learn from them.
How do we move learning forward?	Part 3: Modules 9-11 Part 4: Modules 12-14	In Parts 3 and 4, we relied on our clear vision of where we are and where we're going to intentionally plan tasks, learning strategies, and scaffolds that move learning forward.
What did we learn today?	*Reflections, Cases In Point,* and *Your Turns* throughout Modules	We are building our expertise around the big ideas for teaching, learning, and development in early childhood. Throughout this Playbook, we have created space to reflect and deliberately practice our growing expertise. These reflections and practice spaces help us make sense of what we're learning, how we're learning, and what we want to learn next.
Who benefited and who did not benefit?	Part 4: Module 15	In this module, we examine how learning can be feedback *for us* from learners. Did our tasks, learning strategies, and scaffolds actually work best for our learners at this point in their learning journey? Did our children learn what we intended for them to learn? Did *all* our children learn? Who did not? And now how will we act upon this feedback from learners?

Feedback from our learners fuels our efficacy as educators. By establishing routines for engaging in formative evaluation and analysis as a team, we can act on this feedback to ensure that every learner benefits. We need daily routines, like Lily Swanson's toddler team, for collecting and analyzing ongoing formative evaluation data. We need to identify significant junctures in learning where we will collect and analyze formative evaluation data. This data also serves to drive our decision-making over time.

FEEDBACK FROM LEARNERS AT SIGNIFICANT JUNCTURES

We need to keep our eyes focused on our learning paths and have a clear vision of the characteristics of Visible Learners as well as clarity about what we're teaching, why, and how we'll know if they've learned it. This is true for daily learning as well as learning that takes place over more significant periods of time. By monitoring growth over time, we maintain high expectations while also allowing for children to take different paths at different paces to arrive at the same destination. In other words, we appreciate and value the unique characteristics of early childhood learners: developmental variability, differences in opportunity access and context, and cultural, linguistic, and ability diversity.

Big Ideas

REFLECTION

We closely examined these considerations in Module 5 when we analyzed standards. What do you remember about these three considerations and the ways early childhood standards pose both opportunities and challenges? Record what you remember. Then flip back to p. 90 and expand on your ideas with details.

Developmental Variability	
Opportunity, Access, and Context	

(Continued)

(Continued)

Cultural, Linguistic, and Ability Diversity	

To determine if *all* our young learners make growth, we need to examine the impact of our instructional decisions over time by identifying significant junctures, such as the end of a unit of study or the end of a quarter or trimester. At those times, we monitor children's progress toward mastering the overarching concepts and skills of standards.

Common formative evaluations are one strategy to make learning and development over time visible. Common formative evaluations are used at the beginning and end of a significant period of learning, typically at the beginning and end of a unit of study, in order to document growth over time. They can be specific high-quality tasks or they can be embedded within learning experiences, interactions, and tasks. They can be any format: observation (monitoring chart), photos, videos, children's creations, drawings, writing, and more. In addition, the common formative evaluation should be designed to help the team answer the question: *What was our impact on young learners?*

A note about the social emotional well-being of our youngest learners: Our goal is to collect *feedback from learners* to drive instruction. With that goal in mind, we should **not** create anxiety around any formative evaluation. We should focus on tasks and interactions that fit seamlessly into the daily activities of our classroom or center so that they do not distract or dismay children. In fact, common formative evaluations themselves can be learning opportunities for both learners and educators. As always, our talk about and our interactions during common formative evaluations should reflect positive, intentional interactions where the focus is on learning from our learners. We should position every learner as our teacher and communicate this to learners.

Perhaps you and your team are interested and ready to design a common formative evaluation that is embedded into your instructional day. Here is a protocol to design a common formative evaluation for collaborative, critical, and constructive dialogue about learner growth and development:

TEMPLATES

Protocol Design Template

Unit Focal Standard	
What are children trying to learn? What will mastery of this focal standard look like and sound like? *Establish long-term learning intention(s) and success criteria that embody the focal standard.*	
When and where would we see evidence of mastery? What high-quality tasks do or could children engage in to show what they know?	
What formative evaluation format(s) will we use? *Observation/monitoring chart, photos, videos, children's work, etc.*	
When will we commit to implementing this common formative evaluation before beginning the unit of study? Where would it fit seamlessly into our instructional day?	
When will we meet to analyze this data before beginning the unit of study?	
When will we commit to implementing this common formative evaluation upon concluding the unit of study? Where would it fit seamlessly into our instructional day?	
When will we meet to analyze this data upon concluding the unit of study?	

When using this protocol, the team commits to implementing the common formative evaluation and to meeting to analyze the data before beginning the unit of study. While the task will be implemented before the unit of study, it should still fit seamlessly into the instructional day as another opportunity to learn with and from children. This is why we also consider the variety of ways we could see evidence of the learning rather than merely completion of the task, and this is why we consider high-quality tasks that children already do or could engage in to show what they know related to the learning intention.

Remember, effective feedback is just-for-me, just-in-time, and actionable. This common formative evaluation data is feedback from our learners that must be used to drive the unit of study planning and implementation. When teams meet, this five-step discussion protocol keeps the discussion asset focused and action oriented:

Discussing the Pre-Unit Common Formative Evaluation

Step 1: What parts of these data catch your attention? Just the facts.	(10 minutes): *2 minutes silently writing individual observations, 8 minutes discussing as a group.*
Step 2: What do the data tell us? What do the data *not* tell us?	(10 minutes): *3 minutes silently making notes, 7 minutes discussing as a group.* Make inferences about the data and support statements with evidence from the data.
Step 3: What good news is there to celebrate?	(5 minutes)
Step 4: What are possible common challenges suggested by the data?	(10 minutes): *3 minutes silently writing individual ideas for practice, 7 minutes for group discussion.*
Step 5: What are our key conclusions? How will this data drive our decisions?	(5 minutes)

Source: Adapted from National School Reform Faculty Materials.

Again, upon the conclusion of the unit of study, the team commits to implementing the common formative evaluation and to meeting to analyze the data. The common formative evaluation should fit seamlessly into the instructional day. And again, effective feedback is just-for-me, just-in-time, and actionable, which means this common formative evaluation data is feedback from our learners that must be used to drive the next unit's planning and implementation. When teams meet, this five-question reflection and discussion protocol keeps the discussion asset focused and action oriented:

TEMPLATES

Reflection and Discussion Protocol Template

Question	My Thoughts	Our Collective Thoughts
What is the overall impact of the unit? Is it sufficient, or do we need to make changes?		
What changes did we implement during the course of the unit? What impact did those changes have?		
Which children had negative growth? Why do we think that is? What do we need to do about it?		
Which children had minimal growth? Why do we think that is? What do we need to do about it?		
Which children had exceptional growth? Why do we think that is? What do we need to do about it?		

In order to have a positive impact on children's learning and development, we must know our impact. We must make our impact visible. We must make learning visible. And learning is visible when learners become the teachers and we become the learners.

CASE IN POINT

Alma Hof and her prekindergarten team regularly talk about the differences they saw this quarter with their children. They notice more extended play, more collaborative play, and more language around roles and materials that fit their play scenarios. As a team, they have worked to implement the three characteristics of guided play (p. 159). Their morning meetings often involve games that model the learning intention and success criteria for play with the whole class. This has become a favorite part of planning for the team and of morning meeting for their learners. While they notice growth, Alma and her team want to know if their work to implement guided play is worth it. And they want to be sure *every* child has learned and developed.

The team decides to create and analyze a common formative evaluation so they can see their impact and their children's growth over time. While there are many types of play in their classrooms, they decide to focus on a social learning standard about pretend play. But Alma wonders, "How do you monitor growth in pretending?" Her team isn't sure, but they want to try. They know working together will make taking this risk a bit easier.

The team invites their assistant principal to their planning meeting. Together, they establish a long-term learning intention and success criteria that embody the focal learning foundation.

Unit Focal Standard: "Create more complex sequences of pretend play that involve planning, coordination of roles, and cooperation." (California Department of Education [CDOE], 2008, p. 12)	
What are children trying to learn? What will mastery of this focal standard look like and sound like?	*Learning Intention and Relevance:* We are learning to pretend with friends so that we can play together anywhere and with anything. *Success Criteria:* We'll know we've learned this when • We can make a plan for what we will pretend together, • We can decide roles as a team, • We can choose props as a team, • We can use words and actions to make decisions and play together!

The assistant principal brings an article on pretend play with an observation rubric that describes five stages of pretend play and six components of pretend play, which align with the characteristics of guided play and their focal standard. (Article and rubric available at bit.ly/3xwhcnv; Leong & Bodrova, 2012). They decide to observe using this rubric as well as take photos and perhaps video of the children's pretend play scenarios.

The team commits to observing in the next week and then meeting to analyze their data and make plans for the next quarter.

However, the team enters a debate. They agree the pretend play should just be a regular part of their day. They do not want to stop to do something special or different. But when and where should they observe? Alma says she will observe in the kitchen area of her classroom during centers. But her teammate points out that they also have a mud kitchen outside for pretend play and that he has also seen his children engage in pretend play scenarios with the train set, the playdough in the art area, and the slide on the playground.

What is the value of identifying multiple contexts for observing? How does observing in multiple contexts account for the unique considerations of early childhood?

When and where would you suggest the team observe? What high-quality tasks could their children engage in to show what they know about cooperating in pretend play? Fill in the empty part of the chart below with your suggestions.

Unit Focal Standard: "Create more complex sequences of pretend play that involve planning, coordination of roles, and cooperation" (CDOE, p. 12)	
What are children trying to learn? What will mastery of this focal standard look like and sound like?	*Learning Intention and Relevance:* We are learning to pretend with friends so that we can play together anywhere and with anything. *Success Criteria:* We'll know we've learned this when • We can make a plan for what we will pretend together, • We can decide roles as a team, • We can choose props as a team, • We can use words and actions to make decisions and play together!
When and where would we see evidence of mastery? What high-quality tasks do/could children engage in to show what they know?	

(Continued)

(Continued)

What formative evaluation format(s) will we use?	PRoPELS rubric for observation with photos or video (bit.ly/3xwhcnv; Leong & Bodrova, 2012).

Knowing our impact is an issue of equity. We have an important responsibility as early educators. We strive for a year's worth of developmental growth or learning gains for *every* learner. When we see formative evaluation as feedback *from* learners, when we ask the critical questions, "Who benefited and who did not benefit?" and when this feedback drives our decisions for planning and implementation, then we promote equity of access and opportunity in our classrooms and centers.

LEARNING INTENTION AND SUCCESS CRITERIA FOR MODULE 15

Now that you have engaged with the learning in this module, reread what we intended to learn (the learning intention) and what it looks and sounds like to have mastered learning this (the success criteria). Next, reread the levels, descriptions, and images of the path to mastery (the rubric). Reevaluate where you are right now for each success criteria. Use the box to reflect on the evidence you have of where you are and where you are headed next.

LI: We are learning to make sense of formative evaluation as feedback from learners so that we can ensure that every learner benefits.

SC: I'll know I've learned it when I can

Icon source: istock.com/rambo182

- Explain ways formative evaluation is feedback about the effectiveness of our selection of the right strategy at the right time for each learner, our adaptations of tasks, our interactions, and our communication of clarity.

_____

_____

_____

_____

_____

- Describe ways formative evaluation can be analyzed to determine if our instructional decisions had our intended impact for *every* learner.

_____

_____

_____

_____

_____

- Understand the value of feedback from learners for developing our collective teacher efficacy and equity.

_____

_____

_____

_____

_____

BY DESIGN, NOT BY CHANCE

We began our work in this Playbook wondering: *What matters in early childhood teaching, learning, and development? In what ways should we spend our time, money, and energy to positively impact our youngest learners?*

In each module, we unpacked instructional approaches and strategies with this potential. Seven big ideas for effective teaching, learning, and development in early childhood served as our guideposts. We examined our credibility and self-efficacy, partnerships, interactions, planning and communicating of clarity, learning environment, tasks, phases of learning, formative evaluation, and feedback.

 ## REFLECTION

Throughout this Playbook, we deepened our understanding of these seven big ideas and unpacked ways to implement them in our early childhood classrooms and centers. Take a few minutes to reflect and capture your thinking. When we began our work together, what did you think about each of these big ideas? Now, what do you know?

(Continued)

(Continued)

7 Big Ideas for Effective Teaching, Learning, and Development in Early Childhood

Early childhood educators and their learners work together as evaluators of learning growth for all.		ES = 1.32
I used to think . . .	Now I know . . .	
Early childhood educators and learners have high expectations for learning that communicate equity of access and opportunity to the highest level of learning possible.		ES = 0.90
I used to think . . .	Now I know . . .	
Learning experiences move learning toward explicit and inclusive success criteria.		ES = 0.77
I used to think . . .	Now I know . . .	
Learning experiences and tasks have the developmentally appropriate level or right level of challenge for all young learners.		ES = 0.74
I used to think . . .	Now I know . . .	

Trust is established with all learners so that errors and mistakes are viewed as opportunities for new learning.		ES = 0.72
I used to think . . .	Now I know . . .	
Early childhood educators are continually seeking feedback about their impact on all their children's learning.		ES = 0.72
I used to think . . .	Now I know . . .	
There is the right balance of surface and deep learning in the early childhood classroom.		ES = 0.69
I used to think . . .	Now I know . . .	

As you read your reflective statements, we hope you see your developing expertise around these seven big ideas and feel your growing confidence at implementing these ideas.

Our work does not end here simply because we've reached the end of this Playbook. Every year, we are given the gift of time with new learners and families who present new opportunities for us to meet them where they are, value their unique funds of knowledge, and champion a new learning community that includes and values every learner and family. This fresh start each year is an opportunity to learn from our children and families and to continue to develop our expertise.

And each year, we must continue to hold our ourselves highly accountable for creating and maintaining inclusive, anti-racist, anti-bias spaces, maximizing time, and cultivating intentional interactions with all our youngest learners. We must strive for a year's worth of developmental growth or learning gains for each of our learners.

We know the greatest gains in learning and development occur when learning is visible. This means *early childhood educators see learning through the eyes of their learners and learners see themselves as their own teachers.* When learners see themselves as their own teachers, we have successfully grown Visible Early Childhood Learners. The characteristics of Visible Learners will serve our youngest learners well throughout their schooling and lives.

REFLECTION

What does it mean to grow Visible Early Childhood Learners in your classroom or center? Look back at your reflection from when we began this Playbook (p. 3) and consider all that you have learned, discussed, and implemented. What deeper, clearer understanding of the characteristics of Visible Learners do you have now? And what actionable steps can you take to support these characteristics?

Visible Early Childhood Learners	What This Means Now in My Center or Classroom	How I Can Support This in My Center or Classroom
Know their current level of understanding; they can communicate what they do and do not yet know		
Know where they are going next in their learning and are ready to take on the challenge		

Visible Early Childhood Learners	What This Means Now in My Center or Classroom	How I Can Support This in My Center or Classroom
Select tools to move their learning and development forward		
Seek feedback about their learning and recognize errors as opportunities to learn		
Monitor their learning and make adjustments when necessary		
Recognize when they have learned something and serve as a teacher to others		

We hope our work in this Playbook has spilled out into your classroom or center and into your partnerships with learners, families, and fellow educators. We hope the instructional approaches and strategies are becoming habits of mind, and with deliberate practice, they will become efficient and foundational to your daily planning and interactions. We hope you see learning through the eyes of your learners. And we hope your learning is visible to you so that you can be teachers to other educators as well.

REFLECTION

Our very first work together was to set individual goals (p. 2). You identified the evidence you would need to make your learning visible. Return to those goals now.

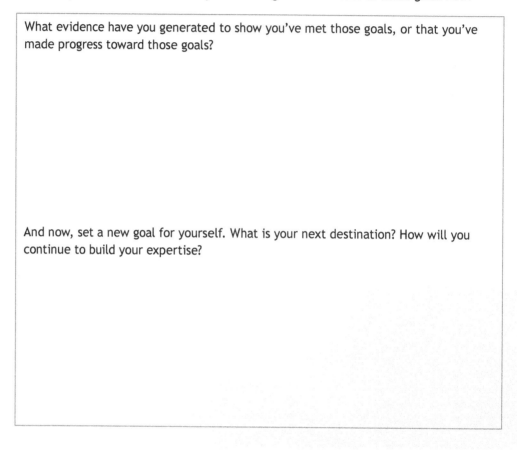

What evidence have you generated to show you've met those goals, or that you've made progress toward those goals?

And now, set a new goal for yourself. What is your next destination? How will you continue to build your expertise?

Teaching our youngest learners is both a privilege and an awesome responsibility. Our youngest learners and their families deserve great teachers—not by chance, but by design. As Visible Learners ourselves, our learning journey continues.

REFERENCES

Almarode, J. T., Fisher, D., Thunder, K., & Frey, N. (2021). *The success criteria playbook: A hands-on guide to making learning visible and measurable.* Corwin.

Antonetti, J. V., & Garver, J. R. (2015). *17,000 classroom visits can't be wrong: Strategies that engage students, promote active learning, and boost achievement.* ASCD.

Australian Government Department of Education and Training. (2019). *Belonging, being & becoming: Early years learning framework.* https://www.dese.gov.au/child-care-package/resources/belonging-being-becoming-early-years-learning-framework-australia-bookmark

Bandura, A. (1977). Self-efficacy: Toward a unifying theory of behavioral change. *Psychological Review, 84*(2), 191-215. https://doi.org/10.1037/0033-295X.84.2.191

Berry, R. Q., III, & Thunder, K. (2012). The promise of qualitative metasynthesis: Mathematics experiences of Black learners. *Journal of Mathematics Education at Teachers College, 3*(2), 43-55. https://doi.org/10.7916/jmetc.v3i2.757

Berry, R. Q., III, & Thunder, K. (2017). Concrete, representational, and abstract: Building fluency from conceptual understanding. *Virginia Mathematics Teacher, 43*(2), 28-32.

California Department of Education. (2008). *California preschool learning foundations, Volume 1.* Author.

CAST. (2018). *The UDL guidelines.* https://udlguidelines.cast.org/

Centers for Disease Control and Prevention. (2022). *CDC's developmental milestones.* https://www.cdc.gov/ncbddd/actearly/milestones/index.html

Clements, D. H., & Sarama, J. (2017/2019). *Learning and teaching with learning trajectories [LT].* Marsico Institute, Morgridge College of Education, University of Denver. https://www.learningtrajectories.org/math/learning-trajectories

Cooper, H., Allen, A. B., & Patall, E. (2010). Effects of full-day kindergarten on academic achievement and social development. *Review of Educational Research, 80*(1), 34-70.

DEC/NAEYC. (2009). *Early childhood inclusion: A joint position statement of the Division for Early Childhood (DEC) and the National Association for the Education of Young Children (NAEYC).* The University of North Carolina, FPG Child Development Institute.

Derman-Sparks, L. & Edwards, J. O. (2019). Understanding anti-bias education: Bringing the four core goals to every facet of your curriculum. *Young Children, 74*(5). NAEYC.

Drake, S. (2012). Creating standards-based integrated curriculum (3rd ed.). Corwin.

Durkin, K., Lipsey, M. W., Farran, D. C., & Wiesen, S. E. (2022, January 10). Effects of a statewide pre-kindergarten program on children's achievement and behavior through sixth grade. *Developmental Psychology.* Advance online publication. https://doi.org/10.1037/dev0001301

Ehri, L. C. (1999). Phases of development in learning to read words. In J. Oakhill & R. Beard (Eds.), *Reading development and the teaching of reading: A psychological perspective.* (pp. 79-108). Blackwell Science.

Fisher, D, & Frey, N. (2021). *Better learning through structured teaching: A framework for the gradual release of responsibility* (3rd ed.). ASCD.

Fisher, D., Frey, N., Almarode, J., Flories, K., & Nagel, D. (2019). *PLC+: Better decisions and greater impact by design.* Corwin.

Fisher, D., Frey, N., & Hattie, J. (2016). *Visible learning for literacy, grades K-12.* Corwin.

Frey, N. (2003). Tying it together: Personal supports that lead to membership and belonging. In C. H. Kennedy & D. Fisher (Eds.), *Inclusive middle schools* (pp. 119-138). Paul H. Brookes.

Frey, N., Hattie, J., & Fisher, D. (2018). *Developing assessment-capable visible learners, Grades K-12: Maximizing skill, will, and thrill.* Corwin.

Gilliam, W. S., & Zigler, E. F. (2000). A critical meta-analysis of all evaluations of state-funded preschool from 1977 to 1998: Implications for policy, service delivery and program evaluation. *Early Childhood Research Quarterly, 15*(4), 441-473. https://psycnet.apa.org/doi/10.1016/S0885-2006(01)00073-4

Goodman, Y. M. (1985). Kidwatching: Observing children in the classroom. In A. Jagger & M. T. Smith-Burke (Eds.), *Observing the language learner* (pp. 9-18). NCTE and IRA.

Hammond, Z. (2014). *Culturally responsive teaching and the brain: Promoting authentic engagement and rigor among culturally and linguistically diverse students.* Corwin.

Hattie, J. (2008). *Visible learning: A synthesis of over 800 meta-analyses relating to achievement.* Routledge.

Hattie, J. (2012). *Visible learning for teachers: Maximizing impact on learning.* Routledge/Taylor & Francis Group.

Hattie, J., & Timperley, H. (2007). The power of feedback. *Review of Educational Research, 77*(1), 81-112.

Hirsh-Pasek, K., Golinkoff, R., Berk, L., & Singer, D. (2009). *A mandate for playful learning in preschool: Presenting the evidence.* Oxford University Press.

Horn, M., & Giacobbe, M. E. (2007). *Talking, drawing, writing: Lessons for our youngest writers.* Stenhouse.

Jimenez, B., Browder, D., Spooner, F., & DiBiase, W. (2012). Inclusive inquiry science using peer-mediated embedded instruction for students with moderate intellectual disability. *Exceptional Children, 78*(3), 301-317. https://doi.org/10.1177/001440291207800303

Kindler, A. M., & Darras, B. (1998). Culture and development of pictorial repertoires. *Studies in Art Education, 39*(2), 147-167. https://doi.org/10.2307/1320466

Leahy, S., Lyon, C. J., Thompson, M., & Wiliam, D. (2005). Classroom assessment: Minute by minute, day by day. *Educational Leadership: Assessment to Promote Learning, 63*(3), 19-24.

Leong, D. J., & Bodrova, E. (2012, January). *Assessing and scaffolding make-believe play.* Young Children.

Libby, M. E., Weiss, J. S., Bancroft, S., & Ahearn, W. H. (2008). A comparison of most-to-least and least-to-most prompting on the acquisition of solitary play skills. *Behavior Analysis in Practice 1*(1): 37-43. doi:10.1007/BF03391719

Lillard, A. S., Lerner, M. D., Hopkins, E. J., Dore, R. A., Smith, E. D., & Palmquist, C. M. (2013). The impact of pretend play on children's development: A review of the evidence. *Psychological Bulletin, 139*(1), 1-34. https://doi.org/10.1037/a0029321

Mardell, B., Ertel, K. E., Solis, S. L., LeVangie, S., Fan, S., Maurer, G., & Scarpate. M. (2021). More than one way: An approach to teaching that supports playful learning (A Pedagogy of Play working paper). http://www.pz.harvard.edu/sites/default/files/PoP%20USA%20More%20than%20one%20way%20working%20paper_FINAL_25%20Jan%202021.pdf

Merriam-Webster. (1999). *Feedback.*

Mills, H. (2005). It's all about looking closely and listening carefully. *School Talk, 11*(1), 1-2.

NAEYC. (2019). *Advancing equity in early childhood education: Position statement.* Author.

NAEYC. (2020). *Developmentally appropriate practice: A position statement of the National Association for the Education of Young Children.* Author.

NAEYC. 2022. *Developmentally appropriate practice in early childhood programs serving children from birth through age 8* (4th ed.). Author.

NAEYC/NAECS/SDE. (2002). *Early learning standards: Creating the conditions for success.* A Joint Position Statement of the National Association for the Education of Young Children and the National Association of Early Childhood Specialists in State Departments of Education.

National Governors Association Center for Best Practices & Council of Chief State School Officers. (2010). *Common Core State Standards.* Authors.

National Research Council. (2012). *A framework for K-12 science education: Practices, crosscutting concepts, and core ideas.* Author.

National School Reform Faculty. (1994). *Protocols and activities . . . from A to Z.* https://nsrfharmony.org/protocols/

NGSS Lead States. (2013). *Next generation science standards: For states, by states.* The National Academies Press.

Office of Head Start. (2021). *Head Start early learning outcomes framework, ages birth to five.* Administration for Children and Families. https://eclkc.ohs.acf.hhs.gov/school-readiness/article/social-infant

Skene, K., O'Farrelly, C. M., Byrne, E. M., Kirby, N., Stevens, E. C., & Ramchandani, P. G. (2022, January 12). Can guidance during play enhance children's learning and development in educational contexts? A systematic review and meta-analysis. *Child Development, 00,* 1-19. https://doi.org/10.1111/cdev.13730

Smith, M. S., & Stein, M. K. (2018). *5 practices for orchestrating productive mathematical discussions* (2nd ed.). Corwin.

Spooner, F., Knight, V., Browder, D. M., Jimenez, B., & DiBiase, W. (2011). Evaluating evidence-based practice in teaching science content to students with severe developmental disabilities. *Research and Practice for Persons With Severe Disabilities, 36*(1), 62-75. https://doi.org/10.2511/rpsd.36.1-2.62

Stipek, D., Clements, D., Coburn, C., Franke, M., & Farran, D. (2017). PK-3: What does it mean for instruction? *Society for Research in Child Development, 30*(2), 1-23. https://doi.org/10.1002/j.2379-3988.2017.tb00087.x

Sweeney, D., & Harris, L. S. (2017). *Student-centered coaching. The moves.* Corwin.

Texas Commissioner of Education. (2015). *TEXAS prekindergarten guidelines.*

Thunder, K., Almarode, J., Fisher, D., Frey, N., & Demchak, A. (2022). *Communicating clarity in the early childhood classroom* [Manuscript in preparation].

Thunder, K., Almarode, J. T., & Hattie, J. (2021). *Visible learning in early childhood.* Corwin.

Thunder, K., & Demchak, A. (2018, November 9). *Taking the time to notice.* http://www.mathplusliteracy.com/taking-the-time-to-notice/

VanHoorn, J., Nourot, P. M., Scales, B., Alward, K. R. (2015). *Play at the center of the curriculum* (6th ed.). Pearson.

Vélez-Ibáñez, C. G., & Greenberg, J. B. (1992). Formation and transformation of funds of knowledge. *Anthropology and Education Quarterly, 23*(4), 313-335.

Virginia Department of Education. (2021). *Virginia's Early Learning and Development Standards: Birth-Five Learning Guidelines.* https://www.doe.virginia.gov/early-childhood/curriculum/va-elds-birth-5.pdf

CHILDREN'S LITERATURE

Carle, E. (1969). *The very hungry caterpillar.* World of Eric Carle.

Daynes, K. (2017). *What are germs?* Usborne.

Farrell, A. (2019). *The hike.* Chronicle Books.

Metzger, S. (2008). *We're going on a leaf hunt.* Cartwheel Books.

Parr, T. (2019). *The family book.* LB Kids.

Pfeffer, W. (2003). *Wiggling worms at work.* HarperCollins.

Storey Publishing. (2018). *On the nature trail: What will you find?* [Backpack Explorer series]. Author.

Tarsky, S. (2019). *Taking a walk: Winter in the city.* Albert Whitman.

Verdick, E. (2006). *Germs are not for sharing.* Free Spirit.

Willems, M. (2007-2015). *Elephant and Piggie* series. Hyperion Books.

INDEX

N22853

CORWIN
A SAGE Publishing Company

Helping educators make the greatest impact

CORWIN HAS ONE MISSION: to enhance education through intentional professional learning.

We build long-term relationships with our authors, educators, clients, and associations who partner with us to develop and continuously improve the best evidence-based practices that establish and support lifelong learning.